ADVANCE PRA

THAT'S

"What poverty is to *Angela's Ashes,* political turmoil is to *That's That,* Colin Broderick's stirring coming-of-age memoir of growing up Catholic in the North during the so-called Troubles. Written with verve and raw honesty, the book is both a captivating saga of personal discovery and the eye-opening story of how one boy experienced this shocking chapter in Irish history."

—Billy Collins, former U.S. poet laureate

"A Northern Irish gutbucket version of *Portrait of the Artist as a Young Man.* Colin Broderick writes with clarity and heart about a time of moral ambiguity, when war and repression were daily facts of life. Religious bigotry, class resentment, a legacy of rebellion—the author expertly peels back the layers of his Irish Catholic upbringing during the time of the Troubles. Must reading for anyone seeking to understand the psyche of modern Northern Ireland."

—T. J. English, author of *The Savage City, Paddy Whacked,* and *The Westies*

"In his searing memoir, *That's That,* Colin Broderick renders the conflict in the North of Ireland with an intimacy and honesty at once brutal, poignant, and unforgettable. Somehow, amid a landscape of ancient hatreds and unblinking cruelties, he manages to unearth the possibilities of hope and redemption. This is a deeply moving story told by an unflinching and eloquent truth teller. Broderick is a writer of extraordinary talent."

—Peter Quinn, author of *Looking for Jimmy* and *Hour of the Cat*

ALSO BY COLIN BRODERICK

Orangutan

THAT'S
THAT

A Memoir

COLIN BRODERICK

BROADWAY PAPERBACKS

NEW YORK

BROADWAY

Copyright © 2013 by Colin Broderick
Published in the United States by Broadway Paperbacks, an imprint
of the Crown Publishing Group, a division of Random House, Inc.,
New York.
www.crownpublishing.com

Broadway Paperbacks and its logo, a letter B bisected on the
diagonal, are trademarks of Random House, Inc.

Library of Congress Cataloging-in-Publication Data
Broderick, Colin.
That's that : a memoir / Colin Broderick. – First edition.
1. Broderick, Colin–Childhood and youth. 2. Broderick, Colin–
Family. 3. Social conflict–Northern Ireland–Tyrone–History–20th
century. 4. Tyrone (Northern Ireland)–Social conditions–20th
century. 5. Tyrone (Northern Ireland)–Social life and customs–20th
century. 6. Tyrone (Northern Ireland)–Biography. 7. Catholics–
Northern Ireland–Tyrone–Biography. 8. Northern Ireland–
History–1969–1994–Biography. I. Title.
DA990.T9B76 2013
941.6'40824092–dc23
[B]
2012040086

ISBN 978-0-307-71633-0
eISBN 978-0-307-71634-7

Printed in the United States of America

Book and cover design by Maria Elias
Cover photographs: (tea bag, grenade, cigarette) © Ocean/Corbis;
(whale tail) © amanaimages/Corbis; (The Flag of Ireland)
© The Irish Image Collection/Design/Pics/Corbis; (schoolgirl)
© Opus/amanaimages/Corbis; (author and cousin on front cover)
© Mairead McClean; (author photograph on back cover) Jon Greenhalgh

10 9 8 7 6 5 4 3 2 1

First Edition

For my parents
Michael and Claire Broderick

And Erica
You are all that is clean of me

I will speak and I will speak
So only secrets I do not know I keep
Will whisper here upon the grass
And follow others through the trees
To the rivers lakes the seas.

Mother. Ireland.

Seen from the window of a plane Ireland is a patchwork quilt, little square fields of green stitched together by thin rows of thorns; spring green, fern green, forest green, pine, sea and shamrock green. From above, she is clean, mystical, magical to behold. That is her first great act of deceit, her lush, rolling beauty the first betrayal of her truth, for on the ground, and deeper still, buried beneath that verdant lawn is her pain; underneath, there is blood.

I assume you've heard bits and pieces of the history of Ireland already, some of the landmark atrocities that have made international news over the years, or perhaps you've heard snippets grumbled over small glasses of amber in the dim light of a smoky tavern in the Bronx, stories of the long and bitter hatred between the English and the Irish, of heroic young men in balaclavas, petrol bombs being hurled into the dark night, monuments of flame on the claustrophobic streets of Belfast, the ghosts of skeletal boys, naked and excrement-smeared, starving themselves to death in the cold cells of the H-Block. And if you did receive your Irish history lesson in a bar from some furtive creature with a brogue, then as the night wore on, you surely heard about his mother also, for every drink poured in an Irish bar leads back to the mother. As you may well know, there is no mother like the Irish mother, and there is no love more wounded and fierce than the love between an Irish mother and her son.

In honor of that age-old tradition I, too, will start with the history. (The mother I will get to in just a little bit.)

In about 6000 BC the first humans arrived in Ireland. They stayed close to the shores, hunting and fishing for their food. Two thousand years later they had evolved into farmers; they grew crops and kept sheep, pigs, and cattle.

Around 500 BC the Celts arrived in Ireland and took to running the show. They were a wild bunch, prone to battles and orgies of food, drink, dancing, and much lovemaking. Their spiritual guides were Druids, and polygamy was embraced if you could afford it; many could. The Celts divided Ireland up into many kingdoms and worshiped many gods, and the *craic* was high and mighty, for a while.

Things went along like that without much of a hiccup until an English lad called Patrick came along. He had been kidnapped and held as a slave for a few years by the Celts and he returned in the year AD 430 for retribution. He began telling the Celts that their lifestyle was evil and that the real God, the one true God up in heaven, would punish them for their debauched ways and sentence them to a place called hell. There they would burn in a molten lava–type substance for eternity once they died. Patrick had the gift of the gab, as they say. Many listened. Christianity had arrived.

Six hundred years later, in 1155, once the Irish had been corralled into a more malleable state with a good dose of Christian shame, humiliation, and fear, Pope Adrian came along, the first and only Englishman ever to hold the papacy. He gave the entire island of Ireland to the king of England, King Henry II. Henry, in turn, bequeathed unto his son John the new moniker Lord of Ireland, and John was welcome to hang on to his new title just as long as he kept paying Adrian and the Vatican an annual fee for the honor of retaining sole slavery rights of the Irish people. It was a sweet deal, and John was just about as happy as a clam at high tide to throw the boys over at the Vatican their yearly bone.

In 1536, Henry VIII had himself anointed the king of Ireland by the Irish Parliament, which was comprised at the time of a bunch of his English buddies. Henry VIII decreed that all the Irish chieftains must Anglicize their names and that all of the English landowners, who had arrived in Ireland claiming all the best land up and down the country for themselves, must now clear their estates of native Irish workers. Of course, this was impossible because the landowners needed to keep the Irish on as slaves to work the land, but the threat of banishment for even the slightest misstep was a wonderful little tool to keep the Irish workers on their toes, and productivity soared.

As you can imagine, by this point the Irish natives were getting a little restless. In 1641 there was a rebellion in the northern part of the country known as Ulster, and twelve thousand Irish were slaughtered for their effort. But they had stirred a nest of bees. Others throughout the country had been awakened to the possibility of defeating the English and ending the horror of living as slaves. England got wind of the whispers and they sent Oliver Cromwell and his army across the Channel to put an end to any buzzing.

In 1649, when Cromwell first arrived in the town of Drogheda, he decided to make a name for himself right away. He slaughtered 2,600 people—the entire population of the town: "I am persuaded that this is the righteous judgment of God upon those barbarous wretches," he said famously, before rolling on down to Wexford and repeating this act.

Over the next ten years, the population of the Irish natives was halved by sword, starvation, and disease. More than 600,000 were killed or died. Another 100,000 were shipped off into slavery in the West Indies. The handful of Irish Catholics still standing were denied voting rights and access to education, and all of their foodstuffs were confiscated and shipped off to England. Then to put the icing on the cake, all land belonging to Irish Catholics was confiscated and given to English Protestants, and that was that.

Thirty years later, there was so much wealth to be gained from the plunder of Ireland's dairy, meat, and grain products that the English started scuffling among themselves for ownership rights. King James II, who had been deposed from the English throne after producing a Catholic heir, made an attempt to win Ireland back for himself from the hands of the new English king, his successor, William of Orange. James had the support of many Irish who believed he would put an end to discriminatory English penal laws (basically a set of English laws that forbade civil rights and housing to anyone accused of being a practicing Catholic) and restore Irish sovereignty once and for all. In July 1690, the two armies met outside Drogheda for the Battle of the Boyne and later in Limerick to give it a lash. William of Orange was victorious. Even today the Protestants of Northern Ireland, "Orangemen," celebrate the victory by erecting enormous bonfires and burning the Irish national flag, just to rub Catholic noses in it every year on July 12.

Things were quiet for a period after that thrashing, but in secret the Irish were regaining their strength and getting ready to take another crack at the throne. In the rebellion of 1798 another 30,000 Catholic Irish were slaughtered in an uprising. The great Irish republican hero Mr. Wolfe Tone attempted a landing with a fleet of French ships and 14,000 French troops ready to join the fray against the English, but they encountered such gale-force storms off the coast of Bantry Bay, County Cork, that they eventually had to turn back. The uprising was quelled. The English eventually caught Mr. Wolfe Tone on another one of his missions up at Buncrana on Lough Swilly, County Donegal. He was imprisoned and upon being denied his request that he be given the death of a soldier by being shot (they sentenced him to be hanged), he cut his own throat in his cell and bled to death rather than suffer the humiliation.

A few years later, inspired by Tone, Robert Emmet also led a small group in an uprising in Dublin but he was caught, hanged, then drawn and quartered.

Daniel O'Connell was the next to take the baton in hand and run with it. After a few chaotic years, he managed to rally enough public support to force the English into granting the Irish the Catholic Emancipation Act in 1829, which meant that we were now bestowed a few basic human rights, such as the right to run for public office and own a little land. A small light of hope glimmered for the first time since Saint Patrick had showed up in town almost fifteen hundred years earlier spouting his great divine vision for the Irish soul.

But the candle was soon extinguished when the potato crop failed a little more than a decade later in 1845, then again in 1846. By 1847 the island of Ireland was engulfed in the darkest period of her history to date. The potato was about the only food the English had left the slaves access to, and suddenly it was gone. Not that there weren't enough foodstuffs being produced in Ireland to keep the population alive. On the contrary, there was an abundance of wheat, meat, and dairy products available, but the English chose to ship those foodstuffs off to the homeland for themselves.

In fairness, the English were not entirely barbaric throughout the period of the potato-crop failure. They did set up soup kitchens around the country where, for the small price of renouncing your Catholic faith and in doing so aligning yourself with the throne, you were granted a small portion of cabbage water. A few poor souls did accept the devil's bargain rather than watch their children die of starvation and were branded forever after as "Soupers." To renounce your faith and accept the English soup meant that you had turned your back on your fellow countrymen and joined hands with those responsible for the genocide.

And make no mistake, this was genocide. To the English the Irish were considered little better than farm animals. After a tour to witness the devastation throughout the country in 1860, the Cambridge historian Charles Kingsley described the Irish he saw along the way thusly: "I am haunted by the human chimpanzees I saw along that hundred miles of horrible country . . . to see white chimpanzees is dreadful; if they were black one would not see it so much, but their skins, except where tanned by exposure, are as white as ours."

During Ireland's genocide, an estimated million and a half were either starved to death or killed by any of the diseases such as cholera, typhoid, and dysentery that blossomed in that black garden of agony, while shiploads of food left Cork Harbour under English guard every day. Another million and a half fled to America, where tens of thousands more died on the coffin ships before they ever reached freedom. The Irish Catholic population had been halved again.

I could go on trying to impress upon you the level of disgust that the English expressed fully and openly for the Irish people as a race (yes, race, for they did not view us as white like they were), but I believe the renowned English historian Edward Freeman captured the sentiment of the day best when he wrote, after visiting America in 1880, "It would be a grand land if only every Irishman would kill a negro, and then be hanged for it."

In 1905, the Irish nationalist political party Sinn Fein (Gaelic for "We Ourselves") was born. We, the Irish people, were determined to rid the island of Ireland of the English oppressor once and for all.

On the twenty-fourth of April, 1916, in the midst of Easter Week, Patrick Pearse, a thirty-six-year-old Irish teacher and poet, stood on the steps of the General Post Office in Dublin and read aloud a proclamation announcing the establishment of an Irish Republic before going inside the building to join his comrade, the legendary revolutionary James Connolly, as well as a small band of armed rebels, to assist in an uprising.

There was an enormous shipment of arms procured in Germany to help in the uprising. The rebel John Devoy, head of Clan na Gael (The Irish Family) of America, had organized the financing of the venture. Another Dublin man, Sir Roger Casement, went to Germany to purchase and accompany the arms to Ireland. Alas, the shipment was seized just days before fighting began (as was Mr. Casement), and after a week of fighting, with Connolly severely wounded, and the post office shelled to smithereens, Pearse surrendered the battle, saying he wanted "to prevent the further slaughter of Dublin citizens." The façade of the General Post Office in Dublin is still pockmarked from the gunfire.

Within a month the British had tried and executed fifteen of the men accused of organizing the event, among them Patrick Pearse, Roger Casement, and James Connolly, the latter of whom had to be strapped to a chair to face the firing squad because of a severe leg injury he had received during battle.

There was outrage among the Irish over the executions

and a renewed vengeance to rid the country once and for all of the British invaders. By 1919, Catholics formed the IRA, the Irish Republican Army. Support was growing among the Catholic masses for a revolution. Things got so heated that the British put together a band of ex-soldiers and mercenaries known as the Black and Tans and sent them over to Ireland to see if they could subdue the savage natives once more.

The English Black and Tans, like their predecessor Oliver Cromwell a couple of hundred years earlier, were given free rein to do whatever they felt necessary to put the Catholics under control again. They roamed throughout Ireland sacking towns and burning buildings. They tortured and shot civilians and priests at random. They threw innocent families into the street and torched their homes.

On Sunday, November 20, 1920, during a Gaelic football match in Croke Park, Dublin, with about five thousand civilians in attendance, the Black and Tans rolled onto the playing field in the middle of the game and opened fire on the crowd. Fourteen innocent civilians–Catholics–were killed, including one of the football players and a man who had kneeled next to the player to give him the last rites. Another sixty-five were seriously injured. Some of the victims were as young as ten years old.

All hell broke loose. The Bloody Sunday Massacre was the final insult for many. The Irish banded together and they fought.

One year later, in January 1922, the great Irish Revolutionary leader Michael Collins signed a much-contested treaty presented by the British government that stated that the

British would give most of Ireland back to the Irish. But at the last minute the British decided to hold on to six northern counties–Antrim, Armagh, Derry, Down, Fermanagh, and Tyrone–for themselves. The south of Ireland was free at last. But many republicans felt that Collins had sold them down the river by not holding out for an agreement that guaranteed freedom for the entire country. Collins was tragically murdered in an ambush within the year.

The Catholics who lived within the six northern counties of Ireland found themselves marooned from the rest of the country overnight. When Collins had signed the treaty, he had envisioned an uprising of epic scale to free the northern counties, but it didn't happen. The free people, in the south of Ireland, did as free people do; they enjoyed their freedom. They had finally been emancipated.

The Catholics living in the six northern counties stayed put. They were not about to be run off their land. They understood that without the six counties, Ireland would be forever incomplete. If they abandoned her, the English border would serve as a noose, all of Ireland would be strangled, and our fighting Irish spirit would be silenced for eternity. Instead, they adjusted to the new surroundings–the increased British security measures, the continued oppression and abuse of their basic human rights–and they quietly bided their time.

Cut to Northern Ireland fifty years later, October 1968; a small band of Irish Catholic activists about five hundred strong got together and organized a few peaceful marches. They were manual laborers, carpenters, farmers, students, housewives, and publicans. They had heard about the great work started by Martin Luther King Jr. in America and they modeled their peaceful movement on his teachings. They figured they had tried everything else; why not give peace a chance too?

Well, if there was one thing an Englishman didn't like to see in Northern Ireland, it was an uppity Catholic out parading in the streets complaining about not having equal voting rights and demanding equality in housing and job opportunities. The nerve. The Brits did what they'd always done: beat them savagely. This time there were cameras present; the beatings were recorded, and for the first time the entire world got a glimpse into the cauldron. The fire had been ignited. Catholics all over Northern Ireland took to the streets and roared, "Enough is enough!" The Troubles had begun.

On the morning of the ninth of August, 1971, the British launched "Operation Demetrius" in the six northern counties. In short, the operation gave the British Army free rein to barge into homes across the north and arrest, detain (without trial), and torture any Catholic civilian they saw fit. Hundreds were swept up across the province. My uncle Paddy Joe McClean, my mother's brother, was one of those men.

In 1972 at a peaceful march in Derry, the police opened fire on an unarmed crowd of civilians. Twenty-six Catholics were shot, and fourteen of them died, most of them young boys; six of the victims were only seventeen years old. The time for talk and peaceful marching was over. It was time for war. The ranks of the IRA ballooned as Catholics all over Northern Ireland felt that all-out confrontation was the only solution.

But amid the chaos of war, much of what happens in a normal life continues unabated: men go off to work, mothers dress their children for school; they shop and cook and hang the laundry out to dry. Boys and girls fall in and out of love, music is played, and into the symphony of chaos babies are born, and they, too, will learn how to walk and talk as children do anywhere, and to them war will feel just as natural as breathing, for a time.

To a child, the rhythms of life are somehow acceptable, no matter how brutal or insane, regardless of where he is born. He will open his eyes to the world, smile in innocent wonder, lift a small hand to grasp the air around him as the very first sounds begin to form—muh, muh, Mammy.

Our revenge will be the
laughter of our children.

—BOBBY SANDS

Begin

I was born in the middle of a snowstorm in a small second-floor apartment on Stratford Road in Birmingham, England, on the second of January, 1968.

My mother, Claire, was just a wee lass of twenty-one, and my father, Michael, little more than a scrub of a lad himself, was twenty-four. By their own accounts they had moved to England from their homes in County Tyrone, Northern Ireland, just a year earlier in search of work and to escape the drudgery of the farm life they had both grown up with. No doubt, as young lovers they also craved a little privacy away from the tight-knit community of the clan so they could freely consummate their passion for each other.

My older brother was born right after they arrived and

they called him Michael after my father, as was customary in Irish families back then.

A year after Michael was born I arrived.

I like to imagine sometimes that I can picture the scene of my own birth as if I were actually there to witness it, as if I had been a spirit who just happened to be passing down the street that particular night in the snow. Huge white flakes drift and dance, softening every sound, turning the drab street into something splendid and magical. The night is pierced by the sound of a woman's cry, and I am drawn to a lighted window on the second floor of a brown brick row house.

Inside the room I see a young woman, she is on a bed clutching her swollen belly. Her cheeks are flushed and she's panting. There is a young man with her. He is dark and slim and when he sits on the side of the bed to calm her, a pair of dimples appear in his cheeks—two dark divots so precisely placed, so perfectly defined that they could only have been chiseled there by the devil himself. He is speaking softly to the young woman, who appears to be little more than a girl now that I see her up close; she has a round cherubic face that she lifts toward him, her eyes pierced with a shock of wounded violence as the first contractions begin to take hold.

Over in the corner of the room, I notice a baby is sleeping in a simple wooden cot. He raises a thumb to his mouth, turns his head away, and goes on sleeping.

"Run like blue blazes," I hear the woman say. "It's coming. Now. Run."

The young man leaps from the bed, grabs a tan coat from

the hook next to the door and he is gone, working his arms into the sleeves as he bounds down the stairs and out into the dark night holding a hand in front of him to shield his eyes from the thick flurries of snow.

At the end of the street he jams himself into a red telephone kiosk and wrestles a twopenny coin and a scrap of paper out of his pocket, his breath rising like steam now as he excitedly begins to talk.

By the time he's back in the room, the woman has gripped the edge of the blanket in two white fists and her face is locked in a tight grimace. She imparts a low, painful groan like an animal as he moves toward her and places a hand on her shoulder and begins imitating her breathing, panting in unison, gripping her hand to pull her back into the room from the edge of that dark ocean of pain.

"I'm here," he whispers. "I'm back. She'll be here soon."

Her shoulders relax and she is breathing again and for a moment she seems to see him again. She smiles as streams of tears drip down her cheeks into the neck of her nightdress and then it begins again and she is bolt upright and cries out in pain.

"Shhhhhhh," he says. "Shhhhhhh, or you'll wake the baby."

With one swift swipe she has wrenched him to her in a headlock, her teeth tight to his ear so she can spit the words directly into his brain: "Don't tell me to be fucking quiet."

There's the sound of a door opening downstairs, the rattle of a bicycle being dragged into the front hallway and tossed against a wall, hurried footsteps on the stairs, and a young girl appears in the room shaking snow off her coat as she rushes to the bed.

"It's okay, it's okay, you can let go of him now," she says, prying the woman's hands from the young man's neck. "I'm here now. Let's take a look at you," she says, slipping her hands up underneath the blankets as she begins to work.

Words like "breech," "flipped," and "push" fill the air with the thick pulse of expectancy and then awoopsadaisy it arrives, blue and bloody, a boy's pink tail between its legs.

The young midwife who delivered me held me up, all nine pounds of me, and with tears in her eyes announced to my parents that I was her very first delivery. The old landlady who owned the flat came upstairs with a cup of tea and some biscuits for my mother and less than a half hour later my mother sat up in the bed and took pen and paper in hand to write her sister a letter detailing the drama of my arrival. My story had begun.

Memory is a game of connect-the-dots. Each dot is a moment of impact; each instant of impact, an emotional stamp on the subconscious. Go first to each place and stake it with a flag on a stick. Here's one. Look, there's another one over there. Take a length of string and run it from one stake to another so you don't forget your place. Watch the map take shape, charting every step of your inheritance, the topography of your pain. Then revisit each place you've highlighted and take a good long look at where the bruise is, take a moment of silence for the child, pull the pin up, let the healing begin.

The Troubles

Two months after I was born, my parents bundled my brother Michael and me onto a plane and flew home again, back to Northern Ireland. My mother's three sisters and three of her four brothers already had children and all of them still lived close to home. It made sense that she would want to be closer to them.

After working for a year in England, my mother in a Laundromat, my father in a tea factory, they had little money saved. Once the plane tickets had been paid for and their furniture shipped home they were penniless, back where they began.

With no money left to pay for a place of their own, they were forced to live with my mother's father again for a spell while my father went looking for a job. It didn't take him very long. If there was one thing you could say about my father, it was that he was a divvil for the work. *You'll never be the worker your father is,* the neighbors would remind me as I was growing up. *With any sort of luck,* I would reply.

Within months of being back in Ireland, my father had secured us a new home to live in and a car to get around in. My brother Brendan was born a year after we got back from England, which meant there were three young boys in our house, or four if you count my father, who was still only a lad himself at twenty-five. My mother was housebound with Irish triplets at twenty-three, not more than a stone's throw from the farmhouse where she grew up right in the heart of Altamuskin.

Altamuskin is almost not a place at all. It's nearly too small and too out of the way to merit geographical definition. It's a stretch of road, with a handful of farms, a small three-room primary school, and a post office. Or, at least, it was back when I was young. The post office has since closed; so it's not as cosmopolitan as it once was. But when I was a boy, Altamuskin was the world. We were home.

Home was a tiny semidetached three-bedroom bungalow–a government-built council house right on the Altamuskin Road, next to St. Brigid's Primary School. To live in a semidetached cottage meant that you shared a wall with your next-door neighbor. The wall that separated us from our neighbor in this particular house was the living-room wall, and because the row house was originally built as temporary government housing the wall that separated our homes was only paper thin and without any insulation to buffer the noise, which meant that we were practically living with our next-door neighbors.

There were strips of these little cottages all over Northern Ireland–four small nondescript bungalows in a row. We were on one end of the strip and my mother's sister Sue lived in the one at the other end with her husband and children. So we were surrounded by family.

On the other side of our living-room wall lived the Mullin family. Sheila Mullin, and her sons, John, Damien, and Christopher. Sheila's husband had died young, so I have no memory of him but perhaps it was because there was no father in the house to keep order that the rest of the family became so memorable. To my brothers and me Sheila Mullin was the friendly witch who lived next door. She was rake thin with long bony fingers and wild, unkempt hair and a toothless maniacal cackle that would collapse into a coughing fit that could only be remedied, it seemed, by getting another cigarette shoved into her gob as quickly as possible.

My parents smoked too back then. Everybody did. It was good for you they said, calmed your nerves, and with armies of hungry, noisy children to be fed and clothed and not enough money to feed them, nerves needed to be calmed.

When my mother would run out of cigarettes, she would bang the living-room wall to get Sheila's attention. That was how they signaled to each other that they were out of something; sugar, milk, bread, or a few tea bags to keep us going until my father got back home with the car. We lived three miles from Sixmilecross, the nearest village, so you couldn't just pop out to the store. The wall was banged three or four times with a fist and then my mother would lean out our front window and Sheila would do the same and they would shout to each other like that across the garden fence.

"Do you have any fags?" my mother would yell.

"How many do you need, pet?"

"A few will do until Machil gets home from work." Machil was what my mother called my father to distinguish him from my brother, so my father was Machil (pronounced Mack-hill) and my older brother was Michael.

"Put the kettle on, pet, I'll be 'round in a minute," Sheila would call back.

All day long tea was drunk and cigarettes were smoked. The women gossiped and laughed, and then they would fall silent as Sheila would read their fortunes in the tea leaves in their cups. My brothers and I were raised at a time where little children were to be seen and not heard, so were hushed and chased outside to run and play, climb trees, dig holes, and play tag. You're it. No, you're it. We were generally ignored unless there was blood spilled.

"Mammy, Mammy, Michael pushed me and I cut my knee real bad."

"Let me see it. Sure it's only a scratch. Here, I'll kiss it better. There now, run along."

"It's still sore."

"Your ear will be sore if you don't get out that door and up that field to play with your brothers right this minute. Will you have another wee drop, Sheila?"

"Ach now, I should be away home to get dinner ready for the boys."

"Sure you'll have another wee drop of tae before you go."

"I'll have one more wee cup."

It is true what they say about the Irish and their penchant for tea drinking. The tea drinking went on morning, noon, and night. The kettle in our house never cooled. Though in the North of Ireland we didn't drink tea, tea was something highfalutin English folks sipped out of delicate china cups with upturned pinkies. We drank tae, T-A-E, buckets of it, reservoirs and oceans of the stuff, we drank tae till the cows come home. We were lucky that the English were not an incredibly intelligent bunch or they could have ended the whole trouble with the Irish centuries ago. All they really needed to do was cut off our tea supply and the women would have organized a complete surrender by lunchtime.

Everyone drank tae, constantly, even the little babies were encouraged to drink tae from the moment of birth. The baby's bottle was filled with tae, lukewarm of course, with milk and sugar because the wee babies love the sugar in their tae. And when the babies were big enough to handle a spoon all by themselves they were set at the table with a cup of bread soaked in tae as their very first meal.

And with the tae came bread and butter and jam. Our diet was simple; if you sat down at the table to eat there was either potato or bread on the plate in front of you. But because the choices were so limited the women took such extra special care in the presentation of those two very basic staples. As a result we became a nation of spud and bread connoisseurs.

Nearly every house you entered carried the bouquet of a freshly baked loaf, each one with its own unique aroma and taste. But it was my mother's older sister Nan who made the best loaf of bread. Her treacle bread especially was a source of envy among every housewife in Altamuskin. Nan's treacle bread could not be replicated. Many tried. They could record the exact ingredients, measure it spoon for spoon, retrace every motion, every degree and minute in the oven, and still never come close to that level of perfection. I am convinced that the missing ingredient was some deeply personal secret that she held; a fusion of pain and love that she unknowingly folded into the bread with her bare hands as she worked, the flower of it bloomed in the cooking and dissolved on your tongue like a mystery.

The pace of life in a close-knit rural community could be slow and monotonous were it not for the elevation of the mundane. Bread was important.

To amuse ourselves, my brothers and I created fresh sport out of whatever was at hand. A game of football would be organized with a ruptured ball we'd found in a ditch. Bows and arrows were fashioned out of sticks we cut from the hedge and strung with binder twine swiped from a hay bale. Catapults were hammered out of the handles of old paint buckets. We dug holes big enough to hide in and fashioned elaborate huts out of straw and twigs, and once in a blue moon when we could find four decent pram wheels we engineered a go-cart and took turns pushing one another around the yard in it until we were called inside for bed at dark.

Sheila's three teenage boys, John, Christopher, and Damien, were like older brothers to Michael, Brendan and me— older brothers who were constantly in trouble, it seemed. My brothers and I were much too young to understand the hows or whys of their trouble, but we were old enough to admire it in them. When you live so far out in the country, trouble, quite often, is your only source of entertainment.

It was not uncommon to see the police pull up outside our little row of council houses in search of one of the boys. Sheila would go to the door and cover for them always, to give the boys time to climb out a back window and slip up through the fields behind our house to hide in a thick hedge. She would stand outside in her bedroom slippers, a black cardigan pulled tightly about her frame, arms folded, a cigarette dangling out of the corner of her mouth, her head tipped back defiantly, telling the police that she had no idea where her boys were.

One particular dry afternoon, just as Sheila was denying to the police that she had any idea where her boys were, John came hurtling up the road driving that beat-up old Hillman Imp of his. He slowed to a complete stop beside the parked police car and blew the horn a few times to get their attention. When the officers, who were talking to his mother, turned to see it was him, they dashed immediately back across the small garden to give chase. But they were not quick enough. John stuck his arm out the car window giving me and my brothers the thumbs-up and a wide, mischievous grin as he dropped the engine into a low gear and the tires bit into the dry tar with a squeal as he tore off again, up the Altamuskin Road, leaving the police frantically bundling themselves into their patrol car out in front of our house in hot pursuit. Sheila shook her head and blessed herself as she joined us to lean over the fence to stare up the road after them.

"They'll never catch him on these roads," she chuckled to us. "He drives that wee car like the clappers of hell."

Sure enough, just a few minutes later we could hear the roar of engines beyond the corner of the road at my grandfather's farm. We rushed back to the front fence to get our feet up on the bottom rung so as to get a good view as John's car came barreling around the corner again and he roared past us with his thumb held high for us to see, disappearing again like a yellow blur 'round the bend at Mary Ellen Corey's house on the far side as the cops came into view far behind him.

"Go on, you dirty black bastards!" Sheila yelled with her fist in the air as the cop car passed, and then to us. "Didn't I tell you they wouldn't catch him?" She cackled heroically before collapsing into a fierce coughing fit, punching her chest with the flat of her fist with one hand and wrestling the cigarette back into her mouth with the other.

The police were black bastards, as were the British Army. In Northern Ireland, to call someone "black" meant they were of the Protestant faith, or perhaps more accurately that they were anti-Catholic or at the very least loyal to the English Crown. The term "black" was a hint of the residue left over from the days of the Black and Tans.

According to the Mullin boys and their mother, the English were evil people who had stolen our land and whose sole purpose in life it was to abuse us Catholics in Northern Ireland every chance they got. We Catholics, on the other hand, as anybody with half a brain could tell you, were good people, God's favorite people, as a matter of fact, if you were to believe the rumors.

But the Mullin boys weren't our only source of enlightenment. We had the gossip of the women–my mother and her sisters–to inform us. The daily tae drinking was a ritual in which every aspect of life in the community was discussed and evaluated. I made it my mission to overhear much of what was said. There were whispers of the local Catholic men who were being lifted by the Brits under internment. I didn't understand internment, but I understood by the concern in their tone that it was bad. My uncle, my mother's brother Pat, was among those men who had been lifted by the Brits. The women managed to keep most of the details veiled as they spoke around the children, but there were still plenty of verbal crumbs that they dropped, crumbs that I hurried off to share with my brothers.

As a boy I was already hungry to pool all the bits and pieces together to form a picture of the whole. I was born hungry for clarity, it seemed. There was so much going on in the adult world that was being hidden from us. I wanted to get to the bottom of it all as quickly as possible, but there were words related to our uncle and the other men who were disappearing that I didn't yet understand, words whispered in bitter tones, I wanted them explained, but was denied. "Torture," "skin grafts," "Provos," and "the Kesh," they were no words for a wee boy to be worrying his head about. Too much information will give a wee boy a sore belly, I was told, before being chased outside with the threat of a good clip on the ear. And make no mistake, a clip on the ear was a very real threat.

We grew up at a time in Ireland when children were beaten, hard and often. To be fair, sometimes we were not beaten, we were hammered, trounced, whaled on, flailed, slapped, punched, kicked, and generally banged about. I don't remember the beatings my father gave me very well, although there were plenty. It has been harder to forget the helplessness I felt when I witnessed my brothers taking a thrashing by his hand. Those images remain more vivid. He could be hard and brutal, but there was always some logic to my father's rage, it seemed; he rarely struck without good reason. Kids had to be beaten, that's how you put manners on them. All parents were at it. The teachers were at it. It was all legal and aboveboard. As long as you didn't hospitalize the little buggers, what harm would it do them?

"It'll tighten ye up a wee bit," is what you were told if you cried.

"Stop being a big girl's blouse."

"If you don't wheesht with that whinging, I'll really give you something to cry about."

We must have been made of harder stuff back then, for I honestly don't think a modern child could endure it. The general rule of thumb was that every child should get a good slap on the ear regardless of their behavior because they were either coming from misbehaving or they were on their way to it.

My mother's wrath was another matter entirely. She was a young girl trapped in a small house with a man and three young boys to feed and wash after constantly. She had the unpredictability of a cobra. When she struck, it was fast and lethal. She lashed out with whatever it was that was in her hand in that instant, a wooden hairbrush, a belt, a broom handle, the flat side of a kitchen carving knife. But more acutely painful than any of that were her tears when she realized what she had done.

They were not monsters, my parents; they were Irish parents in 1970s Northern Ireland. They were parenting how they themselves had been parented. They were parenting exactly how they saw their own sisters and brothers and cousins and neighbors parenting. And nobody passed much remarks on such things.

Every evening like clockwork, at six o'clock we sat to dinner together as a family. We blessed ourselves and a prayer was said and the six o'clock news would start on the television bearing its daily confirmation of the trouble that existed all around us between the Catholics and Protestants in the North. It's a testament to how accustomed we were to brutality as a nation when such a playful word could be attributed to the daily massacre that surrounded us; this wasn't a war, it was a spot of trouble. And perhaps in terms of the horror our small nation had witnessed for a thousand years it was a fitting title for this current phase of our development: the Troubles.

Good evening I am Gordon Honeycombe and this is the six o'clock news.

Daddy, why is his name Honey Comb if he doesn't have any hair?

Would yis wheesht, I'm tryin' to watch the news.

Childer ate yer dinner and let yer daddy watch the news.

I don't like peas.

You have to ate them if yer going to grow up to be big and strong like yer daddy.

Didn't I tell you to wheesht. Michael, turn up that television.

Five British soldiers are dead tonight after a booby-trap bomb exploded near the town of Omagh in County Tyrone.

Northern Ireland is not a big place. The part of Northern Ireland that the English had carved out for themselves was roughly sixty miles from east to west, by sixty miles from north to south. Altamuskin was right smack dab in the heart of it, so nothing that happened was more than an hour's drive away from our home. The towns that were mentioned every evening in the news where bombs and bullets were killing people were usually no more than a few miles away. This town, Omagh, was only ten miles away. It was where we did our family shopping every Friday evening.

What's a booby trap, Daddy?

It's when a bomb is set to go off when somebody steps on a wire or opens a door.

What happens if the wrong person opens the door?

Well then that would be the last door they'd be opening for a while.

If any of you see something suspicious in a hedge don't stand on it for godsake.

Why, could we get blown up too, Mammy?

You'd be blown to smithereens, pet.

Not long after the cops gave chase to John up the Altamuskin Road, he went off to live in England. Maybe he needed to get out of Northern Ireland for a while to let the dust settle, I can't be sure. I didn't hear the details of his departure discussed. There were no good-byes. One morning he was just gone.

Sheila didn't have a phone, so when the police called in the middle of the night from London to say that John was dead, it was our house they called. Normally Mammy would have banged the living-room wall to tell Sheila that there was a phone call for her. But that night Daddy left the house to walk around and knock on her front door. We were told that he was stabbed in the heart by a man in a Chinese takeaway.

I clung to the whispers I heard over the rivers of tae that

flowed in our house in the following weeks of mourning. I tried to make sense of what had happened to the older brother we had lost. I heard rumors that there were people who wanted John dead, that the man who had killed him had suddenly disappeared, and that no one would be charged in the murder. There were rumors that the Chinese man who killed him was being protected by the British police, and it was possible that he may have even been paid to commit the murder. At least, that's how I pieced the story together. Even as a boy it was becoming clear to me that the law belonged to the English, that the police force belonged to the Protestants, and that we as Catholics only had one another to turn to in search of justice. The message was clear; we could only trust one another. We Catholics would police ourselves.

The Holy Ghost

*Good evening. I am Gordon Honeycombe and this is the
six o'clock news.*

*Twenty-one people have been killed and perhaps as
many as two hundred more badly injured in two separate
bomb attacks on pubs in Birmingham.*

Mammy, Daddy, that's where me and Michael were
born.

Would ye wheesht till I hear it . . .

*The Tavern in the Town and the Mulberry Bush pub-
lic houses were targeted last night at about eight o'clock
when the bars were busy with the afternoon crowd. No
one group has claimed responsibility for the attacks but a*

*spokesman for Scotland Yard did say that it seems to have
been the work of the Provisional IRA.*

Did you know that pub when you were there, Daddy?

No, I don't think there were any Catholics in that pub.

Children, bless yerselves. . . .

Why do we have to bless ourselves, they were only a
bunch of Proddies. . . .

Well, Protestant or not, they were somebody's
children, God help them, bless yerselves, you too,
Machil.

In the name of the father and the son and the holy
spirit amen.

On Mondays, my mother and I would go to the flea market in
Omagh, and Wednesdays we drove up to the one in Aughnacloy. I'd have to hide down in the passenger seat of the car in
case anybody saw me when we drove past the primary school.
Then I'd get to help Mammy pick out material for pillowcases
and curtains and Mammy would argue with the men about
the prices. How much for this? For a girl as gorgeous as you,
three pounds, luv. Three pounds? Are ye mad? For that scrap?
What'll ye give me for it, luv? I'll give ye a pound, even though

it's not worth fifty p. Give me two fifty and it's yours. I wouldn't give you two fifty for everything on this table. Come on, Colin. We'll look elsewhere. All right, all right, I'll give it to you for two pound and a hug. How does that sound? I'll give you two pound and you can hug yerself, how does that sound? It sounds like I got robbed.

It was a special treat to get to the flea market. The market was primarily considered an adult affair, women and vendors only. The majority of husbands were gone off to work for the day, and all the children were at school. There was an element of deceit involved for me to be there at all. It was my first real taste of the strange, tingly pleasure of the illicit, and I liked it.

I would have to feign an illness in order to convince my brothers that I had a genuine excuse to miss school for the day, otherwise they would have demanded that they too get to take the day off. I felt bad about cheating my brothers, but my mother was in on the ruse, advising me on whether I should claim head- or stomachache and to what degree I should push my performance, so her complicity quelled my sense of guilt. She would even come to the bed and place her hand on my forehead and claim with a genuine air of concern that I had a terrible fever.

But somewhere along the way my pretend tummy aches became real and with them came very real headaches, and a multitude of trips to the doctor. I had what the doctors referred to as "threatening appendix," which apparently meant that my appendix was threatening to cause trouble but not enough to elicit removal. I had constipation, migraines. Nobody it seemed knew how to stop the pain. The pain was everywhere.

My brain felt so swollen that I feared it might crack the casing of my skull. I was interred in my parents' bedroom for days on end with the shades drawn so that it was as black as a tomb, all light extinguished upon doctors' orders, the family hushed outside the bedroom door for fear I might die. Growing pains, my grandfather Frank called it, and perhaps he was right.

But no matter how close to death's door I might have been it did not excuse me from attending Mass. On Sunday mornings all of Ireland went to Mass. Not even death excused you from going to Mass. If you were dead it just meant you were there early, for Dunmoyle Chapel sat in the heart of its own graveyard.

Inside the church it was customary for all the men to sit in the pews to the right and all the ladies in the pews to the left, in what I can only imagine was an attempt to keep people from fondling one another in order to entertain themselves during the seemingly never-ending monotonous weekly service. There were already a few young couples, like my parents for instance, who had begun to buck the tradition by taking a seat to the left as a family unit.

In the back rows of the chapel and up in the gallery sat the hard men, and the ruffians of the community, bleary-eyed men who waited outside the church gates smoking and giggling until the priest's entrance hymn began, then slipped in quietly to take their place. But attend they did because even they knew that no hangover could excuse their absence on a Sunday morning. The entire community would know that they had skipped Mass. There was an unspoken rule that lay at the moral core of the parish; as an adult you could do what you liked all week, just so long as you could be seen on your knees at Mass on a Sunday morning. Your mere presence at the weekly service was enough to absolve you of all sin.

The old women sat in the back of the church in the pews to the left, fingering their rosary beads with wrinkled, bony fingers, their identities completely concealed by the black shawls they wore about their heads, giving them the eerie appearance of a coven of witches. But perhaps it was only my brothers and I who associated the shawl with witches due to the fact that our mother had cajoled Sheila into wearing just such a shawl one day in an attempt to scare us from going outside the fence onto the Altamuskin Road. We had been playing ball in our front lawn when she appeared, inching slowly up the Altamuskin Road from the direction of the school, a hunched figure clutching a black shawl about her head, her tar-stained fingers clutching the shawl about her chest. We watched in frozen terror as she came right up to our fence and without warning reached over and suddenly tried to grab us over the fence. We ran screaming for the house as she slinked away up the road disappearing as quickly as she had arrived. She'd succeeded to such a degree that my brothers and I were traumatized so horrifically that we were frightened to venture outside the front door for a week. Even the thought of going to bed terrified us. In fact, we were so petrified that my mother had to have Sheila come around and model the shawl again in an attempt to convince us that it had really just been a ruse. But even then I was not convinced because I felt that they were merely trying to trick us into believing it had been Sheila all along to relieve our trauma. We did not wander away from the house unattended for a long, long time after that.

The old men of the community were less terrifying. On Sunday mornings they peeled off their peaked tweed caps and tossed them onto the wooden kneelers to cushion their arthritic bones as they prayed. With their bald skulls revealed they were a vulnerable sight to behold. Even the most treacherous among them were momentarily transformed into harmless elderly beacons of morality; the shiny-domed shamans of our devotional tribe.

Before us all on the altar was our direct conduit to the almighty, the most powerful man in the parish: the priest. When I was a boy, our priest was Father Quigley—a splendid, blustery wreck of a man who roused the spirit of the parish with his absolute unpredictability. It was not uncommon on a Sunday morning to have Father Quigley show up fifteen minutes late for his own service. He would come dashing in the doors of the chapel red-faced, dressing himself in his vestments as he explained the reasons for his tardiness as he ran up the aisle: "Sorry about that, sorry about that now, sorry for keeping you waiting, but one of Miles McCann's cows broke out through a hole in the hedge down the road and I had to try and get it back in again in case it would cause an accident.

"You have to be careful about these things," he would continue, turning his tardiness into a small sermon in and of itself. "It's all right to stop and help your neighbor, you don't even have to like him, but it only takes a couple of minutes now, folks, to stop and put a cow back into a field again, maybe you could save somebody from having a bad car accident or the poor cow from hurting himself, God bless him. We can be good to the animals, too, you know, it's not going to cost you a penny . . . that's what Jesus would want: be good to the animals and be good to each other. He was a simple man, Jesus was, a very simple man. . . . I see a few empty seats up in the front here, if you boys down the back want to come on up to be closer to the altar so you can hear me. Come on up, don't be shy, plenty of room for everybody now. In the name of the father and the son and the holy ghost amen."

Everyone you talked to had a story to share of Father Quigley's miraculous shenanigans in the parish, like the time he arrived at our neighbors' house unannounced at two in the morning because he woke up suddenly in his bed and felt he was needed in that particular house right there and then, and was there to administer last rites to old Micky before he passed. He was our very own Holy Ghost. He had miraculous visions, he could sense or see what it should have been impossible to see. Another afternoon he arrived at my aunt's house, again unannounced, and ran through her living room toward the back hall and the bedrooms saying, "Where's the sick child. There's a sick child in this house, where is he?" And then proceeded to lift my cousin Padge from his bed and carry him straight out the front door and into his car and rushed him to the hospital in Omagh, fifteen miles away, saving his life from a burst appendix—in the words of the doctors, by just a matter of minutes. He appeared and disappeared like a hurricane. He would burst into our schoolrooms all over the parish randomly, in the middle of class, saying, "Stand up now, children.

Jump up and down, jump up and down, and wave your arms about, and say, I'm good and God loves me. Come on, now, say it louder, that's it, jump up, I'm good and God loves me. Wake up and shake up, I'm good and God loves me. . . ."

Before he left the parish my brother Brendan and I went to see him to inquire about becoming priests. I felt during one of my migraines that I had been called by God, that He was speaking to me directly and He was telling me that I must embark on my spiritual quest without delay. The Holy Ghost was in me too, I was convinced of it. My mother was supportive of my newfound devotion and encouraged me to go and talk to Father Quigley about it. Brendan came along, although I felt his heart was not completely in it as mine was.

Father Quigley was digging a vegetable patch in his front garden when we approached.

"Well, what can I do for you two?" he said, seeing us peering nervously over the fence at him while he worked.

"We've decided we want to become priests," I said.

"Oh, why's that now?"

"I just feel like that's what God wants me to do," I said, more than a little annoyed that he had not ushered me off directly to a seminary to begin my studies.

"I'm sure God would be very pleased that you feel that way, but you should just go on home now, the two of you, and play with your friends and enjoy being children."

"But I really want to be a priest," I protested.

"I don't think so, child. Now, go on home and don't be worrying your head about any such nonsense. God would want you to go on home and play with your brothers."

I was devastated as we headed off on the half-mile walk back home again down the Altamuskin Road, thinking for the first time that Father Quigley must indeed be mad, because God had most definitely called me to his ministry and no priest was going to stand in my way.

Of course, there were many in the parish who really did believe he was stone mad and completely out of order and worked tirelessly to undermine his authority with the cardinal, resulting in Father Quigley being moved off to a neighboring parish much to the dismay of many of us children.

After he was gone, we were gifted a new parish priest, the brandy-drinking, golf-playing, self-aggrandizing red-faced terror named Father McNally. Overnight it seemed the parish lost most of its magic, and becoming a priest seemed suddenly a whole lot less appealing to me.

Body of Christ

Good evening. I am Gordon Honeycombe and this is the
six o'clock news.

Three members of the renowned music group the
Miami Showband were killed last night on their way
home after performing a concert in County Down. Two
members of the band who survived the massacre de-
scribed the men who stopped them as being dressed in
British Army fatigues, although it appears from evidence
gathered at the scene that the men were members of the
loyalist paramilitary group the UVF.

Well, the dirty Brit bastards . . .

Machil! Watch that language in front of the
children . . .

What's a bastard, Daddy?

It's a baby who doesn't have a mammy or a daddy.

Do the Brits not have mammies or daddies?

They're the divvil's spawn. Now would yis wheesht
till I hear the rest of the news.

*. . . the armed men then tried to place an explosive device
under the driver's seat of the van but the bomb exploded
prematurely, killing two of the gunmen. The other gunmen then opened fire on the rest of the band killing lead
singer, Fran O'Toole; trumpeter, Brian McCoy; and
guitarist Anthony Geraghty.*

Children, bless yerselves, may the Lord have mercy
on their souls.

In the name of the father and the son and the holy
spirit amen.

When I turned seven, I proposed marriage to the girl of my
dreams. It wasn't a decision I took lightly, this was serious stuff
and the possibility of a rejection was a very real concern. I
fretted over it for weeks, trying to compose the most effective
approach. I could barely sleep, the anticipation was so great.

Margot Kelly was in my class at school. She was a bright,

energetic girl, pretty and clear-eyed. She struck me as a girl capable of just about anything she put her mind to. She had short dark hair and bright rosy cheeks and when she smiled, which she did a lot, my heart danced around in my chest with sheer delight.

On the day I proposed I waited for her in the hallway by the cloakrooms after lunch. When she strolled along, I took a deep breath and stepped out in front of her, essentially blocking her from going any farther. When she stopped in front of me and smiled I almost lost my nerve but I steeled myself, fixed her with a sincere gaze, and forced myself to say the words, decisively and articulately: "Will you marry me?"

"Yes," she said without a pause, as if she too had been thinking it all along. We both stood there for a moment grinning at each other and then we went on to class and never spoke of it again. We didn't need to. It was done. She was mine and I was hers. What more needed to be said?

The other momentous occasion that happened the year I turned seven was that I got to make my first holy communion. Part of what made this occasion so special for me was the new clothes that accompanied it. Mammy took me into Wattersons clothing store in Omagh and bought me a new pair of shorts with a black belt and silver buckle, a crisp white shirt, and a tie the store owner described as robin's-egg blue.

The procurement of the outfit itself was an awfully big deal in our house. Most of the clothes my brothers and I wore had been handmade by my mother from scraps of material she'd picked up at the street fairs in Omagh and Aughnacloy. We didn't have much money. By today's standards we were downright poor. And being poor hurts no matter where you are raised. We were old enough to feel the sting of our classmates' comments when my brothers and I showed up to school on occasion in three matching shirts that looked like they'd been cut from a circus clown's cape. On one occasion, when there was no money for new shoes, she cut the tops of our old rubber mud boots with a kitchen knife and, despite our teary pleas of protest, we were sent off to school wearing those for a month praying that no one would notice. They noticed.

Mammy, I can't wear sawed-off wellies to school, please don't make us wear these.

Be grateful you have shoes at all, we were told. There's children in Biafra would be delighted to have them.

Well, they can have them.

You'll be wearing one of them on the side of your head if you don't get out that door and down to that school in them this minute.

So to have a new outfit, store-bought, that no one else had worn already was a historic event in and of itself. Then, as if that wasn't enough, I was whisked off to Father McNally's house to get my very own prayer book and rosary beads.

At school our anorexically thin teacher, Mrs. Coyle, ran us through the procedure in preparation for the big day. It was an exciting time for us children. Apart from being a welcome reprieve from the usual monotony of school drudgery, there was the very real sense that receiving the Blessed Sacrament of Holy Communion was an induction of sorts into the world of grown-ups. Of course, in order to receive the sacrament we were first required to cleanse ourselves of sin in confession so that we became vessels fitting of the great honor of being a home for the Lord's flesh.

As part of our preparation for the sacrament of confession Mrs. Coyle reminded us that we were all born with sin on our souls. That's why they had to put the water on our heads as little babies, to wash away all the bad things we did before we could walk or talk. Everybody who is born into this world is born with sin already on their soul and they must be baptized right away, she cautioned us, otherwise their soul will be in mortal danger. I was scared when I thought about all the bad things I must have done before I was born and I was terrified that they didn't wash me right to get rid of them all.

"What did I do before I was born, Mammy?"

"You were a sinner just like everybody else."

"Did you sin before you were born?"

"We all did."

"What did I do that was bad?"

"Only God knows the answer to that one."

"What happens if a baby dies before you get to wash all its sins off its forehead?"

"It goes to purgatory and it stays there forever."

"What's purgatory like?"

"It's like a nowhere place about halfway between heaven and hell."

"Can it speak to other little babies?"

"No, it can't see anybody."

"Are the walls red inside purgatory?"

"Sort of."

"Are there any windows so they can see outside?"

"There are no windows in purgatory."

Every night I prayed and prayed to God to make sure that He knew I was sorry for all the bad things I did before I was born just in case they missed one when they'd washed my forehead. I'd seen Mammy washing the spuds for dinner and plenty of times there was still a bit of dirt left that she didn't get.

"What if I sin and I don't know it's a sin?"

"You can go to hell."

"What if I think about doing something bad but I don't do it?"

"You can go to hell."

"Even if I didn't do it?"

"God sees everything, even what you're thinking inside your head."

"But what if He's busy reading someone else's mind for just a minute and I get a bad thought then?"

"God can read everybody's mind all the time."

"Even at night when I'm in bed with my eyes closed?"

"Especially at night when you are in bed with your eyes closed."

Just before we were to make our first confession a blue van stopped outside our house one afternoon and a man came to our door to ask my mother if she would take in a couple of boys to look after for a week or so. We heard him telling her that they were refugees, young Catholic boys from inner-city Belfast, who were in danger of being shot in the sectarian rioting that had engulfed their neighborhoods.

She took the two teenage boys, Peter and Paul. They were skinheads wearing faded denim and tall Doc Martens boots.

At first my brothers and I were terrified of them, but it soon became clear that they were just as anxious as we were in their new surroundings. It turned out they had never been to the country. We taught them how to climb a tree and showed them where we picked blueberries to make blueberry wine. In turn they told us how you could make a petrol bomb using a glass milk bottle filled with petrol and a rag stuffed into the neck as a fuse. They taught us our first curse words—"fuck," "shit," "cunt," and "wank"—and by the time the blue van arrived to take them home again to their families in Belfast, we were prolific in the art of swearing, which was not a talent a boy might want to boast about on the eve of his first holy communion.

Good evening. My name is Gordon Honeycombe and this is the six o'clock news.

Now, everybody be quiet I need to hear this, Michael turn that TV up quick.

A policeman was killed today in a bomb explosion near the village of Sixmilecross.

Mammy, Mammy, Sixmilecross is on the news.

Wheesht.

Mammy, look it's our town on the news.

I know, dear, be quiet till we hear what happened.

The officer was on foot patrol near the small village when a land mine exploded, killing him instantly. Other members of the patrol escaped with minor injuries. The IRA have claimed responsibility in the attack.

Mammy, was that the big bang we heard?

That's right, pet.

And the policeman was killed when we heard the big bang?

That's right, pet, now bless yourselves, childer.

In the name of the father and of the son and the holy ghost amen.

And you wonder why I had to get Sheila to dress up as a witch to keep yis off the road.

On the big day we kneel in the pews, heads down hands clasped and praying. Boys on one side of the chapel, girls on the other. From behind the curtain I can hear Mick McCann telling the priest his sins. I try not to hear because listening to his sins is another sin and I have just enough on my plate as it is.

I close my eyes and try to block out the sound; I only hear him saying the last bit about biting his little brother on the arm but I tell myself it wasn't my fault that I heard it. When he comes out of the confessional box, I want to kick him in the leg for being so stupid talking so loud like that in the confessional box so everybody can hear, and his hair is not even combed right and it's supposed to be the holiest day of your life. He doesn't even look sorry that he bit his brother and I never liked him anyway.

Inside the box I make sure the door is closed just right and the curtain is all the way over so no one can see in and now I can hear Simon McCrory in the box on the other side of the priest telling his sins too. It's too low for me to hear at first but then I hear him even though I don't want to.

"I cut all the hair off my sister Bernie's doll on purpose," he says.

I always knew he was bad. Father McNally tells him to say three Hail Marys and two Our Fathers for his penance and to be nice to his sister in future. Three Hail Marys and two Our Fathers is a lot of prayers. Good enough for him, he deserves them for cutting all the hair off his sister's doll.

I hear the little door being slid across on his side and I straighten myself, keeping my knees together and my back up straight, my hands clasped in front of me and my head slightly bowed so the priest knows I am really sorry and that I am the best wee boy in the whole chapel.

The little wooden door slides back on my side and I catch a glimpse of him through the wire mesh but I duck my head down again so he doesn't think I'm staring in at him, in case he might think that I'm not sorry enough for my sins at all. Arrogance in itself could be considered an affront; best to grovel humbly, perhaps God would see fit to reward me for my effort.

"Bless me, Father, for I have sinned, this is my first confession," I whisper.

"Go on."

"I fought with my brothers, I said a bad word."

"What word did you say?"

"Shit."

"I see, did you say any others?"

"Yes."

"And what might they have been?"

"Fuck, wank, and cunt."

"Oh dear. Go on."

"I took some of the caps from my brother's gun because I ran out of mine and I didn't tell him about it. . . ."

"Mmmm. Anything else?"

"No, Father, that's it." I have the sudden urge to burst out crying because I realize suddenly what a horrible little boy I am for doing all those things. I can't believe that I ever thought God was just going to let me get away with it all.

"All right," he says. "For your penance I want you to say four Hail Marys and two Our Fathers and try to be a good boy in future."

"I will, Father, I promise."

Four Hail Marys and Two Our Fathers, I can't believe it. Four Hail Marys? The way I figured it, that meant that the gun caps had cost me at least an extra Hail Mary. That couldn't be right. About half those gun caps were too wet to even work right in the gun. Surely God knew that part of the story even if I didn't tell it, surely he had seen that I had to take them out of the gun and put them on the ground and hit them with a stone to make them bang one at a time, and now they had made me worse than that horrible hair cutter Simon McCrory. One Hail Mary for six gun caps? It just wasn't fair. By my calculations, there was something flawed in the sin-to-punishment ratio. Brendan could always get more caps, Bernie McCrory's doll would never be the same again.

I took my place on my knees in the pew and said those Hail Marys and Our Fathers as quickly as possible, blessed myself, and sprang back up onto the seat. I didn't want to give anyone the impression that I was some sort of depraved animal. If I wasn't on my knees for long my mammy, who was looking on, would know that I was the best wee boy in the whole world. I wanted to be thought of as a good little boy, a devout and fervent Catholic. Now that my soul was cleansed, my days of sinning were officially over. At least if I died now I wasn't going straight to hell. I could eat Jesus's flesh every Sunday now and just make sure to never sin again.

At the altar Aidan Cuddy kneeled beside me and out of the corner of my eye I could see his big horse teeth when he opened his mouth. In goes the priest's fingers to drop the piece of bread on his tongue, and Cuddy lunges at him like a snapping turtle like he was going to take hand and all with him. I immediately chalked his overzealous devouring of the Lord as the sign of a true sinner if ever I saw one, and there goes McNally's fingers right into the middle of all that smelly Cuddy spittle. So now I had to worry that I was going to get some Cuddy spittle in my mouth when the priest put Christ on my tongue. He's on to me next, lifting the little wafer in his glistening fingers proclaiming in that singsongy voice the priests have . . .

Body of Christ.

Amen, I reply as I reluctantly open my gob and in go the fingers pressing the Body of Christ wafer to my tongue, Cuddy spittle and all.

Jesus doesn't taste like meat. The little wafer the priest places on my tongue sticks to the roof of my mouth the minute I say Amen, and I can't get the tip of my tongue in behind it to pry it free without making it look like I might be chewing it, which is another sin. The body of Christ is to be swallowed without any help from the teeth. A glass of water would have been nice to wash it down.

I have half a mind to go see the priest after Mass and have a chat with him about washing his hands between each person, or at least to keep a wet cloth nearby for when Cuddy opens his big spit hole. But I won't. I'm a big boy now with a clean, sinless soul and a belly full of God ready to begin my new blessed life in the world of the grown-ups.

Peace be with you.

And also with you.

You may go in the name of the Father, the Son, and the Holy Ghost. Amen.

And off I go comforted by the Ghost. He is in me now and around me always and as long as I don't do or say or think a bad thing he will be a happy ghost and keep me happy with him forever and ever Amen.

A Whale in Derry

My name is Gordon Honeycombe and this is the six o'clock news. After another week of trouble with the prisoners in Long Kesh in what officials are now referring to as a blanket protest . . .

Machil, put that television off.

Right after the news.

Now. I don't want the childer watching that while they are eating their dinner.

What's a blanket protest, Mammy?

It's when the Catholic prisoners in Long Kesh refuse to wear any clothes and they wrap themselves in blankets instead.

Packie Donnelly says me and Michael are Brits because we were born in England.

How did he know where you were born?

We had to say it in the class, and I said I was born in Birmingham and then he called me a Brit and Enda McClean called me a wee Brit too.

Tell Enda McClean and Packie Donnelly I'll come down to the school and give them a clip on the ear if they call you a wee Brit again. If anybody says it again you ask them, if a dog was born in a stable would that make it a horse?

Does that mean I'm not a Brit?

No more than Packie Donnelly or Enda McClean, you're not.

Packie Donnelly was the first one at school to tell us there was a killer whale in Derry City called Dopey Dick. I didn't want to give him the pleasure of believing him after what he'd said about me being a Brit, but when I got home from school that evening there it was, all over the six o'clock news; a thirty-foot-long black-and-white killer whale right in the middle of the Foyle River in the heart of Derry City. Even old Gordon Honeycombe couldn't believe his eyes. He looked like he was happy for a change that he got a chance to talk about something other than Brit this and IRA that.

Apparently Dopey Dick had made a wrong turn out at sea; possibly he was following salmon. He wound up swimming all the way up the river into the middle of Derry City. According to Honeycombe, the vibrations of the traffic on the bridge might have scared the whale from returning out to sea again. There was much debate and speculation as to how he could be coaxed back toward the sea before he died. Suddenly he was all anybody could talk about. Dopey Dick was an overnight sensation. Northern Ireland's very first celebrity.

"Mammy, can we go see Dopey Dick please please please?"

"We're not driving all the way down to Derry to see a whale. Do you think we're made of money? Can't you see it right there on the television in front of you?"

"But Packie Donnelly's mammy and daddy are taking him to see it."

"Well, I'm not Packie Donnelly's mammy and daddy."

"But Mammy, this might never happen again, even Gordon Honeycombe said that on the news."

"We're not going."

"Please, Mammy, why can't we go?"

"Because I said so, and that's that."

.   .   .

Suddenly Packie Donnelly was the most popular boy in the whole school.

"When are you off, Packie?"

"As soon as Daddy's finished work on Saturday we're going to jump in the car and race down there."

"Wow. You must be so excited. I can't believe you'll get to see it up close. Maybe you'll even be on the news."

I wanted to beat him over the head with a branch.

Every evening I was glued to the television to see Gordon Honeycombe on the news talking about Dopey Dick and every day I begged my mother harder and harder to take us there to see it but she would not relent. I was obsessed with seeing the whale. There was something so out of the ordinary about it, so magically preposterous that I understood it could never happen quite like this again.

That Friday afternoon, the day before his trip to Derry, Packie Donnelly was like a rock star. Suddenly it seemed he was the most popular boy in all of Altamuskin. Everybody wanted to be his best friend so they could be friends with the boy who saw the whale and I hated him for it. Of course, I was really just sick with envy. I had never wanted anything so badly in all my life and it was killing me that it was he and not I who was going to witness it in person.

To me the arrival of Dopey Dick in the North felt almost miraculous. Suddenly we had a news story that everyone was excited about. This wasn't a two-sided affair, us on one side, them on the other; Dopey Dick was just a whale in the middle of a river, and he didn't give a damn what side of the fence we stood on. Everyone, Catholics and Protestants alike, was free to agree on this one small truth.

I lay in bed that Friday night and I cried silently into my pillow at the injustice of not being able to go see Dopey Dick in person. I was angry with my mother for not recognizing or caring how deeply hurt I was at not being able to go see the whale, and I was furious with God for ignoring my prayers and pleas to override her authority and just make it happen. If He really cared about me, He would see to it that I did not miss this opportunity.

And then, on Saturday morning like a bolt from the blue, God miraculously answered my prayers. Our uncle Frank, Mammy's brother, pulled up on our street unannounced with a bunch of our cousins in the car and I ran to answer the door. It was my cousin Frank. He said his daddy was taking them down to Derry to see the whale and they had room for one more person in the car if somebody wanted to go with them. My head almost exploded into smithereens. It was a miracle: God had sent my uncle to get me. He had answered my prayers.

"Mammy Mammy Mammy, Frank's here and they are going to see the whale and they have room for one more in the car can I go please please please?"

"Why can't I go?" Brendy asked. "I want to go."

"I'm the oldest. I want to go," Michael said.

"But I answered the door. Frank asked me, Mammy. It was me who answered the door and I wanted to go more than anybody else all week, please Mammy I'm begging you."

"All right, Colin can go."

"How come Colin gets to do everything and we never get to do anything? It's just not fair, I'm the oldest and he shouldn't get to go before me. How come he gets to do all the good stuff and we have to stay home?"

"Because I said so, and that's that."

I felt bad for Michael and Brendan, especially Michael because he was the oldest and he really should be going over me, but I knew he didn't want to see the whale as much as I did. I still felt sick in my stomach walking out the door and climbing into the back of my uncle's big blue Peugeot and closing the door behind me. I felt as sick as if I had been the one left at home because I knew my brothers would never get to see the whale now. I understood well the injustice of not being allowed to go, and there would never be another whale like Dopey Dick in the history of Northern Ireland, I was sure of that.

By the time we got to Sixmilecross my uncle Frank had us singing rebel songs and I was able to forget about the boys a bit, and the louder we sang the less I thought about them until I wasn't thinking about them at all. He picked one that we all knew well and we joined in and sang along,

> *Armored cars and tanks and guns*
> *Came to take away our sons*
> *But every man must stand behind*
> *The men behind the wire.*
>
> *Through the little streets of Belfast*
> *In the dark of early morn*

British soldiers came marauding
Wrecking people's homes with scorn

Heedless of the crying children
Dragging fathers from their beds
Beating sons while helpless mothers
Watch the blood run from their heads

Armored cars and tanks and guns
Came to take away our sons
But every man must stand behind
The men behind the wire.

We weren't far out of Omagh when Uncle Frank hushed the whole car from singing. The Brits had a checkpoint set up and we had to be quiet until we got through to the other side. As we slowed down my cousin Enda stuck his tongue out at a soldier pointing his rifle at us in the back of the car and Noel gave him the fuck-off sign with his two fingers—the universal peace sign in reverse.

Frank pulled to a stop and rolled the window down just a crack so he didn't get drenched with the rain coming in. The Brit kept tapping on the window indicating to my uncle that it needed to be down further, rain or no rain.

"Good morning, sir, I need to see your driver's license." He had a very posh English accent, an upper-class accent, the type of accent you might associate with a member of the royal family. The accent never failed to trigger an innate pang of hatred in me. Even as a young boy my body seemed to hum like a tuning fork the instant the first wretched syllable tapped my eardrum.

"Naw ye don't need to see it but I'll give it to ye anyway," my uncle replied as the rain streamed in the open window soaking the inside of the door, the dashboard clocks, his jacket and pants. This was partially where the hatred came from; watching men like my uncle, men like my father, be degraded like this in front of their families on a regular basis at these random checkpoints. These were hardworking family men—good, law-abiding men—going about their daily affairs peacefully in their own country. To see them go through this humiliating ritual week after week, prodded and degraded by pimply-faced young English boys with guns, was almost too much to bear.

These checkpoints were a way of life for us Catholics. The checkpoints served to etch the sectarian line of division even further. We would have to sit there for interrogation and watch as our Protestant neighbors would be waved through the checkpoint with a smile. To add insult to injury the British soldiers would try to flirt with the Catholic women they stopped, including my mother, but with the men there was always the humiliation, especially if there was the opportunity to humiliate them in front of their children. There was sadism in that accent and I grew to hate it.

"Is this your vehicle, sir?" the Brit continued undaunted by the rain hammering down on the roof of the car.

"Naw, I saw it sittin' on the side of the street in Sixmilecross full of children and I just thought I'd steal it and take them for a wee spin with me for the day."

"I see, so these are all your children in the vehicle?" the

Brit said flatly as the rainwater ran in streamers off his helmet down over his face.

"I'm not sure, to be honest with you. Maybe you should ask them that one yerself," my uncle replied dryly. "I don't know who the half of thim are. I never seen them before."

"Right, I'd like you to step out of the car and open the boot, sir."

"I know where I'd like to stick my boot."

"What did you say, sir?"

"I said I hope it doesn't stick, my boot, it's a bit tricky sometimes."

"You trying to be smart with me, Paddy?"

"The name's Frank, it's right there on the license, son, or don't they teach you children to read over there in England."

"Step out of the car and open the boot."

"I don't suppose we could wait till this bit of a shower passes?"

"Out of the car, sir, now."

"I'll tell you what," my uncle Frank said, switching off the ignition and handing the keys out the window to the soldier. "Seeing as you're soaked already, why don't you be a good cub and just scoot around there and open the boot for yourself. . . ."

"I said out of the car. Now!" the soldier yelled.

"Man, you are one twisted bunch of fuckers," Frank said, opening the door to the rain. It was a no-win situation. He had to do exactly as they requested or they would keep us sitting there all day long.

When he got out of the car and stood next to him, Uncle Frank was much bigger and stronger-looking than the boy with the gun, but the boy had a gun and that made all the difference.

When they went around to the back of the car we couldn't hear what they were saying because of the rain thundering on the roof of the car, but it sounded like they were shouting at each other. We waited and stared out at the other soldiers lying belly-down in the ditches around us and up ahead of us, their guns still trained on the car. Then Frank came around and got back in the car and as we pulled away he burst into song again and we joined in louder this time in the hope they could hear us out his open window:

> *Armored cars and tanks and guns*
> *Came to take away our sons*
> *But every man must stand behind*
> *The men behind the wire.*

> *Not for them a judge and jury,*
> *Nor indeed a crime at all*
> *Being Irish means they're guilty,*
> *So we're guilty one and all*

> *Round the world the truth will echo,*
> *"Cromwell's men are here again"*
> *And England's name again is sullied*
> *In the eyes of honest men.*

"Aren't you afraid they might shoot you?" I asked my uncle. I was in awe of his quick wit and defiant response to the man with the gun. He gave me the sense that we were smarter than the Brits, that even if we didn't have guns in our hands to protect us, we could still defend our honor with our tongue. The Brits couldn't take that away from us, and it was obvious that it hurt them. We could use words as our weapons.

"Our daddy's not afraid of anything," Noel piped in. "Isn't that right, Daddy?"

"That's right, our boy."

"They wouldn't shoot you, Daddy?"

"They might if they got me on my own at night with nobody around."

"What about during the day if there was nobody around?" Enda chimed in.

"Well, if they have a local cop with them during the day there's less of a chance of getting shot."

"Would the cops not let the Brits shoot you?"

"If I wound up dead at a checkpoint and word got out that a local cop was there to witness it, then he knows full well that one of ours would pay him a wee visit at his house when he wasn't expecting it, or maybe even leave him a little present strapped underneath the seat of his car and he wouldn't be going on any more foot patrols after that for a while. As long as the cop's with them, there's fuck-all they can do to you."

"God forgive you, Daddy!" my cousin Una piped up in the front seat. "Mind your language."

"Oh, sorry children," Frank said, glancing over his shoulder at all of us boys in the backseat with a wounded expression. "I didn't mean to offend your tender ears, excuse me please. Let me rephrase, if I may. What I meant to say was, as long as the local policeman is present to supervise during the checkpoint, there is absolutely nothing the British soldiers will do to harm you . . ."

"That's better." Una smiled.

". . . the dirty fuckers," Frank concluded with a chuckle, and we all burst out laughing as Una punched his arm in disgust.

We were only stopped one more time after that, just before we entered Derry City, and the Brits there only asked Uncle Frank if we were all the way up from Tyrone to see the whale.

"What whale?" Uncle Frank said without missing a beat.

The Brit regarded Frank for a moment with a look of disgust, knowing full well he was being provoked for our entertainment. He took a quick glance at the line of cars stopped behind us at the checkpoint as if he were weighing the situation and then without another word he handed my uncle back his license and waved him on through as he walked back to the next car stopped behind us.

By the time we parked the car and got to the bridge where the crowd had gathered, I nearly had the fingernails chewed off meself with excitement, and there, out of the middle of the Foyle River rose a thirty-foot-long black-and-white killer whale.

We ran to the edge of the bridge and got our heads over just as he leapt out of the water, tumbling through the air before crashing down again with an enormous splash and sending a spray of water up onto the wall of the bridge. A policeman stood down on the bank of the river with a bullhorn shouting himself silly at the lads in the small rowboats who were down below in the water playing chicken to see who could get the closest to the whale without getting eaten or smashed to bits.

On the side of the river a couple of boys lobbed chunks of red bricks to see if they could hit the whale when it surfaced. A few women screamed at them to knock it off, and then when they didn't an angry man ran down to the end of the bridge and jumped the wall to chase them away. The boys ran for a bit and then they turned and began throwing bricks at the man instead, but at least he had stopped them stoning the whale for a little while.

I looked around to see if I could see Packie Donnelly, but he was nowhere in sight. But I didn't care anymore if he was there or not, I was too amazed at the wondrous sight before my eyes. The whale circled around in the river below us, taking a short sprint, disappearing, and then leaping up out of the water again hurling its great body as high into the air as it could and then curling itself in a transcendent arc as it splashed to the water again. By all appearances it seemed to be enjoying itself. This whale was no dope, I decided. This whale was commanding the attention of an entire country; this was a performance piece worthy of a standing ovation and the whale seemed to be reveling in all the attention it was getting.

After a while, Una was complaining about being cold, crying that her lips were turning blue and her teeth were chattering. So we had to leave the bridge and go off to get fish and chips to warm her up before we headed for home. As we approached the car she threw the last of her chips on the ground and said they were pure rotten, and Uncle Frank had to give her a good clip on the ear to settle her and then we had to listen to her crying all the way out of Derry City. But I didn't care about any of that, because I had seen the whale.

I wasn't at school ten minutes on Monday morning till everyone knew about me and my cousin Noel going to see the whale in Derry. Apparently Packie Donnelly's father's car broke down and he never even made it to Derry after all. My cousin Noel and I were the only two at our school who had seen it and Noel didn't even care about the whale, he just wanted to play football and not be bothered about it, so I was the only one to tell everybody in the primary school what Dopey Dick looked like in real life; for once I was going to be the most popular boy in all of Altamuskin.

My dream of popularity was short-lived. Before I could even share my story in the schoolyard at lunch break, Declan McCrory had decimated my fame, in true Irish style, by sneering that he got a far better view of Dopey Dick on his television set and he didn't even have to leave his armchair to do it. That settled it. Nobody wanted to know anything more about it.

By Tuesday, Dopey Dick had disappeared again, and it was over. He'd slipped away, past the Craigavon Bridge and out to sea in the dead of night. A fisherman standing on the Coal Pier at Moville reported seeing a tail fin slicing hurriedly through Lough Foyle bound for the Atlantic at dawn. Dopey Dick was gone, leaving Northern Ireland in its wake. We were back to business as usual.

Orange Man

As I got a little older there were mornings when I actually looked forward to getting to school a little earlier. If the weather was nice it meant I could join in a game of football with some of my older cousins, and the other boys who lived next door to us who I didn't get to play with outside of school hours.

My cousins the McCanns and the McCleans lived just a short walk down the Altamuskin Road from us, and the Harley boys lived literally on the other side of the fence to the east of our house. Yet the only time I got to play with any of these boys was when I saw them at school or if we happened to be at my grandfather's farm at the same time.

It did not occur to me at the time how unusual it was that our mother did not allow us to cross that fence to play with our next-door neighbors, the Harleys, or that their parents did not allow them to cross the fence to play with us. I accepted the limitations of my freedom without question under the assumption that this was how life was for all other children. I had no evidence in my life to suggest otherwise. The true extent of my mother's phobias would become more apparent as I got older. She was deeply concerned with how we were perceived by our neighbors. There was a certain ideal of what a perfect little boy should look and behave like in Altamuskin, and she was determined that we resemble that caricature as closely as possible. We were Claire Broderick's boys. Wherever we went, we were a visible representation of her talent as a parent. She was going to help us out by making sure our margin for error was severely limited. I would grapple with the ghost bars of Mother's psychic cage for a lifetime.

In the mornings for an hour or so we had free rein of the schoolyard until Baldy arrived. Baldy was what the older boys had christened Master Cooney, our principal, for as long as I was at St. Brigid's. He had a few tufts of hair on the sides of his head, but his crown was as bald as an egg. Baldy never missed school no matter what the weather. When it snowed we would sit on the school wall and watch out for the nose of his red Ford Cortina at the corner by my grandfather's farm knowing that he would always make it, even when there wasn't another car on the road, even when the snow was so bad the local quarry would have to be closed for the day; even when the school bus couldn't make it, he would be there. Because we lived right next to the school we had no excuse not to be there too, unless of course my mother decided she wanted me to stay at home to keep her company.

Sometimes in the mornings we'd see my cousin Gabriel

McCann coming down the hill that faced the schoolyard carrying a couple of rabbits with blood dripping down from their furry ears. He'd swing them over the school wall at us when we'd ask to see them. Gabriel was one of my oldest cousins, old enough to stand with the hard men outside the chapel gates on a Sunday morning, smoking cigarettes and engaging in what always appeared to be the most illicit conversations. He was someone I aspired to be like, so it was important to me that he thought highly of me, too.

"How many d'you get this morning, Gabriel?"

"Just the two."

"How'd'ye catch thim?"

"In a snare."

"What's a snare?"

"A piece of wire attached to a stick."

"Like a booby trap?"

"Like a booby trap without a bomb attached to it."

"Does it catch the rabbit by the foot when it steps in it?"

"Naw. You have to find where they like to run first and then you set a snare for them, and when they run through the snare and the wire pulls shut around their necks, it chokes them."

"Do they die right away?"

"Naw, that's why they're a bit bloody, they're usually still kicking a bit when you get to them in the morning, and then you have to give them a whack over the back of the head with a stick to finish thim off."

I'd seen my uncle Matt kill plenty of rabbits with a stick on my grandfather's farm but those were rabbits infected with myxomatosis, a disease that had been purposely introduced to the rabbit population in the UK in the '70s to curb overpopulation. Once infected, the rabbit would develop horrible tumors, becoming lethargic and in most cases completely blind. My uncle would kill them to put them out of their misery. We had been warned by our mother to stay well clear of the myxomatosis rabbits for fear we would be stricken with similar symptoms.

"Did you hear the bomb yesterday evening?"

"What bomb?"

"The bomb in Omagh."

"I heard it," Mick Corrigan piped up.

"How did you hear it?" I asked. I didn't believe him for a second. I suspected he was lying just so my cousin Gabriel would think he was cool.

"I was outside feeding the cows and I was coming across the field and I heard it."

"How come you heard it and I didn't hear it?"

"'Cause you were probably at home in your bed sleeping."

"I don't go to bed till eight o'clock and I don't go to sleep right away anyway."

"How many Proddies were killed?" Mick Corrigan asked, and then I really wanted to punch him in the face for his hardman act.

"None," Gab said as he casually tossed the rabbits over his shoulder getting blood all down the back of his jacket. "They got them all out in time before it went off."

"That's a pity. The more Proddies get killed, the better," I said, just so he would know I was as hard a man as Mick Corrigan.

"You know our great-grandfather was a Protestant," Gab said, matter-of-factly. "So we might have a bit of Protestant blood in us as well."

"What do you mean?" I asked, horrified at the thought. Horrified that now he'd gone and said something so ridiculous like that in front of Mick Corrigan, who already thought I was a Brit just because I was born in England.

"Our great-grandfather, our mother's grandfather, was a Protestant and he turned to become a Catholic to marry our great-grandmother, so all the McClean family was Protestant once upon a time."

"Broderick's a Proddy!" Mick Corrigan bellowed. "Broderick's a Proddy. Are you going to march with the Orangemen on the twelfth?"

"Watch your mouth, young Corrigan," Gab snapped at him. "Don't make me come in over that wall and give you a beating."

Mick Corrigan shut up then but it was too late. I was a little bit Proddy.

"I don't believe it," I said.

"Ask your mother about it when you get home," Gab said as he turned to leave. "And you, young Corrigan, if I hear you running around shouting that about a cousin of mine I'll come back here and give you a good hammering."

When I got home my mother confirmed that it was true. Her grandfather had renounced his religion and became a Catholic because he loved my grandmother so much.

"Does that mean I'm Protestant, then?"

"No, don't be silly, you were born a Catholic and raised a Catholic."

"But we have a little bit of Protestant blood in us."

"Maybe a little bit, but what difference does that make? Plenty of Protestants are good people too."

"I don't want to be a little bit of a Protestant."

"So don't say you are, and then you're not."

"What if Mick Corrigan says it?"

"Tell Mick Corrigan he doesn't know what he's talking about."

"But now he knows I was born in England and that I have Protestant blood."

"Never mind what Mick Corrigan says. 'Sticks and stones may break my bones but names can never hurt me.' Your great-grandfather did a brave thing for love, and don't you forget it."

The idea that I could be accused of not being one hundred percent Irish was a horrifying realization. The notion that I had even a trace of Protestant, English, blood coursing through my veins sickened me. Protestants were dirty, immoral animals. I'd been hearing it for years in the schoolyard; they were cruel and soulless creatures. A Protestant was the polar opposite of what a real Northern Irishman should be. Protestants were our enemies, our oppressors. I was angry at my grandmother for her cruel legacy. Her love had poisoned us all, tarnished my Irish soul with a vulgar streak of orange. It was a malignant stain on my identity as a true Irishman. There was only one thing for it; I would fight to mask the blemish.

Free State

Master Cooney's class was the last class in primary school before they sent us off to the high school in Ballygawley. There
was no dreaming allowed in Master Cooney's class, daydreaming or otherwise. He had two years to make sure we were ready
to go off into the world from Altamuskin and he was not going
to waste a single second of it.

"Who can tell me what the opposite of parallel lines
are? . . . Donnelly stop picking your nose, it's not lunchtime
just yet. Stand up and straighten yourself for godsake, you're
a disgrace to the human race, stand up man and tell the class,
nice and loud, so everybody can hear."

"Ahhh mmmm."

"Well . . . if parallel lines run side by side for infinity, then
what is the opposite of parallel?"

"Mmm, ahhhh."

"No it's not an mmm ahhh, what the hell is an mmm ahhh? Did you even look at the homework I assigned last night?"

"Yes, master."

"Well, then let's see it."

"I left it at home, sir."

"I see; you done the homework but you left it at home. . . ."

"Yes, master. Sorry, master."

"You must think I'm a fool if you think I believe that for a second. You didn't do the homework, that's why you're standing there looking like an idiot in front of the rest of the class. I want that homework on my desk first thing tomorrow morning, is that understood?"

"Yes, master."

"You think I drive up here from Ballygawley every day because I enjoy your company, Donnelly?"

"Yes, master. I mean no, master."

"Margot Kelly, stand up please and educate Mr. Donnelly over here. What is the opposite of a parallel line?"

"A perpendicular line."

"That is correct, and tell Mr. Donnelly why we think of perpendicular lines as opposite to parallel lines."

"Parallel lines run side by side. Perpendicular lines form congruent adjacent angles."

"Very good, Margot, in other words . . . Mick McCann, stop chewing your pencil and sit up straight in your seat . . . if the two lines look like an L shape, you could say they are perpendicular and these lines will run away from each other into infinity and never meet again . . . Mr. Broderick . . ."

"Please, sir, wouldn't the lines meet if you kept drawing them straight for a long time?"

"No, they will never meet ever. . . ."

"But please, sir, if you wrapped the whole world in white paper and you drew an *L* on the ground and then you went this way drawing that straight line and I went this way drawing this other straight line, wouldn't we meet around the back of the world?"

"Stop talking nonsense. Nobody's wrapping the world in paper, sit up in your chair and tidy that hair of yours; doesn't Mrs. Broderick have a comb at home for that thing? Who can tell me what an obtuse triangle is?"

Good evening. My name is Gordon Honeycombe and this is the six o'clock news.

A total of twelve people have been killed and a further thirty or so badly injured when a bomb exploded last night in a restaurant near Belfast.

In a statement today the IRA have claimed responsibility for the attack and have apologized for the inadequate warning time so that authorities could have cleared the restaurant.

The attack is one of the worst in the history of the Troubles so far and has been condemned by leaders across the province. All of the victims were believed to be Protestant. Seven of those killed were women.

What a friggin' disaster.

It's a disgrace.

Who knows what the truth is, maybe the police are lying; they probably had plenty of warning time.

Machil, that's a terrible thing to say.

You never know, these things happen, who knows what the Brits are liable to allow happen for some bad press for the IRA. So they lose a few, and the IRA look like monsters on the news. . . . I wouldn't put it past them.

Children, bless yourselves, in the name of the father and of the son and of the holy ghost amen.

During that last year of primary school my father had started building our new house. Every spare minute we had, Michael and Brendan and I were there with him, helping out in any way we could. The new site was just down the Altamuskin Road about a half-mile, but it meant that once we moved we would be living right next door to the rest of my cousins, the McCanns and the McCleans.

I couldn't wait to move out of the house the council had given us. I had begun to resent the tiny row house. As I got a little older it was becoming more apparent that it was the kind of house only a Catholic family would have been assigned by the local council offices, whose employees were all Protestant and who saved all the fancy modern two-storied council houses for other Protestants. The nice housing estates in the local towns were almost always predominantly Protestant. But I was not allowed to complain about our little house; as my mother liked to remind me, "Aren't we lucky to have a house at all when all the little children in Biafra have to sleep on the hard ground outside under the stars with their bellies swollen with hunger and not so much as a scrap of a blanket to keep them from the cold."

I was excited about our new house also because we had run out of space. I had two younger sisters now in addition to my two brothers, Noleen and Louise, and my mother was pregnant again with number six. We had outgrown the small cottage.

To save money, my father was doing much of the construction himself. This is what my father did full-time as an occupation and he was good at it. Block work, carpentry, tiling, painting, roofing . . . he did it all, and during the summer holidays and on weekends, my brothers and I joined him in an apprenticeship of sorts. We shoveled and wheeled gravel to fill up the foundations, we carried six-inch concrete blocks and stacked them so the walls could be built, and when we said we were bored or our arms ached, he gave us extra work wheeling clay from one end of the site to another for weeks on end. Within a year of working alongside him, we could drive a nail and use a handsaw and a spirit level. We could mix a batch of concrete or mortar on a sheet of plywood with a shovel. Before we were out of primary school we were budding tradesmen, our small pink hands sporting the first crust of calloused skin along the base of our fingers.

Sometimes on a Saturday morning my brothers and I were rewarded for our effort with ten pence each to spend and Mammy allowed us to walk the three miles into Sixmilecross all by ourselves to get sweets and go to the mobile library for books and tapes.

The village of Sixmilecross had just one street. You came in one end of the town from Beragh and out the other end toward Carrickmore. A good footballer could launch a ball from one end of the town to the other with a single mighty kick. But the village was a bustling hub of commerce in those days. There was a car repair shop, a clothes shop, a hardware store, a bicycle shop, a hotel that nobody ever seemed to go in or out of, a chemist, a Protestant petrol station for Protestant cars, four bars—two for the Protestants and two for the Catholics—a fish-and-chip shop, Eddy Kelly's newspaper shop up the end of the town, and right in the middle of Sixmilecross next to Jack Heaney's pub was Peggy McNamee's sweet shop.

It was understood that the Catholics would support Catholic business and the Protestants would likewise stick to their own. That way we were all saved the discomfort of having to stand next to one another in line at the counter or, God forbid, have to be courteous to one another. Any sign of interaction with the opposing religion could be seen as a threat to local morale or even to the safety of local lives. Catholics and Protestants lived alongside one another, but we remained very much apart.

The smaller local grocery stores were usually split, Catholics for the Catholics, Protestant grocery stores for the Protestants. If you went as far as Omagh, all were free to shop in the larger supermarkets like Woolworths, where there was more space to politely ignore one another.

Catholics had their cars fixed by Catholic mechanics, Protestants by Protestant mechanics. This was serious business. Lives were threatened if it was discovered that a Catholic mechanic was doing trade with a Protestant. Bars were bombed on a regular basis in surrounding towns for similar offenses. Allegiance was paramount to survival. It was critical that you understand the rules. But we had been raised in a circling pattern, Catholics attending Catholic schools, Protestants to their own also, so that by the time we were ten it was deeply ingrained in our nature; every child in Northern Ireland knew exactly where he could be safely and where he was not supposed to be.

The rule was a little more lenient in the case of gas stations, as the business at hand could be taken care of outside of the store at the pumps in plain sight of passersby, although a Catholic would still only avail himself of a Protestant petrol station if it looked like he might run out of gas before he could reach a Catholic-owned one instead. In the case of the bars in the town, though, the distinction was very clear, Protestants to the Protestant bars and Catholics to the Catholic bars. There was rarely an exception to that rule for the obvious reasons: alcohol and a thousand years of sectarian hatred do not mix well.

But there was one shop in town where it didn't matter if

you were church or chapel, and that was Peggy McNamee's sweet shop. Peggy was Catholic herself, so it only made sense that it was the best wee sweet shop in the whole world. All were welcome. A sweet tooth knows no boundaries.

When you pushed open the blue door a little bell would tinkle to let her know that you were there, and after a couple of minutes she would come out from behind a curtain in the back with a cigarette dangling out of the corner of her mouth, a cloud of smoke in thin gray wisps about her head.

The whole shop was filled top to bottom with shiny glass jars and colorful boxes full of sweets. There was every type of sweet known to man: chocolate bars and chocolate bunnies, peanut-butter chocolate, raspberry chocolate, orange chocolate, black chocolate, brown chocolate, white chocolate; licorice sticks and fizz bombs; multicolored gobstoppers; yellow bonbons, white bonbons, red bonbons; lollipops of every size, shape, and flavor you could imagine; there were penny chews and brandy balls, butterscotch squares and peanut-butter brittle, sour-apple gummy bears, lemon drops, and chocolate buttons with sprinkles on top. And for ten p you could get twenty different things if you wanted, and Peggy would let you take all day to make up your mind. Such decisions were important and not to be rushed.

When we had our bags of sweets sorted out, we crossed the street to the mobile library truck that came out of Omagh once a week to service the reading needs of the surrounding community, and if you forgot your book from last week they'd still give you another one to read anyway. I was reading all the

Dr. Doolittle and Roald Dahl books I could find. When I read a really good one, I'd start and read it again right away, but you couldn't expect the same excitement the second time around because you knew all the surprise bits already. But it was still better than not reading at all, and I knew that when I grew up I was going to write stories about talking horses and golden tickets in chocolate bars too.

Sometimes in the summer holidays our father would take us all the way to Bundoran to go to the beach. When we got to the British Army checkpoint at the border of Belleek we all had to be really quiet and behave ourselves because the Brits had to check our father's license and get him out of the car and put him through a rigmarole of questions and open the trunk to make sure we weren't smuggling Provos or Arma-Lites under the spare tire.

But it was never too bad when you were leaving the North of Ireland to travel down into the Free State; it was only when you were coming back home again that the Brits really watched you. They were more concerned about what you might smuggle into Northern Ireland than what you might manage to sneak out.

After you got past the British checkpoint and their barbed-wire fences and their little Gestapo mustaches, you immediately came to another checkpoint right away for the Irish police on the southern side of the border. But the guards on the Irish side were always laughing and smoking cigarettes or over in their little hut watching the television with their feet up on a table and they would wave you on through with a smile or a thumbs-up and a big friendly wink, as if to say, "It's all right, you can relax now, lads."

"Why can't we live down here in the Free State, Daddy?"

"Because all the road signs are in Irish, we wouldn't know where we were going."

"If we learn how to speak Irish, then can we move to the South?"

"How about you learn to speak Irish and we stay where we are with our own people in the North until we can all be free together."

It became more apparent to me later, of course, that most Northern Irish Catholic Nationalists had just about as much time for the "Freestaters" as they did for the English. To many in the Northern six counties, the Southerners had abandoned us Catholics after Michael Collins had signed the treaty and left us to fight the war by ourselves—a war that might easily have been won if the lazy bastards had gotten off their asses and kept the pressure on back in 1922 when the fight was fresh in them.

We smell the sea from miles away. We stick our faces out the car windows to see the first signs of sand along the sides of the road. Someone yells that they see a seagull. A few hungry sheep stand on a rocky crag. The fields are pocked with craters of sand. Then off in the distance the sky and the ocean become one. There is no end to the blue. The first sight of it lighting our faces in wonder as we squeeze together out the rear-door window of my father's orange Datsun.

"Daddy, Daddy, how far does the sea go out?"

"Miles and miles and miles."

"What would happen if you got on a boat and you just kept going in a straight line all the way out?"

"You'd come to America."

"Have you ever been to America, Daddy?"

"Where would I get the money to go to America? I can barely afford to get us to Bundoran for the day."

The main street in Bundoran was lined with every temptation known to a ten-year-old. The pavement in front of every store was an explosion of summer color—yellows, reds, blues, greens, and oranges—in hues so bright, they seemed to have been possible only in the plastic of the oversized buckets and spades and gigantic beach balls stacked shoulder high in the street. There were postcard racks and mouthwatering window displays of thick sticks of pink candy cane, or the green, white, and gold of the famous Bundoran rock. Distracted parents sauntered along, ushering schools of young children slurping on big white ice-cream cones, one or two screaming here and there because they didn't get the bucket or spade they demanded. And over everything rang the tinny ring and ching of the one-armed bandits and the steady flow of a cascade of coins spilling into metal trays drawing every passing eye to the bright arches of blinking lights leading into the dark caverns of the arcades.

Daddy would give us 50p each and we were free to go and spend it any way we wanted. The 2p machines were the best to play because you nearly always won something when the cherries would line up, so you would keep going because you knew that with such measured luck the jackpot was just around the corner.

Daddy liked to play the 5p slot machines, but that's because it was his money and he was better at playing the machine than we were because he was older and smarter. But then one day I found a 5p machine where there were a bunch of coins all wrapped up in a ten-pound note, and nobody must have noticed how close the whole thing was to just falling right down into the little slot if you could just nudge it over the waterfall with the little lever. I watched it closely for a long time to make absolutely sure and I knew that just one more coin would do it. The stack of coins wrapped in the ten-pound note were already hanging right over the lip and I could see clearly that if the lever even so much as brushed it, the money would fall down and it would be mine. But I didn't know how to work the machine right and if I was going to spend 5p all at one time I needed help; I had to get Daddy over there immediately before somebody else could get to it.

"Daddy, Daddy, come over here right away, I'm about to win a whole bunch of money."

"I'll be over in a little bit, I can't leave this machine here it's about to pay out any second. . . ."

"But Daddy, you don't understand, there's a ten-pound note at the very edge of the cliff and if somebody else drops a coin in they're going to get it."

"Just give me a minute. . . ."

"But Daddy, it'll be gone by then."

"I can't walk away from this machine just yet, it's about to pay."

"Daddy, you have to come now quick before somebody else gets this money. Just come over here quickly and show me how to work it. . . ."

"All right, all right, where is it, quickly?"

A man steps up to Daddy's machine before we can even step away, and he drops a 5p coin into the slot and pulls the handle of the one-armed bandit. Daddy pauses to watch as the tumblers drop into place, cherry, cherry, cherry, cherry . . . *ching ching ching ching ching ching ching*. . . . I feel Daddy's hand tighten on mine as the machine explodes into a celebration of bells and whistles and flashing lights. He looks down at me for a moment and I don't recognize him. His lips move to say something but he stops himself, and I watch as he locks his lips in a tight grimace to stop the utterance that almost leaps past his teeth. I watch him swallow the words in a hard lump that I can clearly see as it passes down his throat and into his heart. The man at the machine is scooping out armfuls of coins into cups, he's laughing in ecstatic disbelief as they spill onto the floor behind us and a small crowd gathers 'round to marvel at his success as we turn to walk away.

"Where is this machine you wanted me to see?"

But I don't want him to see the other machine anymore. I want to go back instead to when he was at his own machine and I want to leave him there and see him drop that last 5p coin into the slot and get all that money that should have really been his. But I have to show him my machine now because he has given up so much to come with me, and I can tell by the way he looks at my machine when he sees it that I have been foolishly misled by the trickery of it. I know immediately when I see his expression that the bundle of cash is not going anywhere, but he drops a coin in anyway to let me see how it works and I watch as the little lever brushes the bundle of cash as it sits there right on the very lip of the drop-off like a solid concrete block.

I don't want to go to the beach to build sandcastles and gather shells after that. I don't want a fat stick of Bundoran rock candy to suck on all the way home. I just want to go home. I have a gut-wrenching feeling that something has been lost, not just here with my father in the arcade, but that something more profound has been misplaced. I understand now for the first time that Bundoran is not the magical kingdom that I always imagined it to be. I can finally grasp that the entire enterprise is an illusion, a vast circus sideshow full of con men and tricksters preying on the weaknesses of men women and children alike. It is shame that I have seen in my father's face, shame for not being able to hide the disappointment that the gamble hadn't paid off and that I had borne witness to his defeat. He put his hand on my shoulder and led me out toward the bright sunlight in the open door. I had been roused from the dream of my childhood. There never were any tooth fairies, I could see that clearly now, and Santa Claus couldn't possibly know that I lived in a small council house up on the Altamuskin Road, and Dr. Doolittle could no more converse with the animals than I ever would. I was nearly ten years old; a thin veneer of innocence slipped to the floor of the arcade as the sun touched our faces and the world was not nearly as mysterious as it once was.

A Hawk over a
Freshly Cut Field

Baldy had nose hair you could see from the back of the classroom and long rusty fingers from chain-smoking Gallagher
Greens all day long. He had this knack for smoking them all
the way down to the butt without ever dusting the ash. He'd
suck each and every one past the line of the filter, pacing back
and forth across the room waving at maps and diagrams of
the planets and I'd pass the hours just watching that ash, just
praying for it to fall. I wanted some small thing to break in his
life, anything as retribution for the horror he instilled in me
as a boy. For some reason he had singled me out as an enemy.
Something about me enraged him. Perhaps I was incapable of
obscuring my hatred of him in my eyes. I can't be a hundred
percent sure, but there was definitely something that clicked
in him when our eyes met that was incendiary, so I learned to
avoid eye contact with him at all costs.

"And this up here is Canada," he was shouting one particular summer's day, rapping the map against the blackboard with his knuckles. "Who can tell us something about Canada?" And the ash was drooping until I thought, There is no way in the world he will make it back to the ashtray this time, there is just no way. It's impossible. And then he lifted it again to his lips with not a worry in the world. *Please fall. Please fall. Just this once. Please God let it fall.*

"You. Hackett. Stand up and tell us something about Canada." And it's only hanging by a thread now. It's already begun to crack. Yes, I can see it. It will definitely fall. It's too top heavy. There's absolutely no saving it now. It's doomed. The ashtray is all the way across the room. He'll never make it. But he lifts it one more time to his lips and inhales like this is the last pull of cigarette smoke he will ever breathe.

"It's big, sir," Hackett mumbles. Baldy dips the cigarette back between his lips and draws just as hard again. I don't understand it, a double drag and it's still there. It's unnatural.

"What else, Hackett?" He's moving back toward the ashtray, but he's a long way off. The motion is bound to kill it. Not even the Virgin Mary and all the saints in heaven could save it now.

"It's big and it's green, sir," Hackett blurts suddenly, and Baldy freezes in his tracks to stare at him in amazement. He raises the cigarette to his lips for one more drag, unable to resist the urge to punctuate Hackett's supreme ignorance with a long, silent stare. The ash is toppling as he bites down on the filter, draining the last breath of smoke from its scorched bones.

"What makes you say it's green, Hackett?" He's moving

the last six feet toward the ashtray in a single motion, extending his right arm as he moves so that the ash is forced through the air in a smooth arc all the way into the ashtray, and he'd done it again. The whole damn thing was in the ashtray. It's a miracle. It's an absolute miracle every single time.

"Come on, Hackett, what makes you say it's green?" Baldy says, lighting another smoke.

"I can see it on the map, sir." My heart was sinking for Hackett. I knew what was coming next. Hackett and I were his favorites. He took pleasure in humiliating us in front of the class.

"You can see it on the map. So because Canada is green on the map, it must be green in real life. Brilliant. That's brilliant, Hackett. Isn't that brilliant, boys and girls?" Only two of the new boys and girls laughed. But even they stopped short when they realized that no one else in the class made a sound. The new students didn't understand yet that their laughter was what Baldy had been looking for. He wanted Hackett to be humiliated by his classmates. The rest of us knew. We had been through this routine before. There was a long silence. The girl's awkward cut-off laugh had made it sound like the silence was a planned classroom conspiracy that we had cooked up to turn the tables on Baldy. I knew how he was thinking. I'd spent two years sitting in that classroom for seven hours a day, five days a week. He was furious. He was about to show these new students how things worked under his command. He was going to show them that it was he who was in charge of this little congregation. I could see it in his face, the way his jaw muscles started clenching. *Don't look at him.* My hands flat on the sun-warmed surface of the desk. Head slightly bowed. *Don't move a muscle.* He would be looking for anything from me, the slightest twitch to rope me in. I was his whipping post. I was the one he would turn to, to straighten out this whole uncomfortable little situation.

I could sense him moving across the front of the room, looking, searching, for something, anything from me. *Don't look up. Don't even breathe.* My pencil. It's rolling toward the edge of the desk. I have to catch it. If I catch it, he'll have me. If I don't catch it, he'll have me. I catch it, and in that same instant I look up and meet his eyes. He has me in his sights.

"What are you looking at, Broderick?" This was how it always began. "Is there something funny you'd like to share with the class? Are you sneering at me, boy?" he said, racing the cigarette into and out of his mouth in short, sharp jabs.

"No sir. I'm not, sir." I tried to relax my face to look as neutral as possible, to clear my eyes of any hint of the hatred I felt for him, even though I knew it was hopeless. *Relax. Relax. Relax.*

"What did you say, Broderick? What did you say?" It was all over. It had to be me. It would have been too obvious to pick on Hackett. The new students were about to get a lesson in obedience. He was storming toward my desk.

"Nothing, sir. I didn't say anything. I mean, I didn't do any–"

"I'll teach you not to sneer at me." He was almost frothing at the mouth now. I said nothing more. I had played this game with him before. It was his game. His rules. I had already lost. That was the game. Time would make it all over soon. Soon. Soon. Soon. The cigarette fell from his mouth as he swung his open hand. I had never seen that happen before. *Slap.* He hit me on the left side of my face with full force, knocking me off my chair onto the floor. Now he had everybody's full attention. Silence. Wooden chair legs on the vinyl tile floor. I tried to stand up, but he slapped me before I could make it to my feet. "I'll teach you. How dare you." He was yelling now. I tried to stand but met the force of his hand again about halfway up. This time my chair and my table went over with me. My schoolbag burst open and all my books and pencils flew out onto the floor. I tried to stand again. He had never gone this far before. He was going to make it crystal clear this time. He was the boss. He was the boss. I bent over, picked up my schoolbag, and began gathering my books and pencils. He was seething next to me. I knew he wanted me to cry. He wanted me to at least make some sort of noise when he slapped me, some acknowledgment of his power over me. I reached for a pencil sharpener that had fallen by his feet. He snatched the schoolbag from my hand and flung it in the air, smashing it off the high ceiling, spraying the other students with my books and pencils. He was standing directly in front of me now. I caught his eye and he slapped me again. This time I didn't flinch. I felt nothing. In the center there is a silence. He raised his hand again and it hung there high in the air above his shoulder for a moment wavering like a hawk over a freshly cut field. He swung again, the hand whistling down through the still air like a scythe. I held my eyes fixed on his and then everything went black.

Vampiro

*Good evening. I am Gordon Honeycombe and this is the
six o'clock news.*

*The eleven loyalists known as the Shankill Butchers
were sentenced to life in prison this afternoon for the kid-
napping, torture, and murder of nineteen Catholics in
the Belfast area.*

Daddy, how did they torture them?

They hung them on a meat hook and took a knife to
them and skinned them alive.

Machil!! Never mind how they died. Is that
homework of yours done yet?

But . . .

Don't but me. . . . I haven't seen a schoolbook opened around this house all evening.

But Mammy, I just wanted to know how he did it, that's all.

They're a bunch of bloody animals, that's how they done it, and may they burn in the deepest fires of hell for their actions, God forgive me, and then yis wonder why I don't let yis go out runnin' the roads on yer own. Go on now, I don't want to hear another word about the Shankill Butchers in this house and that's that.

But . . .

Did ye hear yer mother speakin' to ye? Go and get your schoolbooks out before I have to get up out of this chair. . . .

Fergal Kelly was the boy with the red hair and the pale freckled skin who played the organ for the choir at Dunmoyle Chapel. He was the son of Dan Kelly, the wizened old caretaker and gravedigger at Dunmoyle. His mother was among the coven of witches who sat draped in black shawls in the pews to the rear of the church seven mornings a week, though I couldn't have told you which one she was as I don't recall ever having seen her face. Fergal was well known for his dramatic over-the-top Liberace-esque pounding of the keyboard and his three-tiered vocal harmonic renditions of the Sunday hymns.

It didn't take very much to stand out in a small tight-knit community like ours, but Fergal seemed hell bent on being the boy nobody would forget. Many were amused by his antics, some were appalled, everybody noticed. By the time I joined the choir when I was about eleven years old he was already something of a legend. And even though he was about six years older, he and I became fast friends right away.

Fergal also had his own little painting business up and running and he always seemed to have a backlog of local houses to paint during the summer holidays. This was something of a mystery to me because he was so meticulous and so slow at his work that it was obvious he would never catch up to his workload. There were other local painting contractors who could have painted the houses in a fraction of the time for what would amount to basically the same price, but still people remained loyal to Fergal. It was as if they were giving him the work out of some unspoken obligation that I could never quite put my finger on. Every year the job offers continued to flood in, and if a neighbor had to wait an extra year to retain Fergal's services, well, then they just waited and let the chipped paint curl for another winter.

Not long after I started singing in the choir he was taking me along to paint with him. Even though I was only eleven, I already had some experience helping my father out with the painting of our own house, so I had some idea how to use a paintbrush. We weren't going to win any productivity awards but the local housewives seemed to be happy enough to keep us around to drink tea with them three or four times a day. Maybe that was the real service we supplied to many a lonely farmer's wife: a couple of good-natured boys to keep them company for a while during the long days. We certainly knew how to keep them entertained.

Neither of us had any transportation, so we had to rely on the generosity of strangers to drive us to and from work and to and from the local towns for painting supplies. It always amazed me the lengths people were willing to go to for the privilege of retaining the services of our little enterprise.

"Why don't you buy yourself a bicycle so you can get to work by yourself?" I asked Fergal, feeling guilty one day as we waited for a local farmer to quit what he was doing so he could drive us to Sixmilecross for a quart of paint thinner.

"Are you serious?" he replied, incredulous at the mere suggestion, his eyes wide in disbelief that I would even consider such a demeaning mode of transportation for someone as great as him. "The Vampiro on a bicycle? You must be joking."

"It's faster than walking."

"The Vampiro doesn't ride bicycles."

Everybody, including Fergal himself, called him the Vamp or Vampiro because most of his teeth had mysteriously fallen out when he was very young and as a teenager he had been fitted with a row of false teeth that, when removed, revealed his two eyeteeth, or vampire fangs, which he could fold effectively over his bottom lip to terrify little children with whenever necessary.

Our painting empire consisted of two worn paintbrushes, one roller arm, and a tray, and when we needed a ladder the Vampiro just borrowed one. Fergal got whatever Fergal asked for. When I suggested on another occasion that we just walk to Sixmilecross to the hardware store, he cupped his hands over his face so he wouldn't launch his false teeth at me when he burst out laughing.

"You must be joking," he roared. "*Moi!* Le Vampiro! Walk!"

"Aye, why not?"

"The Vampiro does not walk to Sixmilecross, my dear child, the Vampiro has someone drive him to Sixmilecross."

So we never had to walk anywhere. Fergal would simply call someone to come take him to Sixmilecross, or even Omagh, fifteen miles away, and they would come.

Fear of being judged or singled out as different kept most everyone in our small community bound by the chains of conformity, but not Fergal. Fergal thrived in his individuality; there was quite simply no one in a twenty-mile radius, or possibly in the whole world, quite like him. And I, having been raised by a mother whose sole purpose in life, it seemed, was to keep our family well within the confines of social conventionality, was drawn to Fergal like a bee to a honeypot. I saw something courageous in his uniqueness, but it wasn't just that; it became apparent to me early on that Fergal was being allowed to be different. For some reason, the entire community had granted Fergal some mysterious dispensation; even my mother found humor in his outrageousness. Fergal was somehow immune from the bonds that defined the rest of us, so just being with him awarded me with my own small window of spontaneity.

To be fair, he was also a consummate perfectionist when it came to his painting. There were no shortcuts allowed. Every square inch of woodwork would have to be primed and sanded and primed and sanded again until it was like glass. If he wasn't satisfied with the finished product, he didn't try to get by; we painted it again. Even if it meant losing money, we painted it again. Fergal did not care about making money. Customers often tried to convince him that everything had been completed to their satisfaction:

"We're very happy with the job you've done, Fergal, it's just lovely."

"It's not lovely, it needs another coat."

"No, really, Fergal, we love it. You lads have done a grand job."

"No, it is not grand, it's atrocious is what it is. I'll just have to paint it again."

"Ach now, it'll do the finest, don't be worryin' your head about it. What do I owe you?"

"You don't owe me a penny. I won't take one penny for it until it's done properly."

"But it's beautiful, we're very happy with it."

"It's disgusting, it makes me want to vomit, it just won't do."

"Come on now, Fergal, it's great. Just leave it alone now for godsake."

"The Vampiro will paint it again at no extra charge."

"Now, Fergal, you really don't need to. It's not necessary."

"It is necessary. It is absolutely necessary and I will paint it if I have to sneak over here when you are sleeping and paint it in the dark, and that's the end of it."

"Would ye get a way outta that. Sure isn't the job done?"

"The job will be done when the Vampiro says it's done and not one second before. End of discussion."

Fergal didn't smoke cigarettes, and he didn't go to the discos to get girls. Instead he spent all his spare time practicing his guitar or playing piano or helping his dad clean the chapel and mow the lawns and weed the graves.

He knew more about music than any of the boys I'd ever met. I only knew about the music my father had in his record collection and some other stuff like David Bowie and T. Rex that we listened to on Radio Luxembourg late at night when we were supposed to be sleeping.

"Amateurs," Fergal declared, dismissing them with a wave of his hand.

"Even the Beatles?"

"Please, don't insult my intelligence."

"You have to admit Van Morrison is great."

"I will admit nothing of the kind; the man sounds like a sick cow chewing on bagpipes."

"Gabriel McCann says that Van the Man is the greatest singer that's ever lived."

"How could Gabriel McCann possibly know better than the Vampiro. Tell Gabriel McCann I said he should stick to catching rabbits and leave the music to me. Leo Sayer, now, there's a beautiful voice. . . ." And with that the Vampiro leapt from his stepladder and gripping the handle of his paintbrush in his hand as a microphone he broke into a deeply passionate rendition of Sayer's big hit of the day, "When I Need You."

He danced and spun in pirouettes down the driveway, continuing at full volume with his face angled toward the sky, even after old Packie Tierney had stepped out the front door of his house to see what all the commotion was about, and stood there alongside me grinning from ear to ear at the impromptu performance unfolding on his front lawn. For the finale, Fergal was on his knees in the damp grass, his face creased with emotion by the conclusion of the song, and Packie and I applauded and cheered him thoroughly.

"He's as mad as a brush," Packie said to no one in particular, shaking his head and continuing to clap as Fergal rose to his feet to bow proudly in our direction.

It didn't matter to Fergal that knowing every single word of a Leo Sayer love song might not be considered the most valuable talent a boy could possess in the very heart of rebel country, County Tyrone. But Fergal was one of the few lads in our area who had made the decision early on to remain neutral when it came to issues regarding the war; he considered himself to be a man of refined, unbiased taste. He had little time for the boys who insisted on listening solely to nationalistic music from bands such as the Wolfe Tones, the Clancy Brothers, or the Dubliners.

"They think they're hard men, but they're not."

"Some of it's good music," I argued.

"It is good music, if you're talking about its effectiveness as a torture technique."

I didn't dare admit to Fergal that I really liked to listen to the Wolfe Tones too, and that a big part of me wanted to be associated with the hard men of Altamuskin. I admired his individuality, but as I got a little bit older and I began to understand a little more about the war that we were engaged in, I was secretly torn by the desire to be inducted into the ranks of that other swathe of our community also, even though at eleven I was still much too young to be considered a worthy prospect as a soldier.

It was obvious that there were certain families in our community who seemed to garner more respect than the rest. They were families known to all to be very much involved in actively fighting the English. They were considered staunch Provo families, short for Provisional Irish Republican Army families. The boys, older teens, or men in those families always seemed to be better off financially. They drove nicer cars than other boys in their age group, and they carried themselves with a certain air of invincibility that the rest lacked. They always seemed to be employed in the few cool jobs available to a Catholic lad in the North of Ireland, jobs like bartending or working as bouncers in the local Catholic bars and clubs. And even those among them who were not blessed physically with movie-star looks still seemed to manage to be in the company of the most attractive girls around. There was something undeniably radiant about them, something dangerous and unknowable. I was young and couldn't possibly comprehend all the mechanics of it at the time, as so much of it went unspoken, but it was still obvious that they were the hard men in our midst. I saw them on the roads and in the town and at Mass every Sunday in Dunmoyle and I heard the whispers the same as everyone else did. They were the lads and men who were out there with balaclavas and rifles while the rest of us slept, putting their lives on the line in daring attacks against the might of the British Empire, and not one of them owned a Leo Sayer album, I was almost certain of that.

> *Good evening. My name is Gordon Honeycombe and this is the six o'clock news.*
> *A school bus driver was shot and killed this morning by the Provisional IRA outside of Pomeroy in County Tyrone.*

Why did the IRA shoot the bus driver?

Because he was a UDR man.

How come all the bus drivers and the policemen are Protestants?

Because the Brits keep all the best jobs for themselves and the Protestants.

Is that why the IRA shot him?

They probably shot him because he was a bad bastard.

Michael . . . that's enough. Never mind all that and eat your dinner. It's got nothing to do with you. Just

because he was a Proddy doesn't mean anybody has
a right to kill him. It's a mortal sin to kill no matter
what the cause. God rest his soul, he has family somewhere I'm sure. In the name of the father and of the
son and of the holy ghost amen.

Surprisingly my mother let me stay over at Fergal's for a night
shortly after we started working together. It was an exciting
event to stay over at a friend's house, and a luxury that I had
been granted only two or three times before in my short life.

That Saturday afternoon I walked the two miles to Dunmoyle Chapel to meet Fergal, and when I approached the big
iron gates to enter the chapel grounds from the road, I could
already hear his voice booming from within the cavernous interior. He was upstairs in the gallery playing the organ singing
Cliff Richard's "Devil Woman" at the top of his lungs to an audience of empty pews and stunned-looking statues. As I came
up the stairs and slipped into a seat nearby he noticed me and
with a great flourish he brought the song to a close but continued to play on as he stood to the microphone as if to address a
large, adoring crowd.

"Thank you very much, thank you very much," he mum-
bled in a low baritone; his best Elvis impersonation, spinning
colorful little riffs on the keyboard as he spoke. "This next
song is for an old friend of mine. Well, when I say old, he's ten,
OK, he's eleven years old already, a fine young lad from Altamuskin by the name of Mr. Colin Broderick—a great painter,
and a dear, dear friend of mine from way back, almost six, no,

maybe seven, is it seven weeks now? This is a little song I like to call 'Suspicious Minds.'" And with that, Fergal filled the rafters with a thunderous rendition of the King's greatest hit, knowing it was one of my favorite songs of all time.

When he was done, we strolled off down the road, stopping at his aunt's house for a moment to say hello to his cousins who were out playing in the front yard. I went to school with his cousins and knew them well. Sinead came to the fence to show us a necklace of daisies that she'd just made and offered to make me one as well, but her mother, Fergal's aunt, came to the front door just then and called her for dinner and seeing Fergal and me there by the fence, she asked if we'd like to join them. Much to my disappointment Fergal told her that we didn't have time. When her mother called her again, Sinead quickly lifted the daisy necklace from about her own neck and held it toward me.

"Here, you can take mine," she said, and I dipped my head toward her so that she could slip it past my ears. She smiled, seeing it there about my neck, and then she turned and skipped up the garden to her mother.

"I think somebody has a little crush on my cousin," Fergal said as we continued on our walk and I fought not to reveal the truth of his guess in a blush. He was right, of course. Sinead was prettier than most of the girls at our school and if I had not already been betrothed to marry Margot Kelly, Fergal's young cousin would have made a fine wife.

. . .

Fergal's house was down the end of a long, narrow lane with a high bank on either side. The bushes along the lane were so perfectly pruned that they looked like something out of a book of fairy tales. The drooped heads of foxtrots peeked out of the thick green wall with the humility of supplicants. The lane opened onto a graveled yard, revealing a dazzlingly white little cottage opposite a red-roofed turf shed. The turf in the shed was stacked along the open front wall in such a meticulous fashion that I might easily have believed it to be the work of some magical team of elves. The thick rosebushes at either end of the cottage were bursting at the seams with a rich explosion of reds and pinks, and the flower beds at the far end of the yard were awash with huddles of tulips in a near violent yellow. Primroses and moist blankets of purple lilac spilled against the mossy rocks that kept the whole reservoir of blossoms from bursting into the small street at our feet. Even the bees that buzzed from petal to petal feasting on the rich wells of nectar seemed to be infused with some otherworldly intoxicant. Was it any wonder my new friend seemed so special?

His elderly father was there, old Dan Kelly, rolling what appeared to be an empty wheelbarrow across the graveled yard, but he must not have noticed us because he did not acknowledge our presence in any way. He passed by not ten feet away and never broke his stride or turned his head to offer a nod of recognition.

Inside, the cottage itself was so dark that I couldn't see anything beyond the green half-door. So I remained outside alone in the bright sunlight while Fergal went on inside to see his mother. I felt no inclination to follow, as I had not been invited and something about the darkness and the hushed whispers that I heard from within imbued me with the sudden urge to turn again and head back out the lane for home.

When he surfaced again from the house Fergal wore a somber, unfamiliar expression on his face, and even though he did still manage to curl the corners of his mouth into a tight smile to greet me, it was clear to me that there was pain in it.

"Mammy's not feeling well, she has a headache, so we're just going to stay up the field with her sister," he said, and I did not inquire further because we were raised in the North of Ireland to understand that it was not polite to be nosy about other people's affairs. If it was something he needed me to know, he would tell me in good time.

"Your mum and dad are very holy people," I said, not knowing what else to say as we crossed up the field.

"I suppose they are."

"I see at least one of them up there at the chapel every single time I pass by or go in."

"Well, they do take care of the place."

"And they make a nice job of it too."

"I suppose they do."

"They must be the two holiest people in the whole of Dunmoyle."

"They could be worse things, the craturs."

"They could," I said, and let it go at that.

Fergal's aunt Lizzy lived in another tiny cottage down the end of the field, only Lizzy's house was not nearly as well kept as his own. The pebble-dashed exterior walls were a drab gray and the smell of manure from a nearby cowshed hung over the small house like a heavy smog.

Lizzy was sitting in silence at the small wooden table by the front window when we went in. She was a plump woman with a dour, unconcerned face and a thick crop of chin hair clearly visible in the late-evening light that leaked through the smoky lace curtain. She didn't seem to care whether we were there or not.

It was obvious to me by the way Fergal slumped into the armchair in the corner and reached his arm around to pick up the guitar from where it had been propped against a nearby wall that he in fact spent most of his time there in that tiny cottage and not with his parents at the other end of the field.

Lizzy rose from the table almost immediately and dutifully set about boiling water for a late tea. I watched with great concern as Fergal strummed and hummed away over in the corner while Lizzy buttered and jammed the slices of bread, horrified at the thought that I might wind up picking one of her gray chin hairs from my tongue in mid munch. She took a tin box of Kimberley Mikado biscuits off the shelf over the sink and counted out nine cookies onto a saucer. If she were eating with us, that was three cookies apiece. I knew then that I would have to force myself through the beard-hair jam sandwich come hell or high-water if I wanted to savor one of those delectable treats. Growing up in a house of six children, delicacies such as Kimberley Mikados were rare and not to be taken lightly. Fergal hardly spoke a word the entire time.

When the dishes were cleaned and put away, Lizzy loaned me a set of her rosary beads and each of us got on our knees to recite the entire five decades of the rosary, all fifty Hail Marys, five Our Fathers, and Glory Bes and whatever other original little twist she had added at the end of it to make it hers; it was maybe seventy-five or eighty prayers in all, just to prepare our souls for a night's sleep. We Catholics did not do prayer by half.

By the time we crawled up the stairs to the small attic space by candlelight I was exhausted. Fergal undressed quietly and slipped into the bed and whispered good night to me as he turned away to face the wall. I pulled my sweater off over my head, sending a rain of broken daisies to the attic floor. I had forgotten that the chain was still around my neck and felt a little heartbroken at having destroyed such a beautiful gift. I extinguished the candle and climbed into the bed and felt myself begin to drift off into a dark, uncomfortable sleep almost immediately, confused by the great chasm of grief that seemed to have taken up space in the bed between me and Fergal, but my mind was too young to comprehend anything but the ache that it caused me just then, and I slept.

Bury It Deep

Once a year during our summer break my brothers and I would go stay with my father's parents, Johnny and Mary Broderick, on their small farm in a town land called Redergan, just outside of Beragh. Those vacations remain particularly memorable for me for their sheer devotion to simplicity. My grandparents lived in a small white stone cottage with no electricity or running water. Their lives were built on a series of basic daily survival rituals—fetching water, tending the animals, preparing the meals—rituals that had been handed down through the generations, representing one of the last links we had as boys to the true elements at the heart of our Irish heritage: survival, faith, simplicity, perseverance, and death.

My dad's father, my granda, was an easygoing man. He had a full head of silvery hair, yellowed from the constant cloud of smoke that enveloped him wherever he went. Granda was a three- to four-pack-a-day man. If he took a breath, it was through a cigarette filter. We woke every morning in the damp old cottage to the sound of his retching and coughing as his feet hit the stone floor at first light and he reached for the pack to get the first one into his mouth to settle his chest.

I loved being away from home. Granny treated us to full-blown adult-sized breakfasts every morning: fried eggs, bacon, sausage, and baked beans with thick slices of fried bread. She would take our teacups and squint into them through her glasses and make random predictions based on the way our tea leaves had settled, much as Sheila had done with my mother and her sisters. "You're going to have a very pleasant day," she'd say. Or, "I see big changes in the near future." I'd ask her to show me in the leaves where it said this or that, but she'd tell me, "It's not in the leaves but in the way you look at them."

Nobody then or since made breakfast like my granny. Maybe it had something to do with the way she let the lard sit uncovered in that big old black frying pan of hers, only empty-ing it once in a while when the fat threatened to spill over onto the cooker flame. Whatever it was that she did, I have never seen such witchery in eggs.

Granda taught us how to milk a cow, teaching us the im-portance of talking to the cow first to settle her nerves so that she wouldn't draw out and break your leg with a kick as you crossed behind her. He had a short wooden stool that he used to sit next to her as he leaned his shoulder against her bulg-ing belly. He would lay his head against her hide and talk to her as he milked, and she would stand silently, her tail swish-ing playfully from side to side, chewing her cud with an air of contented satisfaction until I would try to fool her by reaching in and slipping my small, weak hands onto her teats to try to replicate Granda's rhythmic strokes. She would turn her big eye on me and snort and shuffle her hooves on the stone floor reluctantly bracing herself for my inexperienced touch, and soon Granda would have to step in again to settle her and slap her on the big shoulder of her front leg and say, "Hup, hup, easy girl, it's all right now. . . ."

In the evenings we sat around the turf fire and listened to the afternoon news on Granda's battery-powered transistor radio and as the daylight dimmed, the house was lit with paraffin lamps that filled the small living room with a thick, gassy smell that fused with the turf fire and the smoke from Granda's cigarettes, giving the room a sort of hazy, ethereal perfume of sleep.

Before bedtime we would kneel on the hard cement floor and Granny would lead us through all five decades of the rosary. The slow, monotonous cadence of her voice lulling me off into a sleep that she would interrupt by tossing a shoe at the back of my head. Then came the litany of saints: "Saint Francis pray for ussssss, Saint Brigid pray for ussssss." And I would bury my head in the seat cushion so that I wouldn't catch my brother flashing me a "yikes" face or rolling his eyes at the way our granny stretched the final *s*. "Saint Dymphna pray for ussssss." But I would have to look, and his face would be there waiting for me when I did, and we would explode with laughter until we were scolded into an unbearable ache of suppressed joy.

One day, Granny and Granda's dog, Judy, lay down in a

heap on the hay-shed floor and my brother Brendan and I watched in amazement as she popped out six small pups one after another. She licked them off and blindly they wormed their way into a clumsy line down along her chest to feed. We ran to tell Granda, who was having his afternoon nap with his Wellingtons off and his socked feet steaming against the warm stove door.

"Granda, Granda, the dog had pups. There's six of them."

"Six of them," he said rubbing his eyes. "They'll have to go."

"Where will they go?" Brendan asked.

"Into a bag."

"What bag?" I asked.

"Just stay away from about them and I'll take care of them when I come out later."

"Why can't we do it?" I asked feeling brave and curious. We grew up in the country so I knew already that pups and kittens were drowned because you couldn't keep them all. It was something the parents did after the children had fallen asleep. I wasn't sure how it worked, but I was ready to give it a try.

"Go on outside and play, you're too young."

"We can do it. I'm eleven now. I'll be going to St. Ciaran's after the holidays," I said.

He eyed us for a moment, lifting his foot to rub his toes. "Are you sure you know how to do it?"

"We put them in a bag and drown them," I said.

"Make sure Judy's locked in the shed before you put them in the rain barrel. She could go for ye if you don't. And then take them away down the bottom of the garden and bury them.

Dig it deep, now. I don't want her digging them up again, so if you're going to do it, do it right. Bury them deep."

We went out and lifted the six small pups into a cardboard box. Judy was too tired to put up much of a fight when we took them out of the shed and locked her in. She got up and followed us, whining and sticking her paw out from underneath the old door.

We loaded the pups into a cloth sack and I lowered it into the barrel of rainwater by the barn door.

"I want to hold them too," Brendan said after a moment, and I let him, feeling a sudden sickness wash over me at the way they were wrestling around inside the bag. He took the bag and held it for a moment, but he didn't last long. Judy started barking and whining a long, painful howl from behind the shed door. Brendan looked at me, and I knew by his face that I would have to finish this. I had said we could do it. I reached my hand in past his into the sharp chill of the water and I took the bag from him. He didn't ask to hold it again. It was a long time before the struggling stopped.

When I lifted the bag from the water they were still, lumped together now in the bottom of the sack like a solid boneless mass.

We took them into the corner of the field past the bottom of the garden and we set them down on the ditch and took turns digging. The ground was hard and full of stones, and a long time later we had only dug a short way.

"That's probably good enough," I said, enthusiastic to get them into the hole and walk away from them as quickly as possible.

"You think it's deep enough?"

"It'll do."

I laid the bag into the hole and we began to shove the dirt over the top of it. That's when we heard the first faint squeal from under the loose earth.

"Did you hear that?" Brendan asked, his face frozen and white. I was silent for a moment listening but heard nothing more. We continued to add more dirt and it came again: a low cry and then another and another and the clay over the bag began to move.

"How can they still be alive? Didn't you make sure they were dead?"

"They were dead," I said. "You saw it."

"How are they alive again?"

"I don't know."

I heard Granny's voice in the distance calling us up for our dinner. There was no time to take them out again and start all over. Granda would see us now and know that we didn't do it right. I jumped into the hole on top of the clay and started stomping it down with my heel as tight as I could. The squeals came again, and louder. I jumped and jumped to make them stop.

When we were done, Brendan suggested we bless ourselves and say a prayer. We stood for a moment staring at the small mound of fresh clay. Then I hung the spade over my shoulder and we made our way back through the potato drills in the garden. Judy barking wildly in the barn. Granny's dark silhouette ahead of us in the small cottage door.

We lose our childhoods by degrees. Inch by inch, time and

circumstance steal the last of our innocence. Some of it will fall away unnoticed; some it will be ripped forcefully from our fingers, other morsels of it we will bury in shallow graves, until only the shadow of youth exists, drifting in our wake like an abandoned ghost.

First Year

As was customary, I started St. Ciaran's High School when I was eleven. I had my first school uniform: charcoal pants, gray shirt, gray V-neck sweater, and a blue-and-gray striped tie. No more sawed-off wellies, homemade trousers, or second-hand shirts for me. Others complained that it wasn't colorful enough, that it was too drab, too depressing, but the uniform liberated me. I felt a sudden sense of comfort from the moment I stepped onto the school bus on that very first morning amid a sea of gray; perhaps the color so closely resembled my own mood that I felt a sense of ease in it, camouflaged from the world.

Out the window of the bus the entire world looked gray. The early morning mist and drizzle had transformed the landscape into a canvas of shadows and ghosts. Trees and fields assumed the deathly hue of a corpse, a charcoal crow sat on a fence, the smoke from a chimney drifted over a slate roof, faded lace curtains hung in the window of a pebble-dashed bungalow, a damp sheep huddled against a rock, an old woman shuffled toward the chapel in a shawl, the hazy breath of a cow hung in the air like an apparition, a farmer in Wellingtons leaned against a corrugated tin shed smoking a pipe, a pillow of steam sat over a concrete slurry tank. In this muted early light not even the grass could retain its true splendor; in the North even the green is gray.

On that first morning on the bus I realized I was also going to have an opportunity to get to know some of the older, harder lads from our community a little better. There were many of them, including cousins of mine who my mother had not allowed me to play with all through primary school because of their dirty mouths and quarrelsome reputations. I was almost afraid to talk to most of them because of all the bad, evil things they might do to me. I sat quietly in my seat about halfway up the bus with my new brown leather schoolbag in my lap, not bothering anybody. But before we got even as far as the White Bridge, the biggest boy on the bus, a boy called Aidan Lafferty who I only knew from seeing at Mass on Sundays, started in on my hair.

"Did your mammy comb your hair for you this morning?"

"No, I combed it myself."

"It's just lovely, it's very neat; do you mind if I touch it?"

But before he could toss it all over the place like he'd already done to Mick McCann's a few moments earlier, my cousin Paul, one of the really bad ones I wasn't allowed to play with, stopped him in his tracks.

"Hey, Lafferty, that's a young cousin of mine you're messing with there."

"I was just going to play with his hair a little bit."

"Well, just go and play with somebody else's hair."

"All right then, I will."

And just like that, I had bus protection. Nobody was allowed to mess with me because I was Paul McCann's cousin. But I was still wary of Paul McCann because I figured he must have been capable of some pretty evil stuff if my mother had never allowed me to be his friend before now. I decided he was probably just setting me up to get me really good later on. I was going to watch out for everybody, especially him.

The first day of school at St. Ciaran's was a day of utter chaos. From the second we stepped off the bus, the entire mass of gray seemed to function like some well-oiled military machine. Antlike gray trails split off from the sea of buses in every direction. As a first-year student there were many new rules I had to follow; I just had no idea what they were. The school was huge compared to the one I just left in Altamuskin, and I felt intimidated by the hundreds of strange faces I met as I tried to navigate my way around the long, room-lined corridors trying to keep up with my class schedule without looking like a complete imbecile.

No running in the hallways.

If you walk on the wrong side of the stairs, you will get yelled at.

If you don't have your tie knotted just right, you will get yelled at.

If you forget your tie, you may get the leather strap.

If you have your sleeves rolled up, you will get yelled at (and possibly strapped).

If you don't get in line fast enough when break is over, you will get yelled at. You may also get your ear clipped and possibly a good strapping with the leather. Or all three simultaneously.

If you laughed too loud while you were in line, you could get strapped, and possibly humiliated by being dragged to the front of the line and given a proper thrashing by hand.

If you farted really loud in the assembly hall and made a bunch of people laugh, like one of the older boys did on that very first morning, you could be sure Master McSorley, the headmaster, would stop right in the middle of the morning prayer and make you own up to doing it and you'd be off to his office in a flash for a really proper seeing-to.

The first day at St. Ciaran's I understood right away that Master McSorley was everywhere. He was around every corner you turned. He was standing next to you every time you even thought of saying a bad word. He was on the staircase when you forgot to walk on the right side. He was behind you in the hallway when you broke into a gallop. He was in the dinner hall when you talked too loud. He was standing in a window overlooking the schoolyard when anybody so much as spat on the ground.

When you arrived at St. Ciaran's for the first time all the children were herded into the gymnasium and sorted like cattle and divided into four different groups; A, B, C, or D. If you were a first-year student you were in 1A, 1B, 1C, or 1D. All the smartest first-year students were in the A class, then all the students who were not quite as smart but not really stupid either were in the B class, then all the troublemakers and the boys and girls who were not so bright were in the C class, and if you were in the D class you were a dunce, you were beyond repair or hope and nobody even bothered with you anymore, not even the teachers.

Right away you got the feeling that it was best to stay well away from the "D-classers" just in case somebody got the impression that you were stupid too. At least, that was how it all appeared on the first day at St. Ciaran's.

Being in the A class meant that somebody thought I was as smart as the smartest boys and girls at the school, which unnerved me because I didn't feel very smart. But my older brother Michael had already been at St. Ciaran's for a year and he was in the A class too and nobody had kicked him out yet. So he was in 2A and I was in 1A. And if you were really lucky and you passed all your tests you would stay in the A class for the next five years, 1A, 2A, 3A, 4A, 5A, and then boom, done, off into the world with no school to go to ever again for the rest of your life.

The only person I knew in my new class from our primary school was Margot Kelly, but once I saw all the other girls at St. Ciaran's, especially the older girls, I wasn't so sure that Margot and I would be getting married after all.

There was only one boy at St. Ciaran's who seemed to be immune from all the rules that the rest of us had to abide by, and that was my good friend Fergal Kelly, the Vampiro, who was in his last year at St. Ciaran's when I arrived. Being that he was somewhat of a genius he was also in an A class, although to be fair even at St. Ciaran's amid five hundred other students he was still very much in a class of his own.

I found him in the schoolyard on my first day making a group of students peal with laughter at his impression of one of the teachers. He moved freely from one group to another sparking laughter as he went. There didn't seem to be a single kid in the hundreds of boys gathered who didn't like him.

He would stop with a bunch of nervous first-year students and have them giggling and chatting up a storm in a matter of minutes before moving on to my cousin Paul's crew, the toughest boys at St. Ciaran's, who were down at the end of the yard by the corner of the dining-room building slipping cigarettes to one another behind cupped hands and he would have them in howls of laughter in just the same way. Because he was my friend, I was accepted by many in much the same way.

It became obvious to me very quickly that the very boys my mother was trying to keep me away from were the very boys I liked the most. In fact, it seemed that the scarier they had been portrayed the more endearing, warmhearted, protective, and genuine I found them to be.

It was an overwhelming first day. So many new faces, rules, names to remember. But it was overwhelming for another reason; it became apparent that first day that my new classmates were accustomed to a lot more freedom in their lives than I was. These boys in my class were my own age and they were already going to the youth club and the Friday-night discos in Ballygawley on a regular basis. They ribbed one another about the girls they liked and compared stories of the girls they had kissed already. I felt the first pang of inferiority as I listened to them talk and I laughed along as if I, too, were accustomed to a rich social life.

I thought of how my brothers and I were not even allowed to cross the fence to play football with our own neighbors, the Harley boys. These were boys our own age, whose garden bordered ours. Three boys we had grown up with who we had spent the first eleven years living right next door to, eleven years of talking to one another over a wire fence that separated their garden from ours, a wire fence that sat atop a three-foot block wall in our front yard.

We had stood on top of that wall facing one another for our entire childhoods, inventing new games of tossing a football back and forth to one another to compensate for the lack of a real game of football. We had stood on the wall to compare Christmas presents, and homework, whispered secrets, and even fought when we fell out from time to time–all with a three-foot wire fence to separate us. In all that time we had never been allowed to have them over to our garden or us to theirs. Eleven years with half a football team of young boys standing on top of a wall in the middle of the countryside surrounded by open green fields for miles in every direction and not one football match together in eleven years? It seemed ridiculous suddenly that I had accepted the limitations of my existence, of our mother's iron fist, so implicitly. There had never been an explanation, no matter how many times we begged our mother for permission to have them over or that we might cross to play with them.

A child will eventually accept anything; that is the nature of innocence and how it is so easily abused.

"The answer is no, and that's that."

At lunchtime I sat at a table with four of my new class-mates and listened to them talk about football matches that they played together in the afternoons, and about their nights out at the local youth club, and about a place they went to play pool in the evenings, and I realized I had nothing fun or excit-ing to add to the conversation. I decided to keep quiet about my life, to lie if I had to, until I understood more.

By the time the bus pulled up outside our little coun-cil house after my first day at secondary school, I had gotten my first little taste that my brothers and I were not like the other children our age. The door to the outside world had been cracked open just a hair. I had gotten my first glimpse of the freedoms other children took for granted. Everyone, it seemed, had more freedom than my brothers and me. But it was only the first glimmer of recognition, and I was still trying to con-vince myself that it probably wasn't as bad as it first appeared.

I felt a twinge of shame getting off the bus to come home and I didn't quite know why. I didn't want to be the boy getting off at this dumpy old council house, to parents who wouldn't let him do the things that other boys my age were doing. And with my shame came a wave of guilt. What a horrible son I was to think such things about my wonderful parents after all they had done for me. I was the most ungrateful boy in the whole world. I went inside, dropped my schoolbag in the hall, ran to my mother, threw my arms around her waist, and squeezed her with all my might.

My shame at having to get off the school bus at our old council house was short-lived. Mammy had just about had it with asking Daddy when we could move into the new house. After three years of work, Dad was still down there every night and all weekend toiling away. He had managed to build the house almost single-handedly. He would come home from his job in the afternoon, have dinner with us, watch the six o'clock news, and then disappear again just as quickly. There were years when it seemed we barely saw him at all. With six young children and a wife in a small cottage, perhaps I would have been tempted to prolong the work also. There certainly would have been little relaxation to be had amid all that chaos.

But he did sacrifice. Every penny he made was being poured into the house. No more summer holidays, no more days in Bundoran, no new records for his collection. All money was for the new house. Not that we had ever been wealthy, but poverty is tiresome stuff no matter how well you are accustomed to it.

But still, when we went to visit the house or help out we could forget all the sacrifice that had gone into it. It was exciting to imagine that one day we would live there, that this wonderful new house was going to be our home. There were four full-size bedrooms with built-in closets and radiators, two bathrooms tiled floor to ceiling, cornices and arches, a huge modern kitchen with a brand-new oil-burning stove, a washroom with a brand-new washer and dryer. There was wall-to-wall carpeting in the bedrooms, a garage, a big bay window in the living room, and a solid mahogany front door. The rooms had been painted, velvet drapes had been hung, a phone had been installed, and still we were living, all eight of us, in a damp shoebox with drafty windows just a stone's throw away up the Altamuskin Road.

Finally our mother could take it no more. She waited until after my father had gone to work one morning before announcing to us boys that we were going to spend the day moving. I was sent running up the road to get my uncle Matt with his tractor and trailer down as quickly as possible.

By the time Dad arrived home from work that afternoon, we had moved into our new house: the beds were made, our clothes were in our closets, the kitchenware was in its place, and his dinner was ready on the table when he came through the door. He had the look of a man who'd just reached into the refrigerator only to discover the last beer was gone. The party was over. But there was nothing he could do about it; we had moved in, and that was that.

Self-Education

Growing up with eight people under the same roof, the bathroom becomes the only place of refuge, and what a bathroom we now had in our new house, free of mold and ice on the inside of the window glass, free of arctic drafts and worn linoleum tile. Once I had that door closed and locked, I was alone. Alone to think, alone to read, alone to stand naked and examine the parts of myself that were beginning to arouse an overwhelming sense of sinful curiosity. I was no idiot; I was well aware that even my thoughts had the power to damn me to hell for all eternity but the urge to explore my manhood was becoming unbearable.

By the age of eleven it had become blatantly obvious that God had decided in all his wisdom to forgo the manly hood of pubic hair that would distinguish me as a man. He was punishing me for the sinful thing that I did with Stella Madden in the old house behind the youth club. I was sure of it. I was going to be bald forever. All the other boys I'd seen in the communal shower stall after physical education class already had a little something going on down there. One lad, Barry McCaffrey, was already sporting something between his legs that looked like a squirrel with a baby's arm hanging out of its mouth. Meanwhile, there I was without so much as a single whisker to display. This was a disaster.

As I lay soaking in the bathtub one Saturday night, shortly after we had moved into our new house, pondering this cruel injustice, I played with the new attachable shower head, marveling at the heady tingling the tiny jets of water produced against my skin. If only I had hair down there I could ask Stella to do for me what I had been doing for her. But I was too embarrassed. What if she saw I was just a baby down there? She might laugh. It would kill me.

Stella was older than me by about five years. She was aloof and guarded. She sat near the front of the bus away from the rest of us rabble. She stayed to herself, her head buried in a book or dreamily staring off out of the window. She gave the impression that she was very much out of place on the bus with all of us children. We, in turn, were respectful of her unspoken appeal that we leave her undisturbed. Even the older boys on the school bus were careful to whisper their observances of her perfectly brushed hair and her pointy little breasts behind cupped hands. She didn't have a boyfriend or seem to care for one. She was commonly referred to as Snow White for the pure untouchable presence she projected, but I knew differently, although she had made me promise never to tell a soul.

It had started just a few months earlier after the youth club let out one night, when we were all milling around in the dark before heading off on the half-mile walk home down the Alta-muskin Road. She had come up next to me and whispered in my ear, "Give me your hand," and she had taken it in her own and guided it up under her skirt. It was dark out and although there were others around us yelling and leaping on one another's backs it would have been impossible to see what was going on between us. She pressed the tips of my fingers up against the soft fabric of her underwear and she held it there as she rode back and forth with little thrusts upon my hand. I could feel her breath close to my cheek and the warm flush of heat between her legs. I let my hand go limp so she could manipulate the tips of my fingers with hers. She had chosen me above everyone else and I was not going to blow it by making a single move or a sound that would scare her away. The thrusts came faster and faster and she gripped my shoulder with her other hand as her breathing came in short deep gasps and then her whole body shuddered and she let out a tiny moan that went unnoticed in the din that surrounded us in the parking lot. For all anybody could see she might as well have been leaning in to whisper something in my ear, and then she was done.

"Thank you," she whispered, taking my hand from underneath her skirt and giving me a quick peck on the cheek. "Promise you won't tell anybody."

"I won't."

"This will be our little secret."

"I'd never tell anybody."

"Good boy."

I had promised to keep the secret, even though I wasn't exactly sure what the secret was. But it was something special, that much I understood–something not to be taken lightly. It was adult in nature and I felt honored to have been chosen at all. I was not used to being chosen for anything. Even when we lined up to play football I was almost always one of the very last chosen for the team. The fact that someone as desirable and aloof as she had chosen me for such an intimate, adult affair thrilled me beyond belief.

She had approached me with the same request on a few occasions since then. And each time her pleasure seemed to intensify and each time I had said nothing. I had simply watched the rapturous expression on her face as she clenched my hand between her thighs and her cheeks would flush and a small skin of sweat would sheathe her upper lip.

The last time it had happened she had taken me into an old storage shed behind the hall one warm summer night. She stood with her back against the wall and unbuttoned her pants and let them slide down around her ankles so that I could see the crisp white patch of her underwear illuminated in the moonlight. She spread her legs and guided my hand up to cup her soft fleshy center, then she placed her hands on my shoulders and began to writhe, saying, "Rub it, harder, harder, right there . . ." as she stared at me, her eyes flickering, her breath coming in hurried gasps–quiet at first, then louder as she threw open her mouth and let out a series of painful groans as her grip on me tightened so hard I thought for sure she would puncture the skin on my shoulders with her fingernails, and still I did not wince as she shuddered and the tension on her face dissolved into a soft smile and she hurriedly grabbed her pants up, buttoned them, thanked me with a peck on the cheek, and ran off back toward the hall again.

The more I thought about it as I lay in the bathtub, the more excited I became. I continued playing with the showerhead, loving the dizzy buzzing that it seemed to ignite throughout my entire body. I couldn't understand what the hell was happening to me. How could something so simple feel so good? I had a niggling suspicion that anything that felt this good had to be wrong or at least dangerous, so I tried to stop. I tried to block the memory of how she had felt beneath her underwear, but it was impossible; the more I tried not to think of it, the more intense this new feeling became. I was becoming overwhelmed by the wondrous warmth of it all. The thoughts of her underwear and the look upon her face forced themselves upon me; I was powerless to stop thinking about it. I tried to take the showerhead away from myself for a second but whatever this feeling was growing within me it was not going to let up for an instant. I was on an upward trajectory, drifting higher than I had ever gone before; something big was going to happen here and I had no idea what to expect, but I was curious, terrified, electrified, my entire body pulsed with joy, and the jets of water from the showerhead danced like angel's feet on my skin. *I should stop now, I know I should, I should* . . . and then it came . . . and my body exploded into a flash of the purest joy I had ever experienced and for a moment I was lost, weightless, euphoric, I had disappeared entirely.

When I finally gathered my senses a little, I looked down and was horrified to see that I was very much still there and now there was something else there also, something white and syrupy that I definitely did not recognize. What had I done? I had broken it. I had broken my penis. I hadn't even sprouted so much as a whisker on it yet and here I had gone and broken it already. I was so sure of this that I was tempted to leap from the bathtub and run screaming for my mother. But another part of me understood instinctively that whatever had just happened should not have happened. I had gone somewhere that I was not supposed to go. I had crossed some forbidden threshold. I had most definitely sinned. I understood now that this is what all the talk of giving in to evil had been about. This much pleasure had to be a sin. Of course I had sinned. I had followed my selfish urge to its ultimate conclusion and now I was lost. The devil had me in his grip and I would spend all eternity burning in hell. I was sure of it.

There was a knock on the bathroom door just then, accompanied by a loud "What are you at in there?" It was my older brother, Michael. He must have heard me. Maybe I had cried out in my moment of bliss and I wasn't even aware of it. I lay perfectly still for a second, terrified to respond. If they found me like this they might rush me straight to the priest's house, or the hospital. What had I done? *I am so sorry, God*, I whispered as I got out of the bathtub and dropped to my knees to beg forgiveness. Michael rapped the door again. "Come on, I've got to take a bath too."

"I'll be out in a minute," I said, trying to sound normal. But he had to know. I was weak and dirty. Everyone would know. How could I ever hide a sin so enormous?

As I moved about the house for the rest of the night I felt

like an alien, as if I had entered another dimension. When either of my parents glanced at me I felt there was a tinge of disgust in it, as though they knew what I had done and that somehow I was lost to them now. I was one hundred percent certain that no one had ever taken their self-gratification to the depths that I had. I was a monster. I deserved to burn in hell. For the rest of the night I struggled to maintain my composure and fought an overwhelming urge to burst into tears. I barely slept a wink.

The next morning at Mass in Dunmoyle, after we had changed into our white vestments, the other three altar boys and I sneaked out the back door of the sacristy to play tag among the headstones in the cemetery. It was a sunny morning and the grass among the graves had been freshly cut and I was relieved by the momentary return to innocence horsing around with my friends. It was short-lived.

"What time is it?" my cousin Noel asked suddenly. None of us had a watch. We stood for a moment to listen. Mass had begun without us.

We could hear the voice of Father McNally, the parish priest, beginning the Hail Mary and the congregation following in unison.

"Holy shit, it's almost time for communion!" Noel cried. "Why didn't he call us? We've got to get in there."

We rushed into the sacristy and dusted some of the loose grass off one another and tried to straighten our hair. We were sweating and our faces were flushed and red from all the running; we were out of breath and panting as we formed a line, clasped our hands, bowed our heads, and filed out onto the altar. I took one quick glance at the congregation for a millisecond, and in a sea of faces I locked eyes with my mother. I could have crumbled then, dropped to my knees on the marble floor for all to see, and begged forgiveness. A single glance from her was more powerful than a bolt of lightning. Just a split-second flash of that face and I understood how worthless I really was. This whole mess was my fault and mine alone. It was I who had kept the others away from the altar, I with my guilt, my secret shame, clawing to retain some sense of the innocence that I had stolen from myself the previous night, and here now was the culmination of that sin: humiliation for my mother, my father, for my family, in front of the whole church, I had let her down and drawn shame upon our family.

Father McNally was raising the chalice and the congregation bowed their heads as one. "Take this all of you and eat it. This is my body which will be given up for you." I got on my knees and bowed my head also as McNally continued the blessing of the gifts.

"Take this all of you and drink from it. This is the cup of my blood, the blood of the new and everlasting covenant. It will be shed for you and for all men so that sins may be forgiven. Do this in memory of me."

It was my turn to accompany him along the rail of the altar, holding the silver spatula beneath the chin of each recipient so as to catch any crumbs that might fall by the wayside as they held out their tongues to receive our Lord's flesh in the form of slim white bread wafers.

As we crossed in front of the altar, the unimaginable happened. McNally fumbled and dropped a piece of our Lord's flesh and I, consumed by guilt and thoughts of eternal damnation, missed it with the spatula as it fell. Instinctively I ducked to pick it up, but before I could reach it McNally whacked me in the chest with his forearm, sending me onto my ass in front of the altar. I sat for a moment stunned as everyone stared.

"It's the body of Christ," he snarled. "You're not supposed to touch it. Only I can touch it." I had no idea. We had never been officially trained as altar boys. I had always assumed that anyone could touch the bread because we took it on our tongue, touched it with our lips, our teeth, our insides, and even our assholes as it passed on the way out again, but apparently, fingers had yet to be added to the "Sacred Body Parts List." Maybe God knew about the unholy things we did with our hands when we were alone.

The following morning the nightmare continued. I had been so preoccupied with the loss of my soul to the devil that I left for school without my shorts and football boots for physical education class. I tried to explain to Master Ward that I had been sick and the bus had come early and our dog had run away and . . . it was useless, but at the age of eleven I still had a naïve notion that I would experience mercy at the hands of a teacher.

He made me stand in front of the other thirty or so boys and hold my hand straight out, palm up, and wait as he casually stepped into his office for the leather strap. I had never received the leather before. It was one of those nightmares you heard about before coming to secondary school but never imagined it would actually happen to you. The strap is a twenty-inch length of thick leather about an inch and a half wide, worn smooth from years of skin contact. Every teacher's strap had its own personality, and I would become familiar with each of them over the next five years at St. Ciaran's. Some were thick, some thin, some were sliced up the middle so the leather formed a forked tongue that would wrap all the way around to the back of your hand with each strike. All of them were sore. Ward's strap was thick and heavy, very matter-of-fact; he didn't need gimmickry, he was the physical education teacher and he had the strength to make each whack count.

"Hold it up, boy," he said with a sneer, and I held it up as he flicked the leather over his shoulder for maximum swing action. This was what happened to boys who played with themselves in the bathtub. Here was the sinful hand held aloft for all to see.

Like all pain, the sting of the strap came not as a shock but as a relief. Yes it was sore, horribly sore, but I was alive; I had endured it.

"Again . . ." he said, and I could see the thrill of it in his face as he, too, found his groove, gripping the strap with tight-fisted determination as he gave in to it, bringing it down with everything he had. The second hurt more than the first, but I was gaining strength. I was the first in our class to receive the strap and I could sense the fear in the rest of them. If it was happening to me now, it could happen to them, too. I was the lucky one. I understood that I could survive it. I would make my mark by bearing it without tears. I had brought the thrashing upon myself. I had sinned in secrecy; now God was forcing my punishment out into the clear light of day.

"Again . . ." By the sixth time my hand was a solid ringing mass, ribbed with thick red welts. I had taken the strap.

At lunchtime I sought out Fergal, the Vampiro, in the schoolyard. If anybody could explain what had happened to me, without announcing it to the entire school in the process, it would be him.

"I did something horrible," I whispered the second I found him, glancing around to make sure we were out of earshot of anyone else.

"I'm sure it can't have been that horrible," he said.

"It is."

"Well then, you must tell me right away. I love horrible stories."

"It's bad."

"Nothing's that bad. Tell me immediately, the suspense is killing me."

"I touched myself in the bathtub and some stuff came out," I blurted.

"Oh, that," he said with a disappointed roll of his eyes.

"I know I shouldn't have . . ."

"It's called wanking. Don't worry about it. It's perfectly normal; normal and necessary."

I was astounded by his flippant response. I had expected horror, not frivolity. This was the damnation of my soul we were talking about here.

"Am I a wanker?" I asked.

"My dear boy, we all are."

"It's wrong. I know it's wrong. Am I going to hell?"

"Well, if you're going to hell for that, you'll have plenty of company, I can assure you."

"Has it ever happened to you?"

"It happens to me every day, a couple of times a day. As a matter of fact, I just did it this morning before the school bus arrived and I'm about ready for another one any minute now. Maybe I'll squeeze one in before the bell goes. The Vampiro is something of an expert in this particular field."

"Really, you're not just saying that?"

"I promise you. It's natural. It's what boys do. All your cousins do it and your friends. Even your auldfella's done it. The priests do it, teachers . . . sure everybody's at it for godsake."

I felt the sun shine again, the darkness lift, the devil release me from his grip. "Are you absolutely sure?"

"I'm positive."

"I'm not going to hell."

"Not for that you're not."

"Well, I'm never going to do it again anyway," I said. "Just in case."

Fergal threw back his head and laughed at this. "Oh, you're going to do it again."

"No I won't, I swear. Never."

"I want you to listen very carefully to the Vampiro," he said as he tried to refrain from giggling at my distress. "You are going to do it again and again and again for the rest of your life, if you're lucky. Don't worry about it. It's one of the few little pleasures we've been granted in life. Enjoy it, savor it. Just don't let your mammy catch you at it. God has a sense of humor about such things, Claire Broderick may not."

Over Fergal's shoulder I noticed the headmaster, Master McSorley, barrel out of the cloakroom doors and cross the yard in what looked like one long step. Fergal also turned just in time to see him reach a boy who'd been cupping a lit cigarette in the palm of his hand. McSorley's open hand clobbered the boy in the face with such brute force that the lad's feet swept a good yard off the ground and by the time he lay stretched on the tarmacadam he was completely unconscious, his legs and his head twitching from the shock of the blow. Rather than pick him up, McSorley plucked the still-burning cigarette off the ground and crushed it in his fist as he yelled at the prostrate boy, bringing the entire two hundred or so boys who were standing around to a complete silent standstill.

"And don't ever let me catch you smoking a cigarette in this school again."

Master Ward, the physical education teacher who'd given me my first taste of the leather earlier that same day, stood in the open door of the cloakroom grinning that sadistic little smile of his, and as he caught my eye for a split second he winked at me before blowing his shrill referee whistle to mark the end of playtime in the yard.

"The Vampiro is of the distinct impression that a personalized stretcher should be mandatory issue with every St. Ciaran's school uniform," Fergal noted, loud enough for many in the schoolyard to hear. "One just never knows when one might need one."

A few boys chuckled at the sheer audacity of Fergal in

the face of such violence, but we understood implicitly that he was the only boy in the entire school who could have gotten away with such a comment. Fergal's immunity was the great unspoken mystery in our midst. Ward blew his whistle again and every head but one shuffled toward the top of the yard to get in line for class. Lunch break was over.

I went back to class for the afternoon with my hand still ringing from the pain. I held my hands under the desk and fingered the thick red welts along my palm. The Vampiro was right. I had found my first escape.

Turf and Spuds

Good evening. This is the ITN news for Northern Ireland. It's six o'clock.

Eighteen British soldiers have been killed in Warrenpoint near Newry in County Down. Witnesses say a civilian has also been accidentally killed by a member of the British Army in a shoot-out that followed the incident. The Provisional IRA have claimed responsibility for the attack.

In other news, Lord Mountbatten and a number of his family members were also killed when the IRA blew up a boat he was fishing in off the coast of Sligo just south of Bundoran.

Lord Mountbatten, an admiral in the Royal Navy, was a cousin of the queen and a mentor to his great-nephew Charles, Prince of Wales, who is said to be deeply saddened by the news. He was killed along with Mount-batten's eldest daughter's eighty-three-year-old mother-in-law, Baroness Brabourne; his fourteen-year-old grandson; and a fifteen-year-old local boy, Paul Max-well, who had been working on the booby-trapped boat when the explosion occurred.

By God they'll make somebody pay for this one. A member of the royal family?

The poor craturs, innocent women and children caught up in the middle of it. Bless yourselves children. In the name of the father and the son and of the holy ghost amen. May the Lord have mercy on their souls. . . .

What's a booby trap, Daddy?

It's a trap for boobies.

That's quite enough auld smart chat out of you, Colin.

What? I was just telling him what a booby trap was.

Machil, can you reach that boy's ear with your hand there.

Ow, I was just trying to tell Brendan what a booby trap was. I didn't know.

No, you were being a smart ass and if I hear another word out of you before you eat the finish of them vegetables, you'll get another warm ear from me as well, I can tell you. Now shush it till we hear the finish of the news.

Now that I was eleven and living in our new house, my mother allowed me to go next door to listen to music with my cousin Des. Life in the McCann house was a lot more permissive than ours. Des had older brothers and sisters who were out of school, working full-time jobs or off living in London. The front lines of the battle for control between parents and children had clearly shifted in the McCann household. Once you had children old enough to start smashing cars and impregnating the neighbors, it took a lot of the pressure off the younger siblings in the home, it seemed.

By the time Des was twelve, he had free rein to do pretty much whatever he liked. That wasn't to say he didn't still get a good hammering from his old man every now and then. Apparently, children still needed a good hammering once in a while regardless. But still, life in the McCann household was a welcome respite from the regime I was battling next door. We could hole up in Desmond's bedroom for hours chain-smoking cigarettes, playing air guitar and head-banging to Black Sabbath, AC/DC, Thin Lizzy, Stiff Little Fingers, and Horslips. For the first time I could feel the faint tremor of something wild shiver within me. Once you taste freedom, the residue clings to your tongue like a thin veneer of hope. We turned the music way up loud and I shook my head until my mother's voice was nothing but a blur.

But the pack of cigarettes that we smoked every day between us was not free and neither Des's parents nor mine were going to foot that bill. We needed to earn that money ourselves. During the summer break I could make three or four pounds a day turning turf in the bog for my uncle Paddy Joe McClean.

Turf is an organic accumulation of vegetation found in areas with a particularly wet climate, like Ireland. It is an early, soggy version of coal. The goal during the summer months was to cut and dry as much of it as possible so it could be used as fuel for heat during the winter months. Turning turf by hand so it would bake in the sun wasn't nearly as much fun as working with the Vampiro, but the possibility of actually getting paid was hard to resist. The new turf machine had just been invented and just about everyone in County Tyrone had gone stark raving mad making turf.

Previously, all turf had been cut by spade, but cutting turf by spade was a slow, tedious process. Even a great man on a turf spade could only cut enough turf to keep himself and maybe a helper in work, but the turf cutter revolutionized all that.

The new turf machine was attached to the rotary arm on the back of a tractor; it powered a blade that could run a four-foot-deep track, laying neat rows of peat moss in perfectly straight lines through the fern. The other real genius of the new turf machine was that it took such a fine sliver of peat from the bog that there were no holes left behind to break your leg in; the bog quite simply closed in behind the tractor so you could come back year after year and cut turf out of the same ground.

Of course, what the new machine did not do was actually turn the turf so that it could be dried by the wind and the sun for burning. That laborious task was the job of every reluctant Irish boy old enough to ride a bicycle. It was one of the very few ways a young lad might earn a few extra pounds of spending money all for himself.

As any Irishman over the age of thirty-five who grew up in a farming community will tell you, turning turf is just about the most painful job on the planet. Every factor of physical discomfort was taken into account.

To begin with, all good turf patches are situated on the top of a mountain with zero shelter from the elements. In all likelihood, the turf in question would be situated so far from any contact with civilization that you had to be transported out there by a third party bright and early in the morning with the promise of a ride home around six in the evening. And that's if you were lucky. Most times the only way to get there was on the "shank's mare," as they liked to say in Altamuskin—or, to those not in the know, on foot.

Once you had been dropped off on the top of a mountain in the asshole of nowhere with no shelter in sight in any direction, you were exposed to whatever mess of weather that particular day might throw at you. If it was rain, and it usually was rain, you had to use your wits to determine what kind of rain it was you were dealing with. In Ireland there are so many different variations of rain that at times it is necessary to invent new terms to define it. For example, a fine mist of rain could be referred to as a mizzle, which meant that it was not quite a drizzle but definitely on the damper side of what you might classify a mist. As far as working outdoors was concerned, mizzle would barely register as a weather factor; you could work through a fine mizzle from morning to night without so much as a pause. You would be a little damp for the duration of the day but not incapacitated. Unless, that is, the fine mizzle came with a few cold gusts of northerly wind, which of course it always did, leaving you a little stiff and generally miserable for the rest of the day, but even with those conditions you could still chalk it up as a good day in the bog.

If the rain upgraded to a drizzle, well, then that was something to be considered. A drizzle might represent the beginnings of a real rain shower on the horizon, but if there was still a patch of grayish blue somewhere visible in the cloud coverage, there might be a chance that it just wouldn't get any worse for the rest of the day. In that case you buckled down and worked away. Home, after all, was now about a forty-five-minute walk away. It was going to take more than just a bit of drizzle to send you off early for the day, home to your mammy, with your tail between your legs, like some big girl's blouse. No, you stayed and thought of the next pound you would have earned by the time you reached the next turf marker about twenty-five feet up ahead of you and you said a wee prayer that the rain would hold off, for if a real rain shower should start, the conditions for working in the bog were downright hellish to endure. The water would run in rivers down the back of your shorts and fill your wellies to the rim. It would curl around your face as you stooped over and blind you while you worked, with the result that you would blacken yourself from head to toe rubbing and scratching at yourself for some measure of comfort.

If it really did happen to rain, well, then you could be excused for straightening your back for a few minutes, maybe even taking a break for a moment to eat one of those delicious bread-and-jam sandwiches you'd brought along wrapped in a paper towel inside a Rover biscuit tin, a mouthful of milk or cold tea out of a bottle to wash it down. You might even have one of the two custard-cream biscuits you were saving for later, for when you would sit down to take a real break for your lunch. In all likelihood, you would not be able to resist the second custard cream biscuit, of course, and you'd eat that one as well; you'd crunch it up and swallow it recklessly, more out of spite than anything else, because you knew now that there was nothing in that lunch box left to look forward to for the rest of the day and you hated yourself for it. You hated yourself for not having had the discipline standing there in that nice steady rain shower to have saved that last custard cream for later. You hated yourself because you knew that if you'd saved it you could have worked toward that damned biscuit all day long. The reward, that custard cream, could have been out in front of you like a carrot to a donkey as your back ached and the skin from the tips of your fingers were ripped and stinging from the constant pulling of the turf out of the coarse bog grass where it lay.

There is something malignant about the weather in that particular patch of Northern Ireland above the border. Even as a boy I was constantly cold. I never warmed to it, never acclimated. I could not figure for the life of me why England would want it so badly. There is a reason that Ireland looks so magnificently green in all those pictures you've seen; it quite simply never stops raining. If I were king of England, I might have carved out a nice chunk of the South of France for my-self instead, somewhere you didn't need to spend half your life working to ensure you had enough fuel not to freeze to death.

Of course, there was always the rare possibility that the sun would shine, and shine and shine and shine. And like your chances of dodging the rain in the bog, the same rules here would apply. There was just nowhere to go to avoid it. So you'd take your shirt off and you'd bake, because as any young Irish boy with half a brain cell knew, that was the only way to get yourself a good tan. You had to go out and suffer a good scald-ing on the first hot day of the summer and then after about a week or so when the blisters had finally all burst and healed and you'd been able to literally peel that first sheath of pink baby skin off your back, chest, and face, you could finally get down to laying down a little color. Once there were no more layers of skin to bubble and peel, the flesh would brown.

If you worked hard, if you didn't waste too much time throwing clods at your brothers, if you managed to get through the day without more than at least one good fistfight, you could make, on a good day, five pounds all for yourself. Of course, a day like that might come along once in a season, but on aver-age a good turf man could still make himself about two-fifty to three pounds for a nine-hour shift if you really put your back into it. Not bad money for an eleven-year-old when you considered a ten-pack of cigarettes ran you about fifty pence at the time, and a box of Swift matches to light them another five.

There were other ways for a boy to make a living for himself, and being a smoker with a burgeoning habit to feed I availed myself of them all. Next to turning turf, gathering potatoes was the most popular occupation of choice. Once a year, around the end of summer, the potatoes were dug and bagged. Fields and fields of them; if you had two legs to keep you upright and one good hand to lift a spud, well, then you were qualified for the job.

All the same weather restrictions for turning turf applied to potatoes, as did the constant back pain from bending all day long, but there were perks to potato gathering that you didn't get with the turning of the turf. For one, the potato field was never too far from a farmhouse, so when tea break rolled around, at least there was the chance you could get a drop of hot water to wet your tea bag. And there was always a good crowd gathered for the day's picking, so there was plenty of competition and entertainment around to help the day pass a little quicker.

If you were lucky, there was a girl or two; maybe the farmer's daughters were out there bending in the clay up ahead. Not that you would have had the balls to talk to them just yet, but even at eleven you were beginning to get the sense that things were always a little less gray if there was at least one half-decent-looking girl around to steal a glimpse at every now and again.

The potatoes were grown in drills the length of the field, and every man had his own section of the drill staked out with a couple of potato sacks. When the tractor passed by busting open the drill, it sent a spray of loose clay and stones and potatoes for about fifteen feet across the earth; it was your job to have all the potatoes in your section cleared before the tractor could turn at the end of the field and make it back again for the next pass.

Like the turning of the turf, there were dreams of real money to be made gathering potatoes. When we first heard that they were giving away five and sometimes six pounds for every sack of potatoes filled, my brothers and I could barely sleep with anticipation. At six pounds a sack we were sure we could make a fortune. We devised a plan of attack: two of us would fill and one man could stack the bags; we could work on rotation so that each of us had a turn from being bent over constantly all day, but the filling of the sacks would never stop for a second. We were convinced that if we orchestrated our plan with precision and determination the poor farmer wasn't going to know what hit him. We would have mountains of potato sacks filled by day's end. They'd have to hire extra lorries to cart them away. It was going to be nothing short of daylight robbery. We almost felt sorry for the shafting the poor man was going to take at our expense.

Of course, we were to learn our first valuable lesson of the workplace on these damp Saturday-morning jobs of turning turf and gathering potatoes: we would never outwit an Irish farmer.

For starters, the sacks we had pictured ourselves filling were similar in size to the sacks of potatoes our mother bought at the market–the big sack, the sack you took to feed a family of eight mouths for two whole weeks. But when we arrived at the field and unfurled the first cloth sack the farmer had shoved in our hands with a grunt, it was like the canvas tarp they used to cover the circus tent. My brothers and I could have stood side by side in this thing with enough elbow room for accordion practice. Then as we tried to recover from this first blow to the plan, we were assigned our strip on the field and we watched in disbelief as the tractor passed by to open the first drill, kicking us out a handful of knobby pink marbles so small that if you peeled them you'd be hard pressed to call it a dinner serving.

Farther up the field we would watch the older pickers packing their cloth sacks with buckets of spuds the size of a child's head. These pickers, we would discover, were friends of the farmer's—men and women who had earned their place at the richest spots in the field long before my brothers and I had hatched our hideous scheme to potato-bag the farmer out of house and home.

It was only as the day wore on that we were able to determine that we had in fact been assigned the weakest stretch of the field—a damp gulley where the tractor wheels spun and the muck clung to the soles of our wellies in big gummy clumps. If we were lucky, we'd have two sacks of potatoes packed between the three of us by the long day's end, and still we would consider it an improvement on a day in the bog turning turf. At least there was the chance of a spud fight. The first one would hit the back of your neck around lunchtime, once everyone was well settled into their day's work—a rotted black shell of a potato with a center of rank water that would burst onto your skull with a dull wet splash. By the time you were upright to take a glance around to see who threw it, there wasn't a man on the field who wasn't bent over busily picking away as if they'd never thrown a spud in their lives. But that was it, the first spud had been lobbed and it was up to you to determine who would receive the counterattack. And so it would go: you set the next big rotten spud you found aside and you waited.

Good evening. This is the ITN news for Northern Ireland. It's six o'clock.

A British soldier was killed today as he crossed a bridge near the village of Aughnacloy in County Tyrone. The IRA have claimed responsibility for the attack. . . .

Mammy, was your brother in the IRA?

What?

I heard that Paddy Joe McClean was in the IRA and that the IRA used to train on your daddy's farm up behind the lough.

Where did you hear something like that?

At school.

From who?

I don't know. I just heard it.

Well, there's not a word about it.

I heard that too, Mammy.

So did I. I heard that the Brits arrested Uncle Pat and tortured him for a week for being in the IRA.

Who did you hear telling these stories?

I heard that the Brits stripped off all his clothes and beat him and hung him up on a hook and he had to go to the bathroom on himself because they wouldn't let him go when he had to. . . .

That'll do, put that television off and finish your dinners.

That's what I heard too, Mammy. The Brits blindfolded him and flew him around in a helicopter for about an hour–

That'll do, Colin–

And when he wouldn't tell them who else was in the IRA they threw him out of the helicopter while they were flying around. . . .

Colin . . .

Did he get killed, then?

Don't be scaring your younger sisters, Colin.

No, Noleen, he didn't die, you know he's not dead,
wasn't he in here yesterday? They flew the helicopter
close to the ground so when they threw him out he
only fell about ten feet before he hit the ground but
he was blindfolded so he didn't know how far he was
going to fall, so he thought he was going to die. . . .

Children, that will do. Your uncle Pat doesn't like
to talk about that anymore. He's involved in the
Workers' Party now, nothing to do with the IRA.

But he was?

Put that television off right now and finish your
dinners. There's not going to be another word about
it. And that's the last time I'll say that. Machil, speak
to your children.

Colin, get up and put off that television right this minute, and the rest of you shut it and eat your dinner,
not another word.

It was becoming more obvious now that I was in high school
that there had been more republican fight in our family when
my mother and her siblings had been much younger. I'd heard

stories about the Old IRA training on my grandfather's farm up beyond the lough from enough different sources to know that there had to be some truth to it. There were whispers too of stories about my mother and her sisters hiding the illicit *An Phoblacht* newspaper in their nightgowns as children when the Brits would raid my grandfather's house in the night. And daring stories of my uncles in getaway cars, driven by a local priest, being chased across the border by the B-Specials, the old reserve police force in the North. I was becoming old enough to recognize that there was a blatant hypocrisy endemic in my own upbringing. I admired and romanticized the old days when our clan was part of the larger fight for freedom in the North and sensed the first bitter pangs of resentment at the life of safety my mother was trying to foist on us at every turn. The brave around us were risking their lives, as my uncles apparently had once upon a time, and now we as boys were being forced to stay at home close to our mothers and drink tea and perform well in school and do exactly as we were told. But it was becoming obvious to me that the only way the English would ever leave is that enough of us would do the exact opposite. This was not a time to be polite, well-behaved little boys; this was a time to fight and kick and scream with everything we had in us.

A Very British Curriculum

It was obvious within the first couple of months at St. Ciaran's that there was nothing being taught there that would hold any currency for me in the real world. In history we studied English history: long, boring wars and lists of dates that needed to be memorized, stuff that I imagined might have mattered to an English boy—English policies and English treaties, mundane details so mind numbing that I spent my days in history class daydreaming of things like leaping off the roof of the school to my death or how I could manage to stroll into the girls' locker room after gym practice when they would still be naked from the showers to see if any of them had hair on their private parts yet. It was infuriating to believe that England had fought all these glorious wars and had all these famous political heroes and apparently Ireland didn't have any history for itself at all. From what I was being taught at school, it was obvious that we Irish had done absolutely nothing of any importance, ever.

It never occurred to me that we were being denied the history and literature of Ireland and that the school curriculum itself might be a part of a more insidious scheme by the British government to eliminate all ties to our Irish heritage.

In English class we were subjected to lectures on English literature and grammar from a teacher so droll, so incandescently boring, that he had been branded with the nickname "Dodo Bird." A man so deathly gray and lifeless it's possible he wasn't alive at all. I know it's not possible, but it does feel like he droned on about the same Thomas Hardy book for the entire five years I took his class.

I was disappointed that the Irish hadn't bothered to write any good books like this Thomas Hardy character. Not that I found Thomas Hardy even remotely interesting, but Dodo Bird seemed to think it was incredibly fascinating stuff, and I took his word for it; he was a teacher, after all.

"Please, sir, did anybody Irish ever write anything?"

"Why, Broderick, have you finished studying Hardy yet?"

"No sir."

"Well then, you'd better get to it; we have exams in four weeks."

"Yes sir."

But it was impossible. Every time I opened Hardy I fell asleep. If I forced my eyelids to stay open I was back to dreaming about girls before I could turn the page.

What I really needed was a girlfriend, a real one, not just one I could pass notes to on the school bus. There was absolutely nothing for it, the time had arrived: I needed to kiss a girl.

All the boys in my class were already courting girls on a regular basis at the Friday-night youth disco in Ballygawley. Monday mornings everybody had a story to tell about some girl, it seemed–stories of how they slipped them outside into a parked car or down the back of the hall to kiss them.

Some of the boys even claimed to have had their hands inside girls' panties already. A thought so wondrous that I spent half my time like some crazed explorer locked away in the bathroom with my mother's Kays Catalogues, thumbing through the ladies' underwear section as quietly as possible, straining to discern any hint of a nipple or a dark patch of hair through the lacy crotch of the models' underwear. I already knew that I was condemned to an eternity burning in the fires of hell, what harm could one more little orgasm possibly do to me at this point.

"Please, Mammy, can I go to the disco?"

"No."

"Please."

"I said no."

"But all the boys in my class are going."

"Well, you're not all the boys in your class and I'm not their mothers."

"But even the real dorks in my class are allowed to go."

"You're not going, and that's final."

"Please, Mammy, I'm almost twelve years old. If I don't go they'll know I wasn't allowed to go and then I'll look like a big baby."

"Well, you aren't allowed to go and you're too young to be gallivanting around discos in Ballygawley anyway. When I was your age you think I was allowed to go to discos?"

"But it's different now. It's not the same as when you were young."

"Not in this house. You're allowed to go the youth club once every two weeks and that's as far as you're going. Your brother Michael can start going to the disco after his birthday and you can go the year after that."

"When I'm thirteen? Please, Mammy, I'm begging you. You can't do this."

"No."

"Please, Mammy, I'll do anything. Please."

"I said no."

"But why can't I go?"

"Because I said so and that's that."

Fridays at school became dodge day. Dodge all conversations about going to the disco. Dodge conversations completely because all conversations led to the disco. Dodge everybody all the time. But there was no avoiding the questions; they kept coming like machine-gun fire day after day.

"Broderick, you going to the disco tonight?"

"Maybe."

"You should come, it'll be fun."

"You going to be there?"

"What do you think?"

"You'd better not miss it this time."

"I'll miss it if I feel like it."

"You're such a wanker, Broderick."

"I know what you are, but what am I?"

"Ha-ha-ha-ha."

Mondays were worse.

"Broderick, why didn't you come to the disco?"

"I didn't feel like it."

"Edel McKenna was there, she was asking about you."

"Well, she can ask, can't she?"

"She wants to go out with you."

"And why wouldn't she? She's only human."

"You're such an asshole, Broderick."

"I know what you are, but what am I?"

"Ha-ha-ha-ha."

It didn't take long for word to get around that the Broderick boys were not allowed to do the things other boys and girls took for granted. It was more obvious now that there were two of us at the school. It hadn't been obvious when it was just Michael not going anywhere, he might just have been that kind of boy. You could believe it of one boy all by himself and you could definitely believe it of Michael. Even at home I had never heard him kick up much of a fuss about anything. He accepted what he wasn't allowed to do and that was that. But after I arrived on the scene, it was obvious that it wasn't just a solitary act of individualistic preference. It was obvious that the Broderick boys were mammy's boys.

Before the end of the first year, the first fights had started.

A boy on our bus called Michael and me the mammy-won't-let-me's. It was obvious in the way that he'd said it and the way the other boys laughed that they had heard it before. It was an inside joke, and we were the only two not on the inside. I tore into him and didn't stop until I was dragged away.

But it didn't matter. You couldn't fight the words back into his mouth. You couldn't fight the laughter from the other boys in the back of the bus back into their mouths. We were the mammy-won't-let-me's and everybody knew it.

I made a decision there and then to keep fighting. I would fight every boy in St. Ciaran's if that's what it took to earn some respect. I was on a mission. If I didn't fight, the humiliation would make my life unbearable. I understood now that I was on the outside of something, some sort of high school camaraderie. I'd always felt like I didn't belong. I'd even found comfort in it on occasion, imagining that perhaps I was special. There were stories of saints who had spent their entire lives being misunderstood. Christ himself had been crucified for his singular vision. Although I found it hard to believe that he had the equivalent of the Kays Catalogues to contend with as I had.

I had the romantic notion that perhaps these were not my real parents at all, that my siblings were not of the same blood as me and that at some point in the not-too-distant future my parents would sit me down and reveal to me the true nature of my beginnings. They would tell me I was adopted, or that my mother had found me in a basket in the Laundromat where she had worked in Birmingham. That would explain the headaches, my general sense of alienation. If it weren't for my friend

Fergal, the Vampiro, I might have believed I was the only one in our whole community who ever felt that way.

He showed up at our door one night pale and subdued. My mother made him tea and told him he was welcome to stay the night if he liked.

"Yes, that would be lovely, Claire. If it would be no trouble," he replied, his face white as milk as he sat on the couch staring down into the cup of tea in his hands, drawing the entire energy of the room about him like a cloak.

"It's no trouble at all," my mother said reassuringly, making no effort to pry into his irrefutable state of despondency. "You're like family in this house, you're always welcome here, always, remember that."

"Thanks, Claire. That's nice to know."

In all the time I had known him I had never seen him so withdrawn. We went to my room and lay on the bed and he asked that I turn out the lights because he had something to tell me and he didn't want me to see his face when he talked.

I put the lights out and opened the curtains so the light from the moon filled the room with a silvery blue sheen as we lay next to each other side by side staring up at the ceiling.

"I had a visit today from Jimmy McCabe, do you know who he is?" he said in a shallow murmur that was completely devoid of all his usual theatrics.

"Sure, I know who he is. I see him at Mass every Sunday with his mother."

"Well, he came to see me today and asked me to go for a wee drive with him because he told me he had something to tell me. I thought to myself, What does this wanker want with me in his car, or what could be so important that he couldn't just tell me without taking me away for a drive . . . ?"

"Right."

"And then he pulls over and stops for a chat up the road and he tells me he's my brother, my half brother."

"What does that mean?"

"It means that we have the same father."

"Your dad is Jimmy McCabe's dad?"

"Yes, but not the dad you think I have. This is where it gets difficult. Our real dad, it seems, is some guy who lives in Australia. I've never met him, apparently."

"But you live with your parents."

"They are not my real parents. They are my grandparents."

"What?" I turned and could see that he had his eyes closed tight in the half light and a little stream of tears was glistening as it rolled down over the side of his face and into the pillow.

"I don't understand."

"I know, I'm sorry, it's a lot to take in, believe me I know. I've been trying to take it in all afternoon."

"So your daddy is actually your granddaddy and your real daddy lives in Australia. So your mammy is your mammy, right?"

"No, my mammy is not my real mammy either."

"Who's your real mammy?"

"You know my aunt?"

"The old lady you live with? Where I stayed with you?"

"No, the other one."

"Sinead's mother?"

"Well, she's my real mammy."

"Sinead's mother is your mother?"

"Exactly. And the two people I live with, my parents, are my grandparents who took me in when their daughter, my aunt, my mother, got pregnant by some guy who was at home on vacation from Australia and was with my mother and Jimmy McCabe's mother and apparently there are others too our age—at least one or two more that he knows about, our other half brothers and sisters."

"I'm sorry. I don't even know what to say." I was horrified, but I was a little envious, too; at least now he had an answer to why he was so different. At least now he had a starting place, somewhere to begin erecting an honest version of himself. The news, with its sense of horror, brought also a sense of relief, as if some part of me had known this truth all along. I understood immediately that this was why the Vampiro had always received deferential treatment in his uniqueness.

"I knew it. I knew there was something wrong with me," Fergal continued.

"It's not you. It's them. There's nothing wrong with you."

"Of course there is, I'm a bastard. They all know I'm a bastard, everybody in Altamuskin and Dunmoyle and Foremass and Sixmilecross and Ballygawley has known all along. Even your parents knew, but nobody said a damn thing."

"You think my parents knew too?"

"Of course they did, everybody of their generation knew. It's been a secret everybody in the whole community has been in on apart from me, it seems. For all these years and everybody's too embarrassed to let the truth come out."

"I don't know what to say about it all. I'm shocked. I can't imagine what it's like to be you right now." But I did share in his disgust; it went against the very fabric of everything they had been hammering into us from birth: "Tell the truth and shame the devil." I had suffered many a beating, the pain of guilt, and the very real fear of perishing for eternity in the flames of hell for even minor displays of dishonesty, and here they were, our parents, teachers, and priests–the punishers–complicit in a unified hypocrisy.

"I know. Thanks, Colin. But it's all right, I know what I have to do now. . . ."

"What?"

"I'm going to become a priest."

"Why bother? The priests probably knew too; they're no better than the rest of them around here." I could picture the faces of those we had worked for over the years and how they had treated Fergal and me, and I couldn't help but feel a sense of rage begin to boil deep within me, for every act of kindness we had been shown was suddenly tinged with a hint of con-descension and pity in my memory of it. Is that why so many had employed us to paint their houses? Were they really just being nice to the "poor bastard child"? And how would I ever trust an adult to tell me differently now that they had proven themselves to be such masters of deceit?

"I have to. They all think I'm a bastard. Everybody around here has known I'm a bastard all my life. I have to do some-thing to show them I'm not a bastard."

"But you didn't do anything wrong. You don't have to do anything for anybody. Fuck them all and what they think."

"No, I've decided. That's what I'm going to do. I'm going to see McNally tomorrow to start the process. I'll probably go to Maynooth, they have a big seminary there. It's all settled."

"So my best friend is going to be a priest?"

"Yup."

"The Vampiro in a collar."

"Father Vamp."

It made perfect sense that he would want to replace one false self with another. Perhaps that was the real mark of maturity, I thought, finally deciding which mask suits you best, and wearing it.

Savage

By my second year at St. Ciaran's the children who rode the Altamuskin school bus had earned a reputation as the most notorious troublemakers in all of St. Ciaran's High School. It was a remarkable achievement because St. Ciaran's had no shortage of troublemakers in attendance. The rear windows of our bus had been smashed so many times from our constant wrestling and slamming one another around that the Education Board was forced to weld protective steel bars over the windows to keep us from spilling out onto the road while the bus was in motion. The Education Board responsible for the financial damage we inflicted on the bus was, of course, a British organization. We would have been beaten half to death by the men of our community if we'd purposely so much as chipped the paint on a car owned by a local Catholic, but the bus was considered fair game.

Our bus driver, Harold, a timid, graying middle-aged man, lived constantly on the verge of a nervous breakdown from the abuse, which was all right with us because he was a Protestant. Only Protestants got to have a cushy job like driving a school bus or an ambulance, or as an office clerk in one of the many government buildings in big towns like Omagh or Dungannon. Nearly all our fathers, the Catholic men, had to work out in the frost and the rain, building houses or running after cows or digging holes.

Even the Protestant farmers operated in a class all their own. It became obvious as I grew a little older and spent more time helping my grandfathers on their land that the Protestants of Northern Ireland had long since divvied up all the best land for themselves. The Catholic farmers, both my grandfathers included, spent their lives struggling to eke out an existence on rocky slopes barely fit for a goat. The Catholic farmers had land on the sides of mountains and the middle of wet bog land, land that would have been parceled off for the Catholic peasants once upon a time.

The Protestant farmers by comparison had lush, rolling, green pastures—flat land fit for the finest dairy farming. And because they had the finest pastures, they also bred the finest animals and grew the best crops. And because they were able to generate so much income from the land, they could easily afford all the latest equipment to do the bulk of the work for them: milking machines, the latest state-of-the-art tractors, humongous harvesters. On weekends they hitched horse trailers to their Range Rovers and went off to hunt or race or whatever it was that rich Protestant people did with horses.

Meanwhile on Saturdays and Sundays, like every other morning of the week, both my grandfathers were still letting their cows file into the byre one at a time, and settled their stiff, bony asses down onto short wooden stools to relieve the cows of a gallon of milk apiece by hand. After a lifetime of daily struggle neither of my grandfathers owned a car or a tractor, never mind the luxury of a milking machine or, God forbid, a show horse.

When the local Protestant farmers passed us by on the roads in the latest-model Range Rovers, they did little to hide their disdain for us in their sideways glances. It was no secret that they regarded us Catholics as little more than savages. We had a thousand years of an oppressive history as a testament to their hatred.

Not even the young Protestant boys spent their weekends, as we did, turning turf or gathering spuds for pocket money. They didn't need to. Instead, they studied and played cricket and went off to college. When we saw them in town, their shoes gleamed, their trousers were pressed to a fine crease, and their jackets were not stained or patched at the elbows. From the moment they were old enough to walk they carried themselves with an air of entitlement. They understood that they were destined for the finest universities and the cushiest jobs that our community had to offer. At that time, I did not know one single member of our extended family or even of our neighbors' families, for that matter, who'd had the privilege of a college education. Not one. So it was only fair that old Harold our bus driver was made to suffer a little. He was the only

Protestant we children had access to. It was only fair that he should be forced to share in our discomfort.

After they caged the bus windows to keep us from slamming into them, we took to smashing them by flinging coins through the bars until we'd managed to shatter the glass. Then they resorted to installing reinforced glass behind the steel cage, but we broke that, too. We were being shuttled to and from school like wild animals, and poor Harold was blinking and twitching like a man on the verge of a massive seizure.

Master McSorley stood us in the gym one morning and made an impassioned appeal to end the madness. He clenched his fist and called us a bunch of irresponsible savages, but his emotional plea only served to fuel our sense of chaos. We had taken the school bus and apparently there was nothing much they could do about it. Apparently Harold was too afraid for his own life to name names. And rightly so: his predecessor had been shot and killed by the IRA driving that very same bus on that very same route only a few years earlier. Harold had inherited the dead man's job driving a school bus full of savage children into rebel country. I'd have kept my mouth shut too if I were him. That evening on the ride home we rejoiced in our victory, cigarettes were smoked, heads were smashed, and a general jubilant free-for-all ensued for the forty-minute ride.

The school bus was the real classroom. That was where you learned about how things operated locally. Without too much being said, you got to understand the difference between the UDA (Ulster Defense Association) and the UDR (Ulster

Defense Regiment) and between those Protestant paramilitary units and the foreign British soldiers. The uniform was much the same but the Brits were English soldiers; the UDA and the UDR were mostly local Protestants who wore the camouflage fatigues for part-time night duty.

The UDA were hell bent on dispensing their own brand of tit-for-tat justice in Northern Ireland. They were ruthless and unpredictable in their violence against Catholics and were allowed to operate legally under the protection of the British government for more than twenty years.

The UDR, the Ulster Defense Regiment, were Protestant men also, who worked day jobs, quite commonly as bus drivers like our own Harold, and would then go out on patrol at night to earn an easy second wage setting up roadblocks on quiet country roads to harass Catholics and gather information for the British Army. Because they were notorious for their abuse of Catholic drivers, making them stand out in the rain and verbally humiliating them in front of their wives and children, UDR men were a prime target for assassination by the IRA.

To protect their identities, the men who enrolled for duty would be stationed far enough away from their own homes that they might elude recognition by one of their Catholic neighbors. For instance, a Protestant neighbor of mine might be stationed in a county twenty or thirty miles away, and even then, when they went out at night they rubbed black shoe polish on their faces to further deter recognition. But no matter where they went, some were still recognized. And it was common knowledge that the minute any Protestant was pinpointed as an abusive member of the UDR, he became a walking target. He was liable to get shot answering the door to his home one night, or blown to bits in his own booby-trapped car, or indeed shot in cold blood as he worked his day job. No mercy would be shown. That was why the previous bus driver of our school bus had been murdered by the IRA.

UDA, UDR, UFF, UVF, RUC . . . they all spelled the same word for us: enemy.

We were taught by the older boys on the bus that no Protestant could be trusted. None. Not the local farmers, nor our bus drivers or petrol pump attendants. It didn't matter how nice they seemed, it was to be assumed that they were all murdering scumbags who worked in collusion with the British forces, and we were to give them no personal information. We could be courteous if we wished, bid them hello, but it was under strict advisement that we were never to be seen having an actual conversation with one of them. We stayed well clear of their women, also. It was made perfectly clear that Protestant women were particularly cunning. We were led to believe that they had no scruples, no moral compass to guide them, that they would let you sleep with them in a heartbeat just so they could loosen your tongue to extract information. Men had died from secrets whispered across a pillow.

We were educated by the older boys on what to say and what not to say at a British Army checkpoint, or a police checkpoint. We were taught never to give them any information that they did not already have—nothing, not even your own name—we were to lie at all costs.

"Be wary of the friendly Brit, he's just trying to squirrel information out of you."

"If you see a strange car on the road, record its number plate."

"Memorize the license plate numbers of local cop cars so you can recognize them when you meet them on the road at night."

"Know the registration differences in cars from Belfast or Derry; sometimes the Brits will send one of their own driving into the community undercover to gather information. If you see a strange car on the road, mention it right away."

It was also about this time that I began to get a good sense of which men in our own community were involved in the IRA. Names were whispered behind cupped hands with the threat of a severe beating, or a kneecapping, if it were revealed that I told a soul. Every boy by the age of twelve had a fairly good idea of who was involved and who wasn't, and it was understood that those men and their families deserved our respect and our discretion to survive. Their lives were literally in our hands. It was powerful information for a child to possess, and it felt good to be trusted with it, to be a part of something larger than my family or the confines of my school. Their bravery was becoming one of the only things that made sense to me. There was a clarity in their purpose and I clung to that.

Good evening. This is the ITN news for Northern Ireland. It's six o'clock. Northern Irish political activist Bernadette McAliskey is clinging to life this evening after an assassination attempt on her life by members of the Ulster Defense Association.

Well, the dirty rotten bastards.

The men entered her home outside the village of Coalisland in County Tyrone early this morning, apparently taking the door down with a sledgehammer before bursting inside the cottage, where they shot her seven times in front of her three small children. Thirty-four-year-old McAliskey and her husband, Michael, who was also shot several times, were airlifted by helicopter by a British Army patrol of the Third Battalion to a hospital in Belfast. Questions remain this evening as to what the battalion were doing watching the house and how they could have let the gunmen enter without attempting at any point to stop them. Locals claim the battalion has been camped outside McAliskey's home observing her comings and goings for the past week. McAliskey has been in the news of late as a leading spokesperson in support of the hunger strikers within the Maze Prison, who are fighting for prisoner-of-war status. She has been drawing a lot of heated criticism from loyalist politicians across the North.

Bernadette McAliskey was well known and well liked in our community. Even the youngest children in our house had heard her name spoken in beatific terms. She was a local girl, one of our own, raised just a few miles up the road from where we lived. She was our Joan of Arc, articulate and fierce in her outspoken denunciation of the British regime. Even my father, who was usually successful in suppressing his rage over the afternoon dinner table so as not to provoke my mother's wrath, could not conceal his frustration at the news.

"They couldn't stand to see a Catholic with an opinion. She was too smart for them, she was making too much noise, she was showing them up by telling the world the truth about what's going on here, so they had to try and kill her. The poor girl. Can you believe this, the friggin' British Army sat right outside her house and covered for their buddies in the UDA to break down the door and go in and shoot her in front of her children. The whole thing was a friggin' setup between the Brits and the UDA and they screwed it up. They're enraged that a Catholic woman was smart enough to play them at their own game. The dirty bastards."

"And they'll get away with it too," my mother added with a bitter stoniness, for she, too, was heartbroken and horrified at the news. Here was a woman her own age–a local woman–and her husband, Michael, gunned down in their own home in front of their children like a pair of animals while the people who were supposed to be protecting them sat outside and allowed it to happen. Here was how the McAliskeys had been rewarded for their outspoken nationalism.

McAliskey, who rose to prominence in 1969 as Bernadette Devlin, when she was the youngest person ever to be elected to a seat in Parliament at the age of twenty-one, is said to be in grave condition this evening . . .

"Right," my mother said, choking back her own tears. "Everybody put your knives and forks down for a minute and let's pray for Bernadette and her husband and for them poor wee children who witnessed it. Bless yourselves. In the name of the father and of the son and of the holy ghost amen."

Paris-Bound

It was during my second year at St. Ciaran's that one of our teachers announced that our class, out of the twenty classes in the school, was one of only two chosen to take the trip of a lifetime to Paris. The news was met with a wave of excitement and enthusiasm the likes of which had never been witnessed in our short lives. Not since Dopey Dick had slipped beneath the Craigavon Bridge had there been a more coveted adventure at hand.

Not only would we be the first students to get to leave the country, to visit the great art galleries and cafés of Paris, but the sheer sexiness of the entire endeavor served to catapult us instantaneously into a position of minor celebrity among our peers. The remainder of the students at St. Ciaran's were so unified in their envy of us that our spirits were temporarily buoyed by the sheer force of their jealousy.

We had two months to bask and revel in the glory of it all. But my worst fears were realized when I bounded through the door that very evening thinking that if I approached my mother with a show of unbridled enthusiasm, I might trick her somehow into forgetting, for a moment, that she had any say in the matter. This was, after all, a school outing. The teacher had said we were going, it was educational, it was final.

"Mammy, Mammy, Mammy, you're never going to believe it we're going to Paris, our class and one other class got picked out of the whole school to go on a trip to Paris . . ."

"Well, you're not going."

"But Mammy, everybody's going, I have to go."

"Well, just because everybody else is going doesn't mean you're going."

"Mammy, please, I swear I'll be a good boy and do whatever you want. Please, you have to let me go."

"You're not going."

"But all my friends are going."

"Well, you're not."

"But why, Mammy?"

"Because I said so and that's that." Those two words from my mother's mouth were beginning to haunt my entire existence. It was becoming more and more apparent that my mother was going to inflict on me and my brothers her own skewed sense of parental dominance.

I'd heard snippets of stories from my older cousins that our grandfather Frank had raised my mother and her siblings with an iron fist; beatings had been administered generously. As his grandchildren we only ever knew him as sweet and funny but apparently he had been tyrannical with his own brood. Little freedom had been granted any of the girls to socialize. The children were awake at dawn and expected to work–hail, rain, or shine–seven days a week to preserve the farm. My mother had been only fifteen when she watched her mother, Minnie, die of stomach cancer in that house. The impact had left its mark; she was not going to lose anyone else she loved. She was going to keep us as close as possible, where she had some control over our fates. Whatever psychic or physical bruising she sustained as a child ran so deep that no amount of common sense would deter her from uttering those two dreaded words: "That's that."

The words "That's that" from my mother's lips meant no; never. It meant that the decision had been stamped in stone, it could not be undone. She had spoken the truth and it could not be unspoken, it could not be otherwise. It did not matter if it defied all logic or reasoning, for in my mother's eyes there was only one absolute truth and that was hers. It was a truth that she held about her like a steel cloak; no one would ever penetrate it. Good mother that she was, she was going to protect us.

"You are not going to Paris, and that's that."

For the next two months my migraine attacks increased in frequency and intensity. Those two words hammered the inside of my skull like a mallet in an oil drum. I lived in a constant state of rage and fear. Fear that I would be found out, that now even more children would know me as one of the mammy-won't-let-me's. I would never live it down if I didn't go on that trip. I refused to believe that I was out of options. I prayed and begged God with all my might to turn this nightmare around.

I prayed like a boy possessed. All carnal activities ceased at once. If I caught myself having even so much as the first signs of a sexy thought, I fell to my knees at once and petitioned God to remove it. If there were a God in heaven, he would hear me.

At school it was all anybody wanted to talk about, day in and day out. It was the only thing I could hear anymore.

"Only six more weeks now and we'll be on our way."

"I bet you I won't get seasick."

"I can't wait to stay in a hotel."

"Are you going to kiss Margot Kelly when you get there?"

"Maybe we'll kiss some French girls instead."

"Ha-ha-ha-ha."

"Hey, Broderick, did you bring in your approval letter yet from your parents?"

"Naw, not yet."

"You'd better get it in soon or you won't be going."

"I just keep forgetting it."

"You'd better not forget it much longer or you'll be left behind."

"Some chance of that happening."

"Ha-ha-ha-ha."

In the last two weeks the teacher in charge of the trip had started taking me aside and asking me if everything was OK. Why hadn't I brought the letter of approval? Why hadn't I brought a single penny of the trip money we had been asked to bring in more than two months beforehand? I assured her that everything was under control, that I had just forgot, that

I would have the money and the letter from my parents in just the next few days.

I was running out of time and the minutes were clicking by like the hand of a ticking time bomb. I couldn't picture my life going on if I was not on that bus with the rest of my classmates. I begged and cried and lied and threatened and fumed silently into my pillow at night. Just days before the trip I was considering my escape: I would run away. There was no other option. I would meet my class in Paris. I would stay in Paris forever. I would become a street urchin, a pickpocket, the Artful Dodger de Paris.

And then it happened. With just hours before my humiliation was to become public, one of our friends, a boy who was going on the trip, was killed by a car while out riding his bicycle in the afternoon. Peter McCrystal was a boy I played football with in gym class, a boy I didn't know very well, but well enough.

It was as these things are when a young person dies in a small community. It was as if the entire school had lost a brother, as if every mother for a ten-mile radius had lost a son. He was a child of our community and he was suddenly gone. Word spread from tongue to tongue like whispered flames until the whole parish burned in a unified blanket of searing grief. All but one boy, that is, who had suddenly, miraculously been granted a window of freedom from which to escape the locked cage of his own small death.

It was too late for the school to postpone the trip to Paris; there was an enormous funeral to attend, a day of mourning, a parade of St. Ciaran's students—his classmates and friends—in a procession to the chapel. Anybody who really considered themselves a friend could not possibly go gallivanting off to Paris to enjoy themselves in the midst of such catastrophe. I had been saved. Peter had taken the fall for me and I would never forget the boy I knew "just well enough," for I was sure that God had answered my prayers and sacrificed him so that I could live. I could believe again.

H

On the first of March, 1981, a young Irish prisoner named Bobby Sands refused his first meal in protest of the treatment of Irish political prisoners being held in Her Majesty's Prison Maze. The prison was situated inside Her Majesty's Royal Air Force Station of Long Kesh, just outside the town of Lisburn, about ten miles west of Belfast City, about forty miles from where we lived in Tyrone. The prison was more commonly known to locals as the H-Block, due to the shape of the cell blocks built within the complex.

The letter *H* would be forever after seared on the collective nationalist conscience, stamped in bold capital so we would never forget what it stood for; *H* for H-Block, *H* for Hunger, *H* for Horror, *H* for Hate.

The 1981 hunger strike was the culmination of an ongoing campaign for prisoner-of-war status that had begun a few years earlier back in 1976 when a handful of Irish prisoners had refused to wear the prison clothing in the Maze. The blanket protest, as it was known, had led to the dirty protest. The dirty protest, started in 1978, was when the Irish prisoners, protesting physical abuse by the British guards, refused to slop out and began to smear their waste on the walls of their cells.

By October 1980, the first hunger strike had started in the H-Block. By December, three women in nearby Armagh Women's Prison had joined the men in their refusal to eat. The protest ended after fifty-three days when the British government appeared to concede to the demands to recognize political status for parliamentary prisoners. Among the five simple demands the prisoners sought were the right not to wear prison uniforms; the right to organize educational and recreational pursuits; and the right to one visit, one letter, and one parcel per week.

Bernadette McAliskey and her husband had been shot in January of 1981 for her outspoken support of this first strike. Both of them had miraculously survived the assassination attempt. By March, the protest was launched once again into the public domain.

The boy who led the strike, Bobby Sands, was a twenty-six-year-old Catholic who had been given a fourteen-year sentence in the H-Block for possession of a firearm. His hunger strike quickly became news around the world.

The sight of this handsome young long-haired Irish poet challenging the might of the British Empire with nothing but his naked, starving body as a weapon was also a potent brew for the oppressed souls of a nation. British prime minister

Margaret Thatcher found herself drawn out into the open in a showdown that was playing itself out in the presence of an international media frenzy. She alone could save the boy's life with a nod of her head, and the entire world sat riveted to the news reports to see who would break first. Over the next days and weeks another twenty-two young Catholic Irish boys joined in the hunger strike, the dates of their first refusal of food deliberately staggered so the campaign could continue on long after the first of them had starved to death.

It was topic number one both at school and on the daily news. Images of skeletal, long-haired men wrapped in blankets, cell walls smeared in shit, hordes of Catholics marching in the streets all across the North in support. These were our boys. They were doing this for us. They were going to show the Brits what real Irish men were made of. They were going to show them that they didn't possess a weapon in their arsenal to equal our spirit. They were going to show them once and for all that we could never be beaten, not as long as one among us stood and breathed.

Our very own archbishop, Tomás Ó Fiaich, the man who performed my confirmation among countless others, further humiliated the British government when he said, after visiting the cells in the Maze Prison, that he hadn't seen men forced to live in such inhuman conditions since he had first witnessed "the spectacle of hundreds of homeless people living in the sewer pipes in the slums of Calcutta."

By the summer of that year, every Catholic schoolboy could recite the names of the first hunger strikers: Bobby Sands, Francis Hughes, Raymond McCreesh, Patsy O'Hara, Joe

McDonnell, Martin Hurson, Kevin Lynch, Thomas McElwee, Kieran Doherty, and Michael Devine among them. Twenty-four-year-old Martin Hurson grew up less than ten miles away, near the village of Cappagh. I was at school with his cousins. We considered these men our brothers, our neighbors, our heroes.

The extent of their crimes was never once discussed. It was understood implicitly that each one of them had been sentenced by a court system that we as Catholics refused to recognize. The entire system was British-run. There was quite simply nothing just about the rule of law for a Catholic in the North of Ireland. The Brits were in the position of judge and jury. We all knew that when the Brits decided they wanted a young Catholic boy off the streets, they simply arrested him and charged him with whatever crime they liked. If they wanted him in prison, they imprisoned him; if they wanted to torture him, they tortured him, as they had done to my own uncle and countless other locals, including the young hunger striker Martin Hurson who had been arrested and tortured in our local RUC barracks in Omagh when he had been only nineteen years old. If they wanted you dead, they shot you. Legal battles were all but pointless; we didn't have Catholics employed on a local police level, never mind the judicial level. Bobby Sands and his comrades were simply demanding that they be recognized as the prisoners of war that they were, and in turn be treated with the level of humanity they were entitled to under the terms laid down in the Geneva Convention.

The older boys at school came back from the protest marches wearing buttons bearing the faces of our heroes, and we huddled around the lapels of their denim jackets in the schoolyard as we listened to stories of stones thrown and plastic bullets dodged and stories of those that weren't dodged. Every week it seemed another civilian Catholic protester was shot and killed by a plastic bullet at the marches; scores more were badly injured. The shootings were indiscriminate, passive bystanders were killed. Men, women, and children fell, a twelve-year-old girl in Belfast walking home from the store carrying a carton of milk in her arms. A fourteen-year-old girl in Belfast also returning from the shops. A fifteen-year-old boy in Derry. There was even a thirty-year-old woman shot in the head from an RUC police vehicle. All were dead—and many others with them. We were accustomed to such horror stories, it wasn't the first time the British had killed Irish children with plastic bullets in the North, but this fresh wave of heartless brutality rattled even the hardest in our midst. No Catholic among us was safe any longer.

Thatcher knew that the hunger strikers were reinvigorating the republican movement all across the North and still she would not relent. Her refusal to compromise made her the most hated oppressor in Ireland since Cromwell had rolled through town three hundred years before her. As far as we were concerned, she was single-handedly starving these lads to death.

When Bobby Sands was miraculously elected to a seat in Parliament while starving to death on a prison bed, the North erupted in a triumphant burst of unbridled veneration. Here was the proof of what one man could do. A boy with no other weapon than willpower, determination, and a belief in what was right was commanding the attention of foreign leaders from every corner of the world from his prison cell. Suddenly, anything was possible. He had shown us our worth. The fiery blood of our Celtic ancestors still coursed in our veins. Without firing a shot he had proved we were still warriors.

Every Sunday there were prayers for the hunger strikers during Mass. Our local priest gave one memorable sermon on how the Catholic Church did not consider it a sin to kill a man if the man was killed in the line of war.

And as we dipped our fingers in the holy water font to bless ourselves on the way out the door, a man stood at either pillar of the chapel gates holding out copies of *An Phoblacht,* the illicit, republican-run newspaper, so we could get an untainted view of what was really happening inside the Maze Prison.

Taking the *An Phoblacht* in your hand at the chapel gates was a statement of solidarity with the republican movement and the IRA itself. It was illegal in the North to be even in possession of the weekly publication. The men who stood there selling them were neighbors of ours, men we knew well, men who risked arrest as did anyone who bought a copy if it happened to be found in your car at a checkpoint. But the men who sold it didn't need to wear masks to hide themselves among us. There wasn't a man, woman, or child leaving that chapel who needed to be told that they should not breathe a word of who they saw there. Here again was the unspoken bond of the community, collusion in silence.

Inside there were biographies and photographs of every man on strike, calendars marking the days since they had first refused food, updates on the struggle to force the British government into a compromise, and an occasional poem from the pen of Bobby Sands himself, words he'd scrawled on toilet paper with a smuggled ballpoint refill.

Thatcher never budged.

When Bobby Sands died after sixty-six days on hunger strike, the North erupted. For three days straight Catholics rioted in the streets all across the province. I was only thirteen—too young to attend any of the marches that were held in his honor, but old enough to feel the hate that had been seared into the hearts of every boy in the schoolyard. And as we watched each of the other ten young men drop off one by one over the next two months, we learned to reserve a small cold corner in the winter of our hearts for revenge.

The strikers' demands had not been met but this boy had won my admiration. Finally here was a Northern Irish identity I could aspire to. To many a lad throughout the six counties Bobby Sands was nothing short of a modern-day Christ. He had martyred himself to draw international attention to our plight. To me he was a beacon of manliness. The first true Northern Irishman. *H* for hero.

A Herd of Baby Elephants

The first girl I fell in love with was Erin O'Rourke.

I first saw her from across the hall at a Friday-night disco in Ballygawley. She was standing alone, swaying to the sound of Roxy Music's "More Than This." Her face had such an instantaneous spectral pull on me that the room seemed to crumble and fall away around her. I was momentarily paralyzed as I watched her. I had never witnessed such beauty. She had short brown hair spiked in a bold, punkish wave. Her dark eye makeup was drawn all the way out to her hairline, accentuating the pale white skin of her round and smiling face. I watched her, mesmerized by the way she rolled her head, dipping her large silver-hooped earrings to touch the padded shoulders of her black knee-length coat, the crescent of her full, wide mouth highlighted in dark-maroon lipstick. I was in love.

When the song ended, she turned to the door as if sensing someone's arrival. I looked too, and there in the doorway stood Jerry Keane. Jerry was much older than me—almost twenty. He was one of the coolest boys ever to graduate St. Ciaran's. He was legendary in his coolness. He wore it like a pair of old jeans. He was just cool.

Seeing him there, she smiled and skipped excitedly down the hall to greet him with a passionate hug. When he leaned down to kiss her, my entire body ached. He draped his big, loose arm around her shoulder, casually tucking her to his side as he languorously plucked a cigarette from behind his ear to light it, and they left like that, without a word to anyone.

It's not that I had been completely without prospects in the romantic department up until then. The truth was I'd gone through the mechanical process of kissing lots of girls from St. Ciaran's, but in that moment when I first saw Erin it was obvious that everything that had gone before had been mere childish fumbling in the dark.

Over the next couple of months I lived for just a glimpse of her. By this point my mother was allowing me to attend about one Friday-night disco a month, or whenever the mood struck her to relent to my constant begging. After I saw Erin for the first time I had good reason to beg. Once, about three weeks after I first saw her, I made eye contact with her, but when she caught me staring I turned away quickly, horrified at the thought that I had revealed in my expression how pathetically in love with her I was.

Weeks later at the Christmas disco, someone tapped my shoulder and when I turned around, it was her. She was standing there with a sprig of mistletoe held over her head. I met her eyes but I could not move. The sight of her beauty so close to me was overwhelming. She took a step toward me and without a word she pressed her lips to mine and she kissed me. Her mouth opened and mine opened to greet it. Something sacred and electrifying passed between us and we collapsed into each other as if this union had been ordained by the universe. Her arms folded around me and her body pressed up against mine and as we continued to kiss I put my arms around her and we clung to each other like that until we dissolved into each other, until I was awash with such a wave of bliss that it felt like we might have disappeared completely.

When Jerry finally arrived sometime later in the night to see her, we were still there, wrapped around each other where we had first started, lost in some oblivion. A friend of hers tapped her on the shoulder and that was the first moment that we broke from our kiss, as if we had been called back from a dream. But we did not part from each other. She looked at him blankly as if she had no idea what words might transcribe to him what had just occurred. He seemed to understand implicitly that there was nothing to be done about it and without a single word he turned, taking a smoke from behind his ear, and slipped out the door again just as casually as he'd arrived.

From that night on I was consumed with the image and feel of Erin in my every waking moment. I ached for her, I was sick with longing for the sight and touch of her from the moment I woke in the morning until I fell asleep with thoughts of her at night. My heart thundered like a small herd of baby elephants in a stampede.

I scribbled her name in every spare inch of blank paper in my notebooks. I scrawled her name in pen on the palm of my hand so I could see it there and know that it was real. I wanted to share my newfound bliss with the world, but my only real confidant, the Vampiro, was off at Maynooth becoming a priest so I no longer even had him to turn to for counseling. I was like a delirious foreigner in my own body. I burned with a secret so profoundly euphoric and terrifying that I was more than a little convinced that I had, in fact, gone completely mad.

My mother found out about my new relationship through my older cousin Padge, who congratulated me in our kitchen one afternoon with a hearty slap on the back.

"You're some boy," he said with a wink. "Jerry Keane's girl? Erin O'Rourke? The best-looking girl in town? How the hell did you manage that one?"

"What wee girl's that, now?" my mother said, noticing the interaction as she filled the kettle for a cup of tea.

"Oh, this is no wee girl, Claire. Colly here is dating one of the finest young women in all of Tyrone." Padge grinned, folding his hands across his chest in mock seriousness as he leaned against the stove to warm his ass.

"How old is this young woman?" My mother laughed, but I could sense an edge in her voice. I had kept any mention of Erin from her, knowing in my heart that she would be enraged by the age difference. I tried to divert Padge away from my mother's interrogation, but he was oblivious to the menace in her tone.

"I don't know rightly, Claire. She must be eighteen or

nineteen if she's a day. How old is that lovely woman of yours, Colly?" Padge asked, continuing to needle me.

"I don't know," I lied. "She's not much older than me, maybe sixteen."

"Right, I don't know too many sixteen-year-old girls who look like that." Padge laughed. I glanced at my mother's expression tightening around the corners of her mouth and I knew it was too late; the damage was done.

"Well, eighteen's way too old for you," she snapped. "What kind of an eighteen-year-old woman goes out with a fifteen-year-old boy?"

"It's not like that. You don't know anything about her. We're in love," I blurted, enraged at her accusatory tone as I made for the door.

"We'll see about that," she said before I could get the door closed behind me.

That Friday evening, with my heart on the verge of detonation from the pent-up anticipation of seeing Erin at the disco again, my mother casually dropped the ax on my plans.

"You needn't think you're going out to the dance tonight."

"But I have to go."

"You're not going."

"You can't keep me from going anymore, I'm fifteen now."

"Well, until you're eighteen you'll live by my rules, and you're not going."

"Please, Mammy, I have to go. I told all my school friends

I'd be there tonight," I said, being careful to exclude any mention of Erin from the argument.

"Well, you're not going."

"Please, Mammy. They'll be waiting for me. Everybody in my class is going tonight. We've been talking about it all week."

"No."

"But Mammy, they'll make fun of me and call me a big baby for not going, please don't do this."

"You're not going, and that's final."

"Please, Mammy."

"I said no."

"But why, why can't I go?"

"Because I said so, and that's that."

"You can't do this to me."

"I can do whatever I like, and you'd better watch who you're talking to like that or I'll give you something else to complain about in a second."

I was done for. There was no way to contact Erin and let her know that I would not be there. Michael had decided not to bother going either, so there was no way I could even get a message out to her. Because she didn't go to our school, no one I knew, knew her. She lived more than seven miles away. There was no way to even get a call out to her, even if I could find a phone number for her, without my mother hearing every word. Besides, that wasn't even an option to consider; I had long since stopped telling anyone that my mammy won't let me. I had learned over the years that the only solution was to lie.

"I really didn't feel like going."

"Discos are for big babies and sissies."

"Who wants to go to a dance with a bunch of first- and second-year students anyway?"

"I'd rather be at home playing darts, listening to Meat Loaf, and smoking cigarettes."

At fifteen and with a minor reputation for being ready to fight at the drop of a hat, there could be no further mention of "Mammy."

I lay on my bed and fumed. I screamed into my pillow and clenched my fists until my knuckles hurt. Erin would think that I stood her up. If she felt remotely like I felt, she would find it incomprehensible that I was not there waiting to rush into her arms. I hated my mother with a hate that was as pure and sharp as a razor blade. My stomach balled itself into a knot and I writhed on the bed with my hair clenched in my fists. She would never stop until she had destroyed me. This is what Irish mothers did, they destroyed their sons.

I resolved to spend the next week convincing my mother through my indifference that I did not care whether I ever went to another disco again as long as I lived. In order to be allowed out, she would have to believe I wanted nothing to do with this girl.

When I got to school on Monday morning, my friends told me that Erin had been there at the disco on Friday and she had waited all night for me to show. She had watched the door all night and when I didn't arrive she had approached them and asked if anyone knew where I was.

"That's just Broderick," they had told her. "Sometimes he comes, sometimes he doesn't."

"I don't get you, Broderick," my good friend Gary McKenna scoffed. "Why wouldn't you go to the disco when you have somebody like her waiting for you? There's something seriously wrong with you, Broderick. You know that, right?"

"She'll be there next week, won't she? Where's she going?"

"What an asshole."

"Ha-ha-ha-ha."

For the next week I was like a ghost in our house. I did my homework on time, cleaned the house enthusiastically after dinner every evening–sweeping mopping, yes Mam, no Mam, three bags full Mam–the whole week. Then on Thursday night I made a plan with Michael. He would act as my envoy. He would approach my mother and say that he wanted me to go with him to the disco. He would tell her that it was more fun for him if I was there with him. Michael was always in her good books and she would find it hard to disappoint him. It worked.

When I entered the hall that Friday night, she was there waiting with that bright, beaming smile. It took every ounce of energy I had not to run at her like an eager child. We found a quiet corner and never left each other's arms for the next few hours until it was time to go.

"Why didn't you come last week?"

"I missed my lift and there was no way to get here from where I live."

"I thought you didn't want to see me."

"I thought about you every single moment we were apart."

"Me too."

By the following afternoon, my mother knew all about it. I could tell by the way her eyebrows inadvertently twitched into an acute arch after she had just hung up the phone that she already knew I had been with Erin.

"So how was the disco last night?"

"Good."

"Just good?" Her left eyebrow cocked to such a severe angle that it appeared suddenly like an arrowhead poised and quivering above her eye, and I knew that with one wrong move from me she might release the tip of it into my heart.

"Yes, just good," I lied, and rose instantly from where I had been sitting reading my *NME* music magazine by the window and crossed by her to leave the room.

"I suppose she was there?" she called after me as I moved for the door without a word. "Don't think you can pull the wool over my eyes and get away with it. She's no good, that girl, and you'll have nothing more to do with her if I have anything to say about it. She's too old for you."

I continued on out of the kitchen feeling the first arrowhead nip my skin as I pulled the door behind me. I was done for and I knew it.

The following Friday after a prolonged week of longing

and dread, when I finally approached my mother to plead my case about going to the disco, she mocked me with a sneer.

"Ha, you must be joking. You can go up to your room and listen to your music or read or do whatever else you want to do, but you're not leaving this house and that's that."

I pleaded in vain for a few minutes and even turned to my dad, who sat silently on the couch hiding behind a newspaper. But it was worthless; he had long since deferred all judgment on such matters to my mother. I stormed out of the kitchen, slamming the door behind me, and heard him yell after me, "If you slam another door around this house, I'll come up to that room after you."

I went into my room and sat on the edge of my bed for hours, unable to wrap my head around the injustice of what was happening to me, unable to move with the hurricane of rage that whirled in my skull threatening to shred all that was left of my will to live. I listened to my family banging around through the house: the thud of the dartboard from my brothers' bedroom; my two little sisters giddily playing with their dolls across the hallway in their bedroom; my five-year-old brother, Gerry, the child of the house, the brother I shared my bedroom with, opening the door every twenty minutes or so and closing it again whenever he could see that I was still in no mood for chitchat or games; and from down in the kitchen, where my parents were sitting, came the exaggerated laughter of some Friday-evening comedy show on the television.

In a family of eight people living under one roof, there was no space to be totally alone with your thoughts, ever. And even if I was alone, the noise in my head had been increasing ever since I had been in primary school. Trapped at home without the freedom to come and go as other boys and girls my age did, or even to express myself honestly without the risk of punishment, I had developed a noisy inner life of fantasy and escape, a place where I was free to roar. I was going to leave that house the first chance I got. I was going to escape my parents and the parochial small-minded mentality of Altamuskin as soon as I possibly could. It was hard to imagine that others around me lived with this same stadium of chaos blasting away between their ears. Was I the only one whose head felt this way? Was I the only person under that roof who felt trapped and alone there?

The following evening when the phone rang, I knew instinctively that it was Erin.

"Why didn't you come to the disco last night to see me?" she asked.

"Sorry. I couldn't get a lift."

"Will you be coming out next Friday night?"

"Yes. Definitely."

"Are you sure? You don't have to go if you don't want to, you know."

"I want to come. Believe me. I'll be there."

There was a knock on the door and my mother's voice behind it.

"Are you done with that phone yet? I need it to make a call."

"I'll be done in a minute."

"Who's that?"

"Nobody. I have to go now. I'll see you next Friday night."

"Say you promise."

"I promise I'll be there."

"All right then. Bye. I miss you."

"I miss you too."

Good evening. This is Scene Around Six. *Here is the news. The funerals were held today for the two men who were shot and killed by the SAS near the town of Coalisland in County Tyrone. A spokesman for the British Army claims that the men were armed; a spokesman for the IRA claims the boys were unarmed.*

The bloody animals, they shot them two cubs for doing absolutely nothing.

Machil.

The two men have been named: Colm McGirr, who was twenty-three, and Brian Campbell, who was just nineteen years old. At the funeral of Brian Campbell at St. Patrick's Church in Clonoe, County Tyrone, local priest Father Joe Campbell told mourners that the circumstances of Brian Campbell's death should be called into question. He demanded that the basic right of life should be respected by all. It was only when this was done, he said, that there would be a true foundation for justice and genuine peace. Another priest, an uncle of the man who died, also took part in the Mass. At the graveside the coffin was flanked by an IRA color party and a volley of shots was fired. A short time later in Coalisland, at the funeral of Colm McGirr, Sinn Fein assemblyman Martin McGuinness put the tricolor on the coffin. A black belt, gloves, and beret were put in place by Gerry Adams, the MP for West Belfast and president of Sinn Fein. In the Church of the Holy Family the circumstances of the shooting were referred to by Father Brian McCreesh, a brother of one of the IRA men who died on hunger strike. He said faceless, nameless strangers had violated the law of nature by striking down Irishmen in their native land.

Of course they did, as usual. This is Thatcher and her bloody shoot-to-kill policy at work. The murdering auld hoore, may she go straight to hell.

In the assembly there was condemnation of what were called disgraceful scenes at today's funerals. Ivan Foster of the DUP said that if the Catholic Church was opposed to the IRA, their opposition should have been demonstrated today. John Cushnahan of the Alliance Party said he wouldn't deny any man the right to a Christian funeral, but he distinguished that from what he called the glorification of terrorists by clergymen.

Terrorists? There's only one crowd of terrorists in this country, and that's the Brits themselves, over here terrorizing and shooting innocent, unarmed children in our own bloody country, the dirty shower of bastards. ·

Machil, that'll do.

The bloody animals.

The poor wee craturs, nineteen and twenty-three, sure they were only boys.

Children put your knives and forks down and bless yourselves.

Why did they shoot them, Daddy?

Because they were Catholic and Thatcher told the Brits they can shoot who they like over here.

Could they shoot us, too?

They can shoot whoever the hell they bloody well like, it seems.

Brendan, get up and put that television off for a minute and everybody stop eating and bless yourselves and let's say a wee prayer for the two boys. In the name of the father and of the son and of the holy ghost amen.

If I had been daydreaming through my days at school before I met Erin, I was now in a constant state of absenteeism. I sat in class and stared out the window at the sheets of rain as they rolled over St. Ciaran's playing fields, and the boys out there all muddied and cold chasing a small white ball with such determination that their screams and yells could be heard all the way up where I was in the middle of a droll history lesson. What did it all mean? What did it matter if you caught the ball or if you didn't? It was just a ball for godsake. And as for the history lesson, would I really need to know the exact dates and policies of Herbert Asquith's coalition government? Where was any of this information to serve me? And to whom would I repeat this long list of English dignitaries whose very names sat on my pink Irish tongue like a razor blade that I was being forced to swallow and regurgitate at will?

After dinner that Friday evening, my brother Michael washed and dressed to go out and I got down on my knees on the kitchen floor in front of my mother and I pleaded.

"I'm begging you, let me go just this one time. I will do anything . . ."

"You're not going, and that's that."

"Please."

"I said no, and that's that."

It was hopeless; she would never concede. A girl like Erin, a girl men found irresistible, was to be feared in a small community like ours: who knows who she might seduce next. This was still a time in Ireland when sex outside of the confines of marriage was very much a taboo subject. Women were still expected to be virgins or, better still, sexless. When my mother had been young, girls like Erin were being locked away all over Ireland in the Catholic Church–run Magdalene Laundries, the Vatican's answer for wayward girls. The Magdalene Laundries were still open for business when I was a teen. My mother was never going to allow me to see her.

I turned to my father as a last-ditch attempt.

"Dad, talk to Mammy. Please, please, let me go. You were my age once, remember?"

"You heard your mother, you're not going and that's that."

I went to my room and lay on the bed and hatched a plan to see her. I had to see her. I was suffocating without her. There was no reason to continue if I didn't see her. If I didn't see her, I would die.

When I got up the next morning I asked my mother if I could go see my friend Mark McCann, who lived just a few fields away.

"As long as you're back by dinner, and be careful around that farmyard. No riding on the tractor."

I hurriedly walked the ten minutes to Mark's house over the fields. As soon as I saw him, I announced immediately that I needed him to cover for me if my mother called. Then I turned again and I took off walking down the Altamuskin Road just as it began to rain. I buried my hands deep in my pockets and turned my face against the biting cold and leaned into the wind. I had made up my mind. I was going to see Erin, and nothing was going to stop me.

It took me about two hours before I reached the small country store where she lived with her parents.

When the bell tinkled over the door, she looked up to see me standing there soaked to the skin, a puddle of water forming about my feet on the linoleum floor.

"I'm sorry," I said. "I'm getting your floor all wet."

She ran out from behind the counter and threw her arms around me and kissed me furiously and suddenly I could breathe again.

"Tell me you didn't walk all the way here in the rain."

"It's not that bad."

"You're crazy."

"I'm sorry, I couldn't help it. I needed to see you."

And then she kissed me again.

An hour later, after being toweled off and kissed and hugged into a delirious stupor and successfully deflecting all inquiries about why I hadn't come out to see her the previous night, I told her that I would have to go again, never once mentioning that I had to steal away from my mother to see her.

As I headed out on the road again from the little shop the rain picked up just where it had left off. A dark continent of cloud seemed to have settled over the entire Northern Hemisphere and a savage wind roared at me from every angle over the open plains of bog land until my skin burned with bitter sheets of rain as I walked.

By the time I reached McCann's, it was almost dinnertime and I was nearly blind and deaf from the thrashing I had suffered at the hands of the storm. Rainwater squished out of the tops of my shoes. Not a single car had offered to give me a ride in more than fourteen miles of rain—so much for Irish hospitality. But I was elated. I had seen Erin and my mother was none the wiser. They hadn't beaten me just yet.

My euphoria was short-lived. Within the week I was denied seeing her again.

"You're not going out to see that tramp."

"She's not a tramp."

"She's a dirty tramp."

"You can't say that about her, you don't even know her."

"I know enough to know you're not going near her, and that's that."

It was a hopeless situation. I couldn't tell her that my mammy wouldn't let me go. The humiliation would have killed me. And I could think of no other excuse that could explain my failure to see her once a week. It was obvious that any boy in his right mind would be at the disco on a Friday night if Erin O'Rourke were his girlfriend. Unless, of course, there was something else wrong with that boy—something more sinister, something that nobody else really knew about him. It could be quite possible, and totally believable, for instance, that a boy like that didn't really like girls at all. A boy who would rather stay home and listen to Duran Duran in his room on a Friday night rather than be in the arms of someone like Erin O'Rourke would have to be gay. What other reason could exist? What other conclusion could she or my school friends, for that matter, finally come to? They would either consider me gay or they would know my mammy wouldn't let me out to be with her; either option would destroy me.

I spent that night and the next day planning the phone call I had to make. Then at about six o'clock the following evening I sneaked the telephone into the living room and sat on the floor with my back to the living-room door, took a deep breath to brace myself, and I called her.

"Hello, Erin."

"Hey, it's you. Are you OK? What happened yesterday? Why wouldn't you come out to see me? I waited for you all night."

"I have something I have to tell you."

"What?"

"I want to break up with you."

"What? Why?"

"I'm sorry to do this on the phone. I should have come out last night to tell you to your face."

"I don't understand. Why? Did I do something wrong?"

"No, it's nothing to do with you. I just want to be single, that's all."

"But why?"

"No reason."

"I thought you really liked me."

"I do, but I want to end it now that's all."

"Are you sure? I don't understand this."

"Yes, I'm sure. Bye, Erin. I have to go now."

"Bye, Colin."

I hung up the phone and sat there with it in my lap for a long time before I was able to move, stunned at the brutality of what I had just done to save myself from further humiliation. Then I got up and went out for a walk, down old Johnny White Paddy's lane and up the Altamuskin hill in front of our house, lighting one cigarette off another, gathering stones as I strolled and flinging them straight up into the night air high above my head. Closing my eyes for a moment, standing perfectly still, and bracing myself knowing that at any second one of them could come crashing down and pierce my skull as it plummeted from the darkness. I picked larger and larger stones, hurling them as hard as I could up into the blackness and waiting for one to bring me an answer to the pain, to halt that familiar voice that continued to speak to me even then, in that remote darkness, but the rock never came to take me away, and the voice was there to mock me with each failed attempt: "You're not going, and that's that."

What'll It Be?

During my last year at high school I was allowed to go to Kelly's Inn for the first time. Going to Kelly's Inn on a Friday night was like an initiation into manhood. Kelly's Inn was a real bar, the most popular bar to be in on a Friday night for a fifteen-mile radius. There was a dance floor and a DJ, notorious local drunks and troublemakers, Provos and wannabe Provos, and the best-looking girls in all of Tyrone. I had been hearing stories about Friday nights at Kelly's Inn since I was in primary school.

I was nervous as I strolled in with my brother Michael and our friends the McNamee brothers from just up the road. My cousins Paul and Des were there when we entered, at the bar with pints in hand. Most of my friends were accustomed to Kelly's; they had been going there on and off for years already.

"Well, would ye look who it is?" Paul said, grinning, as he

saw me sauntering in trying not to look like a complete idiot. "They finally let you out with the big boys, did they?"

"They finally did."

"Well, in that case, let me buy you your first drink in Kelly's. What'll it be?"

"I don't know. What's that you're drinking?"

"A pint of Harp it is. Lawrence, another pint of Harp over here when you get a chance, and whatever the boys here are having as well."

"Oh Jesus, McCann's finally buying a round, is he?" Brendan McNamee teased.

"I haven't seen you dip your hand in your pocket for a while either, McNamee, now that you mention it. Must be all going into that new car of yours."

"I still have enough for the next round, don't you worry about that, McCann." And so the ribbing would continue. It was good to be there at the bar in the midst of it all. Men talking like men talk, a match flares, smoke rises, somebody laughs, a girl walks by with a smile.

"Hold up a wee minute there," said the bartender, Lawrence McGarvey—a neighbor of ours and a lifelong friend of my parents—as he leaned out over the bar to get a good look at me up close as if he didn't recognize me already. "How old are you, young Broderick?"

"Old enough."

"You are in me arse old enough. You're still at school."

"That lad's been having a pint in here for the past six months and you're only noticing him now?" Paul said, winking at me to let me know this whole debate about age was nothing but a comical charade.

"If he has then I'm a blind man, because that's the first time I've seen that face in this bar."

"Come on now, Lawrence, give the man his pint and don't be making a show of him here in front of all his friends. If he gets into any trouble, I'll take all the blame."

"Well, on your head be it . . ." he said, releasing the pint from his hand into mine. "And don't you tell Claire Broderick I served you a drink or she'll have me guts for garters. Do you hear me?"

"I hear you, Lawrence."

"They'll be up here at the bar ordering drinks out of their prams shortly."

I took the pint and all the boys took theirs and raised them.

"To Colly's first pint," my brother Michael said, and we all clinked our glasses and put them to our lips and I tasted the first bitter swallow of Harp Lager run down my throat as I got my back slapped by an audience of hands.

I had tasted a sip out of my father's Smithwick's bottle as a boy, but never a full, deliberate swallow of beer before, not until that very moment: fifteen years old, at the bar in Kelly's Inn. It tasted like shit, truth be told, but I loved it.

Before the first pint was drained I could feel its warm, slippery tentacles creeping up the walls of my insides and wrapping themselves around the pleasure zones in my brain and running at will throughout my body, caressing the very places where I had been hurting my entire life, throwing open the windows of my heart and letting the great breeze of possibility rush in. I knew right there and then that I would never stop. This was the altar at which I would pray. This was the ocean of wisdom wherein I would swim. This was the key that unlocked the heavens. This was finally a reason to live, a reason to love, and suddenly I was whole for the first time in my life. I had escaped my prison cell and I was free. . . .

Three pints later I was slow dancing with a girl called Noleen Campbell. A tall, willowy, dark-haired girl from my school class, a girl with high, classically formed cheekbones and skin so dark and smooth she didn't look Irish at all. And I was no longer concerned about how my feet were moving or that she was a good half a head taller than me, or about how I might approach her for a kiss; I simply wrapped my arms around her and we swayed around the dance floor to Wham!'s "Careless Whisper" and we kissed without speaking and I was in love again.

Before the night was over I was drinking vodka and Cokes, I may have cried a little, and then there was a brief period of time when I seemed to disappear and then reappear again sitting on the wall of our neighbor's house and I was calling for my brother Michael to help me because I couldn't stand up and he was coming toward me across the Altamuskin Road in front of our house with his finger to his lips trying to shush me, and suddenly I was on my back in the neighbor's lawn, laughing hysterically because I had fallen and I couldn't seem to move at all and the stars were swirling in the sky above me.

When I woke the following morning I was in my bed,

fuzzy-headed and a little stunned by how quickly the night had passed. I had no memory of actually coming into the house or undressing for bed. It was my first association with time travel; I had blacked out. I liked it. If alcohol was going to help me spend less time living with the noise that was in my head, then I was all for it.

Good evening. This is the ITN news for Northern Ireland. It's six o'clock.

    A British Army UDR soldier was killed this afternoon in a bomb attack in County Tyrone.

Somebody put that television off now.

Wheesht just one minute till I hear the headlines.

Louise, get up from the table and put that television off now.

The IRA have claimed responsibility in the attack, which took place outside of the village of Castlederg . . .

Louise.

I'm puttin' it off now, Mammy.

Well hurry up, then. We can do without it for one minute while Colin gets his birthday cake. Are you all ready?

Happy birthday to you, you were born in a zoo,
with the elephants and the monkeys and the
crocodiles, too.

Yeahhh.

Well, how does it feel to be sixteen?

Old.

Five months later I sat for my final school exams. On the back
of one of the test forms, I used the time allotted for the exam to
scribble a rambling essay voicing my displeasure at the entire
educational system.

To my surprise, Master McSorley appeared in the classroom before the end of the exam to collect the papers himself.
When he came to my desk he picked up my exam paper and
noticed right away that none of the questions had been answered. He turned it over and read the title of my essay at the
top on the back page: "The Reasons I Have Not Taken This
Test, by Colin Broderick." He slipped it into the armful of other
exams and moved on to the next desk without a word. I was
done with school.

Slane Burned

There are six of us; six teenage boys. We are sitting in a car at the roundabout in Ballygawley. It is late at night and we are stoned. Simple Minds' "New Gold Dream" plays on the stereo. We are just returning from a hundred-mile round-trip to Belfast, where we must go to buy our hash. Two of us are rolling joints. A couple of joints are already in circulation.

The car is a hive of warm feelings and thick smoke. I run the lighter under the quarter ounce of hash, crumbling a fine powder of it off into the tobacco-lined paper in my lap. The lights of an occasional car roll past and slip off the roundabout on their way to Aughnacloy, Dungannon, Omagh, or beyond. Someone giggles, someone says yes, and someone else says turn this one up a little bit . . . there is a loud rap on the driver's window startling us into a volley of curses. It's the fucking Brits, someone whispers. The car is surrounded.

There are about six or seven British soldiers with their rifles casually aimed at the car windows. What do I do? someone says. Screw down the window. The joints are cupped into the palms of hands or ground out on the floor of the car. All hash is slipped from pockets and dropped discreetly to the floor. There is enough hash here to have us all thrown in jail for the rest of our lives should they decide to frame an arrest that way.

The driver rolls down the window and a thick cloud of hash smoke belches into the face of the soldier who has knocked. He sticks his big fat uninvited head almost all the way in the driver's side window, holding a bright flashlight that he casts around the interior of the car from face to face. No one in the car speaks.

"What are you boys up to, then?"

"Nothing," our driver says.

"Nothing?" the Brit says, recalibrating the word into a sharp nail he contemptuously spits back at us in his English vernacular. "So wot are you doing sitting 'ere, then, at the side of a roundabout in the middle of the night?"

"We were just on our way back from Belfast and I was tired. I pulled over to take a little break."

"Right. Sure you did. Give us your license then, son."

Our driver hands over his driver's license and we watch in silence as the Brit stands to examine it with his flashlight. He leans back down and holds the light in our driver's face again.

"So, you're telling me that you boys were just coming back from Belfast and you decided to stop here innocently for a rest when you live only another five miles down the road from here. Is that it? You expect me to believe that, Paddy? Who are you boys waiting for here? Who do we have in here? Get out of the fucking car. All of you. Slowly."

My heart is racing. We are lined up on the grass shoulder and told to keep our hands away from our pockets.

Four of the soldiers set about searching the car and others search us, as each of us is grilled in turn about our whereabouts, our names, and our addresses. Everyone lies automatically: a false surname, a false address, a false date of birth, just as we had been taught to do. Give them nothing they don't already know.

"Where were you?" one of them said to me.

"I don't know."

"'Course you don't. What were you doing there?"

"Knitting."

"You like to knit, you fucking fairy? What's your name, Paddy?" He got up close and spat the name at me in that thick English accent of his, taunting me with the derogation of my heritage. Patrick was not my name, nor was it Paddy, Pat, Pauric, Patsy, Packie, Padge, or Podge: my name was Colin. Paddy was the name the Brits used for us, the bastardized version of Patrick–Saint Patrick, our Catholic patron saint of Ireland. He knew the strength of the name to cut, like calling a black man a nigger to his face, or a Jew a kike, the name hurled and repeated and kicked in your face like dirt.

"That's right."

"You wot?"

"I said that's right. Paddy. You got it. Good guess."

"You being smart with me?"

"No, you got it. That's my name, Paddy."

"Paddy what?"

"O'Shaughnessy. Paddy Patrick O'Shaughnessy."

"Is that a real name? Spell it."

Over their shoulders I see a soldier in the back of the car holding between his finger and thumb the quarter ounce of hash that I dropped. He is holding it up, examining it in the light of his flashlight. I try to imagine what my parents will say when they get the phone call that we have all been arrested. How quickly everyone in the parish will hear that we have been arrested for drugs. No one has ever been arrested for drugs in our parish. I wonder how much time we will spend in jail–years maybe. I can hear the priest bellow the word "DRUGS" from the pulpit, giving the word its long-awaited debut to the ears of the parishioners. I watch in amazement as the soldier tosses the hash back onto the floor again and turns his focus again to the seat, running his hands into the cracks, pulling at the cushions looking for the guns, ammunition, grains of fertilizer.

They keep us standing there for more than half an hour, and miraculously find nothing.

"OK, I don't know what you lot are up to or who you were waiting for here, but I do know you're up to something. We'll be watching you lot from now on, you can be fucking sure of that. Go on, get out of 'ere."

We get back in the car and when we pull away, everyone is able to locate their hash. Fresh joints are rolled. The music is back on. We are talking and laughing at their ignorance, at how they had held the hash in their fingers, examined it and tossed it away without the slightest suspicion of what it was, and we are proud of ourselves because it feels like that was one minor battle that we won fair and square.

Good evening. This is the ITN news for Northern Ireland. It's six o'clock.

An RUC unit on patrol this afternoon in the town of Ballygawley narrowly escaped in a rocket attack directed at them by the IRA.

That's what all the helicopters were about this evening.

I hope that's some of the same bastards we saw last night at the roundabout.

Were they stopping at the roundabout last night?

They were.

Wheesht a minute till I hear the news.

Police have recovered the RPG from a nearby field and are scanning the area looking for clues.

Mammy, we seen the helicopter landing down in McCann's field after school, and all the Brits got out with their guns and disappeared into the hedges.

I know you did, Louise, and what did I tell you about that, when you see the Brits landing in the fields? To come into the house right away.

But they were over in McCann's field, not ours. . . .

I don't care, that's close enough. You never know when something might happen. They could accidently shoot you when they're jumping out of the helicopter. . . .

Would they shoot us?

Not as long as you eat up the rest of that cabbage. Then you'll be big and strong and there'll not be a gun in the country strong enough to shoot you with.

Now that I was sixteen and done with school, my parents allowed me to go to my first big concert at Slane Castle. Slane Castle was the largest outdoor concert venue in Ireland. Once a year, roughly fifty thousand teenagers from all over Ireland converged on this tiny southern village to see the most famous bands in the world perform on the lawn of an old castle.

Throughout high school I had been tortured by the stories of friends and cousins who had been already, been to see acts like U2, Thin Lizzy, the Rolling Stones, and Simple Minds. It wasn't just that they had been to see the bands themselves, it was the stories they brought back of the three-day party that had accompanied each trip: the late-night bonfires, the random hookups, the sheer debauchery of the whole enterprise.

My brother Michael and I caught a ride with our friends the McNamee brothers. We made a stop at a liquor store in Aughnacloy, and between the four of us we filled the trunk of Brendan's new Ford Escort with cases of beer, boxes of cheap white wine, plastic bottles of cider, and bottles of vodka, whiskey, Cointreau, and Tia Maria. Once we had passed through the British Army border checkpoint at the bottom of the town, we turned the music up and started into the cans of Tennent's Lager right away. It was my first weekend away from home without adult supervision, and I was not about to miss a single minute of getting hammered.

It was one of those bright sunny afternoons that happen maybe once or twice in a young person's life when for a few brief shining hours it seems like anything in the world is possible. The sun was high in a crisp blue sky, the music playing loud, and we were four close friends in the Free State of Ireland on a Friday evening with three straight days of fun ahead of us. Beer was spilled, songs were sung, busloads of tourists were mooned, and by the time we reached the little town of Slane three hours later, at least three of us were completely hammered.

For miles out, the traffic was slowed, young kids with backpacks and long hair and tie-dyed T-shirts filed along the sides of the road, raising their beer cans or plastic cider bottles in the air, toasting anyone who cheered from a passing car. Two-fingered peace signals were raised in salute and we turned the stereo all the way up and yelled along with the lyrics of "Someone Somewhere in Summertime," and in the dusk of that great evening as we finally found a field to park in somewhere on the north side of the village, I experienced joy for the first time. The kind of exalted joy that could inspire a young boy to weep and hug his friends and tell them for the first time and without any reservation that he really did love them, and make great proclamations of how this was just the beginning of things and that this is how it should always have been and would always be from here on in, and that there were things that he knew but didn't know quite how to explain, but the important thing was that they understand something about exactly how he was feeling, something about this great moment in time when we were all young together in this very field on the eve of something monumental . . . And then I fell to my knees in the dry grass and was sick–wave after wave of nausea and coffee-tasting Tia Maria on its way back up again and the boys laughing and goading me along: "What was that you were saying about something great about to happen? Is this it? Is this the big thing? Ha-ha-ha . . ." And the field spun and a small crowd of people cheered and I rose to my feet and did a small pirouette before the ground swung fiercely up at me again, whacking me suddenly in the side of the face, catching me completely off guard, and then my brother's voice saying, "It's all right, young fella, we have you now," as he and Brendan McNamee raised me again and got under my arms to help me along as we were swept into the thick throng of kids marching toward town.

When we entered Slane, the town was in chaos. Gangs of boys ran screaming through the crowd with their fists in the

air. We were knocked and jostled in the fray. I allowed myself
to be swept along with them. They were Northern lads with
thick Belfast accents. Brendan and I linked arms with them
and skipped down the middle of the main street yelling the
lyrics of a rebel song we knew well: *"A nation once again, a nation
once again and Ireland long a province be. A nation once again."* But
when I turned to speak to Brendan, he was gone. In his place
I found a stranger on either arm. It didn't matter. I was drunk
with the abandon of it all. The push of the crowd insisted we
go forward. I went forward, carried along with the force of the
tide, liberated, cresting a great sea of Northerners. We were
twenty across, arm in arm, wave after wave of us. We tipped
our faces to the sky and we roared the lyrics of the song: *"A nation once again. A nation once again and Ireland long a province be.
A nation once again."* All the scattered voices suddenly slipped
into key and we were no longer a chorus, we were one unified voice. *"A nation once again. A nation once again and Ireland
long a province be. A nation once again."* Suddenly it was as if the
potency and magnitude of our cry had miraculously turned
some psychic key and as the tumblers fell into place the door
was flung open wide, releasing a flood of latent primordial bar-
barianism. There was a volcanic eruption of violent tension.
Years of repression and anger and hatred crashed through the
peaceful façade, shattering the warm flowering of love in the
little town, and we were unified in a colossal symphony of rage.
No one led the way. No one needed to bark an order; our own
harmonious rage conducted us to violence. We surrounded an
empty Garda police car and we flipped it on its head. Windows
were kicked in, a match was lit, and the whole thing roared

into flames right there in the middle of the street in the little village of Slane.

The entire crowd seemed to suddenly explode into a mass rioting mob, a swirling vortex of savagery down the streets of this historic little village, overturning every car as they moved, smashing glass, leaking petrol, turning the street into a forest of flame, and I was swept along in it unleashed, untethered, ferociously alive for the very first time in my life, until I realized I had lost sight of the boys I had been with and the whole town was being torn apart by an angry mob.

I kept staggering along down the middle of the street, blindly making my way through the throng. The crowd thinned on the road and I saw that I had walked clean out the far side of town by about a half mile. Night had fallen in the country, and when I turned around I could see the pockets of flame roaring up past the silhouettes of the rooftops in the little village as Slane burned.

The following morning I awoke next to a tent. The flap peeled back and my cousin Des crawled out over me where I was lying in the grass.

"How the hell did you find me?" he laughed as he sat next to me.

"I thought you just found me."

"You didn't know I was here?"

"I didn't even know you were in Slane."

There were a bunch of other lads with him from home crashed out in and around the tent also. My cousins Paul, Frank, Noel, Eamon, and Shea McClean were all there, and a lad called Mark the Bard. Mark's real surname was Mullin. His grandfather had been a local poet of some note, so they were known as the Bards to distinguish them from the other Mullin families in our parish. The Bards were the most notorious family of nationalists in our whole community. They made no secret of it. I'd seen his brother Brian standing next to Gerry Adams at our chapel gates. Another one of their brothers was serving a long stretch in the H-Block on a sectarian murder charge.

Mark the Bard was just about as hard a man as you were likely to meet in the entire province. He popped open a warm can of beer and handed it to me for breakfast. I took a pull on it and watched him as he slipped a half pint of whiskey out of his back pocket, cracked it open, and tipped it to his head. The other lads followed suit. Someone threw a packet of smokes my way. I took one and threw the pack onto the next. Before long my brother Michael and the McNamee brothers had found us, and we all settled in to get good and drunk before the concert began.

They informed me that the rioting had gone on all night. The local Slane police had barricaded themselves in the station house as hundreds of riot police had been called in from surrounding towns to quell the mayhem. The news had gone global. Lord Henry Mountcharles, who owned Slane Castle, made a statement to the effect that it would probably mark the end of the annual music festival being held in the small town.

"It's not the first time this place has burned," the Bard said.

"Did they burn it last year too?" I asked.

"You don't know much about your own history." The Bard grinned. "This is where they fought the Battle of the Boyne, right here in these fields. They were camped out right where you're lying there on the side of this bit of a hill."

I knew the Battle of the Boyne had some connection to the Protestant celebrations on July the twelfth, but that was about the entire extent of my knowledge.

"This is where it all went down," he continued. "In 1690, the Catholic king James fought the Protestant king William of Orange, right here. You've heard of the Orangemen, right? They march on the twelfth of July in the north every year?"

"I know the Orangemen march on the twelfth," I said, not wanting to appear completely ignorant.

"Well, this is where it happened, right here in Slane. The Protestants against the Catholics for control of the British throne, right here, three hundred years ago. If it had gone the other way there'd be no war in Northern Ireland today. It would have ended here." He paused to take another pull on his bottle of Jameson. We were all listening intently now. He had our full attention. "But it didn't," he said, capping the bottle again and hitting it a tap with the palm of his hand. "It didn't go that way."

The rest of the weekend went by in one great quest for oblivion. By early that Saturday evening Santana and UB40 had roused the forty thousand teenagers into a unified, cider-and-hash-soaked swaying mass of crimson euphoria as they lulled the crowd into a long rhythmic chant of *"Red red wine, stay close to me-e-e"* just in time for Dylan to burst onto the stage with "Highway 61 Revisited," sending this devoted congregation into a volcanic eruption of ecstasy. Halfway through his set, when Van Morrison joined him onstage for "Tupelo

Honey," we were openmouthed and speechless; girls wept and boys stood staring at the bright stage against the lush green valley beyond in rapt reverence, knowing that we had been gifted just a little slice of musical history, and by the time Bono strolled onto the stage late in the night to sing "Blowin' in the Wind" with Dylan, we knew we would never see another concert as good again.

Apprentice

Now that I was done with school, I had my first real job. For twenty-six pounds a week I was an apprentice electrician, working for one of the most reputable electrical contractors in all of County Tyrone. A very respectable and much sought-after position it was, too. The kind of a job a young Catholic lad should be on his knees thanking the good Lord for in County Tyrone.

But with the new job came the first inkling of responsibility. It was up to me to get out of bed and somehow get myself to Carrickmore every morning by eight thirty. Not an easy task, because at sixteen years of age I could have slept until dinnertime every day if they'd let me. And not an easy task because Carrickmore was more than five miles away, so I had to try to get up in time to thumb my way into Sixmilecross to catch a ride from a coworker who passed through town at about eight. If it was raining when I left the house, it meant I would be wet for the day, for as ridiculous as it must seem we did not own an umbrella. Nor had I ever in my life seen an Irish person in possession of an umbrella. Here in one of the most precipitous climates on the face of the earth we had learned to take the rain as it fell. If you were a workingman you were just going to get wet, and often. That was just the nature of things in Ireland when I was a boy.

Being the fresh new apprentice on the job also meant that I was the one they'd send down into a two-foot-wide pipe at a quarry to drag a length of thick cable through dirty water and muck, or up into a dark and musty attic to catch a face full of cobwebs while fishing wire through the dusty insulation, or to stand at the top of a ladder against a hay shed, outside in the freezing cold, holding a cable until my hands and ears turned numb. You learned quickly not to complain about any of this. To complain about the cold only opened you up to a fresh barrage of insults and put-downs about not being man enough to handle it like everybody else. So you kept your big mouth shut about the cold.

Within a month or so I was becoming so proficient I could second-fix an entire council house by myself in a day. The second fix involved trimming the bare wires coming out of the freshly plastered walls and ceilings and affixing the wall sockets, light switches, and light fixtures. Sometimes I was so enthusiastic that I could almost complete a second house, wiring every outlet and light fixture before it was time to wrap it up at six o'clock. I was doing as much work as guys who had been with the company for years, and they were not very happy about that.

But I was determined to better myself as quickly as possible so I could ask for the raise I needed to organize my own transportation. The twenty-six pounds I was making couldn't get me through the weekend; five pounds to my mother toward my room and board, ten pounds on a Friday night to buy a pack of smokes and catch a buzz at Kelly's Inn, and if I was lucky I would have enough left over to get me out again on a Saturday night, but by Sunday morning I wouldn't have the price of a bottle of Lucozade to swill after Mass for my hangover. I'd be back to borrowing money for another five days till payday.

There was also the added pressure of knowing that at any moment I could be subjected to some form of humiliating initiation treatment on the work site. I knew it was coming, but the fact that I didn't know exactly when it was going to happen kept me in a state of high alert and mild terror. I had already been subjected to some of the more painful methods of initiation, one of which involved someone sneaking into the house where I was working and throwing the switch on the power while I was handling live wires upstairs, sending a bolt of 240 volts up my arms and into my neck muscles and knocking me on my ass, or to the other side of the room. Two hundred and forty volts is enough power to kill a man, but chances are a boy could survive it if you only switched the power on and off again real quick. But it left you jittery for a while and you learned the first painful lesson: that you were never to touch a wire if you were not one hundred percent sure that it was dead.

But that was playful entertainment compared to the real initiation they had in store for me. I witnessed the real initiation only a few weeks after first starting on the job.

A boy who started work alongside me as an apprentice was snatched by the older men in the tea room one morning and was dragged kicking and screaming outside, held down on the cold dirt, and stripped of his pants and underwear. Then he was held, legs pulled apart and pinned to the ground, while another man painted his balls and his ass with green Cuprinol wood preservative and the rest of the crowd of about fifteen grown men stood around watching on in peals of laughter, mocking his little dick and shriveled ball sac.

Anybody who has ever worked with Cuprinol will tell you it does not wash off your skin, but rather fades away after weeks of continued washing. To have your entire tackle publicly varnished with a coarse brush was not as much an initiation process as it was sheer torture.

I lived with the constant dread of my own initiation, and after a couple of weeks I was beginning to wish they would just leap on me and get it over with. The anticipation and the stress of having to constantly watch over my shoulder for an attack was turning me into a nervous wreck on the job.

My turn came one cold wintry morning just after we were sitting in silence in the tea room after our breakfast. A big rough-looking man who worked for one of the other contractors sprang from where he was sitting and yelled, "Get him."

Without thinking I spontaneously stood and put my hands on my hips and said, "Good. I want you to start." There was a pause for a moment as my assailant tried to comprehend what had just happened.

"What the fuck did you say?"

"I said I want you to start. I want you to be the first to pull down my zipper and take my trousers down. I want you to see it first." I could barely believe the words were coming out of my mouth. I had not planned a word of it, but it was miraculously holding him at bay, so I kept smiling at him.

"Holy fuck, he's a queer."

"He's not a fucking queer," someone else said with a laugh. "He's pulling your fucking leg."

"He's a faggot."

"He's not a faggot."

"Well then, you pull his fucking trousers down then if you're so sure."

"I don't want to pull his fucking pants down."

"Can somebody please pull my pants down?" I smiled.

"Fuck you, you little queer. If you're not careful, I'll give you a box in the mouth."

"Mmm, I might enjoy that."

A man I worked with, Eugene Coyle, began to applaud.

"Well done, young man, that's the finest piece of acting I have ever seen on a job site."

The big man sat down again and I sat down too and went back to reading my newspaper. Nobody ever touched me on a site again after that. Neither did they ask me out for drinks. But that was all right by me. I was growing accustomed to feeling like an outsider. As far as I could see, the intelligence of a man seemed to diminish in degrees the larger a group he belonged to. I would take my chances alone.

Within about four months I had quit the job because I couldn't survive on the pay. I had nervously approached my boss in his office one Friday afternoon to ask him to consider giving me a raise. He'd responded with a giggle and a shake of his head confirming without a word that there wasn't a slim chance in hell that the possibility was even on the horizon. I was too young and insecure to have any sense of my own self-worth, so I left his office without even trying to argue my case.

My next job was working as a housepainter. I had plenty of experience in this particular field since my days of training with the Vampiro. Apparently, word had gotten around that I could handle a brush and I got a job with one of the top house-painters in all of Tyrone, a man called Brian McHugh. It turned out Brian was almost equally as crazy as the Vampiro, so we got along famously. He liked my work and paid me well for it. In a matter of months I was able to buy my first car and go out and get drunk three nights a week. Pretty soon after that I got offered a job working as an apprentice carpenter to Mickey McCann, a local cabinetmaker, working for ten pounds a day. So I quit painting and took that job instead. I already had some experience from my days of apprenticeship with my father building our own house. But what did it matter? Carpenter, painter, candlestick maker—the days were long and gray and my feet were always wet and my toes and fingers stung from the cold and there was never enough money to get me out to a bar seven nights a week no matter how much I worked.

I couldn't wrap my head around the hard men, men like my dad, who stepped out of the car in the morning onto the work site raring to get at it. He'd walk straight over to an icy puddle and break the skin with the heel of his boot before immersing his hands in the frigid ice water because it was a sure way of getting them warm. And if that didn't do it, the work surely would. For hard men like my dad it was only a matter of horsing into it and you'd be breaking a sweat in no time. But I never did. I never warmed to it.

No matter how hard I worked, I was always cold. Mornings with the rain coming in sideways as I sat on the roof of some new house, not able to feel the nail that sat between my finger and thumb, with an entire ocean of slate to go down before nightfall. I couldn't even go sit in the car to have my tea so I could warm up a bit. That kind of sissy behavior was absolutely forbidden. I had to sit outside with everybody else, with the damp arctic wind creeping down the neck of my sweater and up the leg of my pants, and keep my fat face shut about the cold as I ate the few cheese and tomato sandwiches that my mother had taken the trouble to pack for me. And I held that cup of lukewarm tea in my shaking hands for the twenty minutes it took for my body to seize completely and then my father would rise—it was always my father to rise first from the tea—and take an armful of slate on his shoulder before skipping back up that ladder onto the roof again for another five-hour stretch in the evening.

"You'll never be half the worker your father is."

"With the help of God."

But if you didn't suffer the job, and if you didn't clean

yourself up for an hour on a Tuesday morning to go down and sign on for your dole check, there'd be no Friday nights at Kelly's Inn. You got up and you suffered because it was the only way you were going to have money in your pocket for drink and smokes and petrol. When you needed a shirt, you bought a shirt and wore it till it was done. A pair of jeans would last you nearly a year if you didn't tear them in a fight; a good pair of leather shoes, six months.

On Sunday mornings you put on your uncomfortable clothes for Mass. A pair of pressed trousers with a crease in the front and a white shirt and tie and a clean sweater that you wouldn't be seen dead in on any other day of the week, and you sat in the pew with your back straight and if you had to yawn you suppressed it so your eyes got all teary. And you spent the entire fifty minutes staring at whatever girl's ass was kneeling at the pew in front of you and you asked God to forgive you for this sin of fornication in His holy house, for even if you thought about it you had sinned, just as sure as if you'd leapt over that railing and rode her through the Act of Contrition.

And sometimes if your head was a bit fuzzy from the heap of vodka you poured into it the night before, you could swear that the lips on the statue of the Virgin Mary had just quivered a bit and that she was just on the verge of opening that pouty little mouth of hers to address the congregation because you knew in your heart and soul that such things happened and happened often everywhere, and that one of these days it would only make sense that you would witness one of these miracles for yourself.

And when you came out of the chapel gates, you bought

your copy of *An Phoblacht* because you were a hard man now with your own hard-earned money in your pocket and you bought a small bottle of Lucozade as well, out of the back of Eddie Kelly's newspaper van, and you nudged in beside a few of the old-timers to lean against a gate or a fence across the road from the chapel to puff for a bit and nod your head and wink and give auld smart chat to lads you knew as they were on their way out past you.

And once in a blue moon you might stand in that very same spot and listen for a while to this fiery young republican politician by the name of Gerry Adams, with a speaker strapped to the roof of Brian Mullin's old red Ford Escort, as he held court with a microphone about why it was time we all voted Sinn Fein and how important it was that we all stick together as good Irish Catholics and rid the Northern six counties of Ireland of the English oppressor once and for all. And you were embarrassed and angry at the way your mother and father would continue on past Mr. Adams and down to the car park without stopping for a moment or two, to pay a wee bit of respect for his effort, because they were middle-of-the-road now, politically speaking, because our mother's brother was Paddy Joe McClean—the same man who had been tortured by the Brits during internment was a Workers' Party man now, or a Sticky as I'd heard him called when he was not around to hear it—and as far as my mother was concerned, Paddy Joe and the Workers' Party were a more respectful bunch to side with because they believed in peace and equality for everyone; they did not condone violence in any form. And if my mother believed in my uncle's politics, then I very much wanted to hear the alternative, because I was determined not to be on her side about anything ever again.

As a young Catholic boy, you knew the word on the street was that the Stickies were weak and their approach was naïve, and that the only way to rid ourselves of the English oppressor was with the language of Semtex and ArmaLites; that was the only language these English bastards really understood—a language this young, fiery Gerry Adams seemed to be well versed in. Here was the orator we young Catholic boys had been waiting for. Here was the man to give voice to our frustrations. And if my neighbor Brian the Bard was standing next to him to vouch for him, well then that was good enough for me, because Brian the Bard was one of the hardest men in all of Tyrone and he kept it no secret where his allegiance lay.

On Friday nights I washed up and squeezed into a pair of faded, skin-tight jeans and fixed my hair so I looked a bit like David Bowie—starved and a little sick. The McNamee lads would swing by and we'd head on over to Kelly's Inn for a heap of beer. And I would drink more than I should, more than was necessary, until I was legless.

On the way home the boys would wait patiently in the car while I slipped into Lisa Monaghan's house for tea. We'd kiss and make out on the couch and I'd touch her over the top of her clothes and we would rub our bodies against each other until we were on the verge of passing out with the sheer hellish bliss of it all. But I was careful not to go too far with her because she was a nice girl and I liked her a lot and I didn't want her to think I was some sort of filthy brute, some sort of a sick degenerate pervert, by trying to put my hand down into her panties.

No, I saved that for another girl, who wasn't so nice. Another girl I slipped out of the bar when nobody was looking and she didn't stop me when I laid her down on my coat on the grass, and she didn't stop me when I lay on top of her and kissed her hard and put my hands up her shirt and down into her pants, and she didn't stop me when I put my hand between her legs, and she didn't stop me when I clumsily tried to get my thing in there, and she didn't say anything, even when I wasn't quite sure if I was getting it in the right place at all, or if I was doing the thing that I was supposed to be doing correctly.

And she didn't say anything when I was done and she didn't say anything once we were about to go back inside again, and she didn't complain when I let her hand slip from mine without even a good-bye, and she was kind enough to let it all happen that way because she knew I had a steady girlfriend already and that the thing between her and me would just be that one thing. And I never was able to tell her that I loved her too, loved her for being the one who let me do it that first time without a word, loved her for being warm and patient and open to it all, loved her for taking the boy in me and turning me into a man, loved her for being even more special than all the other girls I'd ever kissed, and I definitely never got to tell her that I had loved her from the very first time I had seen her sitting ahead of me at Mass almost three years earlier. And afterward, after that night, I never did kiss her again because I knew too many others who had and I hated myself for being part of that group also and for not being man enough to set myself apart from them by telling her how I really felt, to give her the meager gift of my honesty and the little dignity that admission might have bestowed.

Just Like Your Uncle

Good evening. This is the ITN news for Northern Ire-
land. It's six o'clock. A mortar attack on a police station
in Newry last night has killed a total of nine members of
the RUC. The police officers were having their dinner at
around six o'clock yesterday evening in a temporary can-
teen on the base when the fifty-pound mortar shell struck
the building. A further thirty-seven have been reported
badly injured. The attack marks the largest loss of life in
a single attack on the RUC police force since the Troubles
began in Northern Ireland.

"Maybe now they'll go home to their own bloody country," I said. I had become more vocal in our home about my
hatred of the English. I was growing more and more frustrated
with my mother's peaceful attitude toward our oppressors. As

far as I could see, the only language the British listened to was the language of violence. To me, any other approach smacked of weakness. I understood that if the Catholics stopped expressing their rage the English could consider the occupation complete. The moment we stopped fighting them, Northern Ireland could be marked down as another successful acquisition for the Crown.

"They are home," my mother replied. "The police are just Northern Irish Protestants; they were born and raised here like me or you. This is their home as much as it's yours or mine."

"They're all the same, Brits, police–a bunch of scumbags, and good riddance to them."

"That will do."

"Well, it's the truth. I hope they kill them all, every last one of them."

"Colin, that's enough."

"What? I can't say I hate the Protestants? Who cares about them, they're a bunch of dirty pigs. Why are you defending them?"

"There'll be none of that talk in this house. God have mercy on their souls, the craturs. In the name of the father and of the son and of the holy ghost amen."

The car that I'd bought gave me a new freedom. I might not have been old enough to leave home yet but my mustard-colored Austin Mini 1000 helped me escape for at least a few hours a night when I could afford the gas to get away. My drinking had increased also. I was up for any distraction that might help me bide my time until I was of legal age to move out of my parents' home and leave Altamuskin for good.

One Saturday morning, my mother flipped out because I was too hungover to get out of bed and go off to work with my dad. He was gone by the time I got out of bed, but she was there waiting for me when I came through the kitchen door, my head musty with vodka.

"This is the last time this happens in this house. I will not sit here and watch you turn yourself into a drunk."

"Is this necessary?"

"You're damned right it's necessary. I have a brother dying of alcoholism this very minute and you boys are not going to do the same." My mother's brother Brendan McClean was a very successful businessman, but at forty-two he was drinking himself to death. She would go to his house with her sister Sue to beg him to stop before he killed himself, and they would return red-eyed and empty with nothing to say. It seemed to me as I listened to my mother that Brendan had good reason to have another drink if this was the kind of pathetic nagging he had to put up with from the women in his life. I had a good idea of how he felt.

"Well, you don't really have a say in whether I drink or not, Mum."

"Don't you tell me I don't have a say in what happens in my own house. You are seventeen years old, and until you are eighteen, you will damn well do exactly what I say, is that understood? That room of yours smells like a brewery."

"You can say what you like, but I'm just telling you that it doesn't matter at this point."

"Don't you dare think I can't tell you what to do," my mother said, racing around the table and sticking her finger up under my nose. "I am in charge in this house, and as long as you live here you'll do exactly as I say and that's that."

When she lowered her hand I stormed outside, got in my car and left a trail of burning rubber from our front gate for about twenty yards down the road. I drove with my shoe flat to the floor, slapping the car up through the gears, feeling the rip of the tires as I screeched the tar on the dry road around corners. I would have driven straight into the middle of an ocean to escape my mother and that house. Here I was, old enough to work, old enough to drive, old enough to drink, old enough to feel like a man and still she treated me like a child. It was unfathomable to me that she possessed the legal right to insist I stay living at home under her control. I went on down through Sixmilecross without cooling the motor for the town speed limits and out toward Beragh, my knuckles white on the steering wheel, my skin taut with rage.

I was about a mile out of Beragh, rounding a blind corner at over eighty, when I drove straight into a British Army check-point. I swerved to miss the soldier stationed in the middle of the road with his hand raised for me to stop. I stood on the brakes and brought the car to a screeching halt, the tires leaving two long black streaks behind me on the tar like a pair of exclamation marks.

By the time I had stopped, there were three rifles drawn on me at close range. I threw my hands up to cover my head and waited, expecting the first blast through the windshield. Men had been shot for a lot less in the North. But the shot did not come, and when I looked in the mirror the soldier who was standing in the middle of the road was coming toward me at a brisk pace. I could see his face in the mirror as he drew within a few feet of the car, his dark little mustache like something a child might have scrawled on his face with a crayon.

"Wot the bloody hell do you think you're at, then?" he yelled before he had come to a stop beside my window.

"What do you think *you're* at?" I yelled back, delighted to have someone in front of me to finally vent my rage on verbally. The words that had been trapped in my throat for the past ten minutes leapt past my teeth like an eruption.

"Don't you yell at me, boy."

"Fuck you, don't you shout at me, you fucking asshole."

"Who the bloody hell do you think you're talking to like that? You almost killed me and a bunch of my men."

"Well, maybe next time you'll think before you stand like a bunch of baboons in the middle of the road on a blind corner when you hear a car coming at eighty miles an hour."

"We can stand wherever we bloody well please. . . ."

"And I can drive wherever I bloody well please. . . ."

"Get out of the car."

"Fuck you."

"Get out of the fucking car, Paddy. Now."

He grabbed the door before I could get it locked and had me by the shoulder, dragging me. Once I was out, he slammed me against the side of the car and stood back locking his hands into a good grip on his rifle.

"Oh aye, you're a big fuckin' man with that gun!" I yelled,

daring him to smash me in the face, or shoot me even, anything to release me from this explosion of rage.

"You think I need this gun to put manners on you, Paddy?" He had a gun; I only had my tongue.

"If you didn't have that gun to protect you, I'd kick your ass from here back to your own country where you belong."

"This is our country, Paddy."

"No, this is Ireland. You're from England; that's the country shaped like a large turd on the other side of the Channel."

He flipped his rifle around and shoved the barrel up under my chin hard.

"You want me to blow your fucking head off?"

"Go ahead. See if I give a fuck."

"You think I fucking won't? You think anybody would bloody well stop me?"

"Well do it, then. Do it. What the fuck are you waiting for? Go on . . ."

A few of the others had gathered around, and one of them stepped in before my new friend's trigger finger "accidently slipped."

"OK, OK, that's enough, break it up, break it up. Get in your fucking car, you, and get the hell out of here without another fucking word. Go on, you heard me. Get out of here."

As I got in my car and pulled the door closed, my buddy with the mustache leaned in the window to whisper his parting words.

"I'll fucking get you one of these nights, Paddy."

I gave him a little wink as I started the car and took off

down the road toward Omagh, noticing suddenly the shake in my hands as I tried to light my smoke. No matter where I turned I was penned in, it seemed. At home I lived under the iron will of my mother; outside of that I was surrounded by an army of foreign invaders who would like nothing better than to see me dead. No wonder alcohol was becoming so important. It was the only window I could fully escape through.

That afternoon when Dad returned from work, Michael and I were summoned to the kitchen and our brothers and sisters were chased from the room.

"The drinking in this house is going to stop right now," my father announced when the room had emptied. My mother, whom I'd avoided since our fight that morning, stood behind him at her station by the sink, her cheeks pink and bright from being out in the cold hanging the laundry. "You're going to get in your car and you're going to drive up to the priest's house, and you're going to tell him that you want to renew your pledge."

"I'm not taking my pledge again," I said, and felt my heart give a little skip in the refusal. I had taken all the pushing that my body could handle. Just a few hours earlier I'd stood up to a man who'd shoved a gun under my chin, what more harm could they do to me at home? From here on out I would push back no matter what the cost.

"I'm not asking you," my father said as sternly as he could manage without raising his voice. "I'm telling you. The two of you will go out that door and get in that car this minute, and there won't be another word about it."

"Go on, now, take yourselves on out of here and get up the road," my mother added, and Michael moved past me for the kitchen door without a word.

"Well, I'm not going," I announced, folding my arms and leaning back against the range, bracing myself for the first slap.

"I said you're going," my father barked, taking a step toward me.

"Come on, Colin, let's go," Michael coaxed, opening the back door to leave.

"Get out that door right now without another word," my mother snapped.

"I'm not going," I said, resolved to stand my ground at last. My father took another step forward and clenched his fists. He was only three feet away now, almost within swinging distance, and I knew by his face that I had pushed him to the edge. "Go ahead hit me. Go on, do it, beat me all you want, you can drag me out the door and bring me to the priest's house against my will if you want and you can have him stick a probationary pin on me if you like, but I will drink again because that's what I'm going to do and you can't stop me."

My father moved to hit me, but my mother stopped him. "Go on," I continued, for the first time knowing that I could handle any beating they could administer; I'd taken all kinds of beatings and survived them all. Physical pain couldn't hold a candle to the mental anguish I'd suffered through my teens. I was ready for anything they could throw at me. "Do whatever the hell you like for the next year!" I yelled. "Go on, you can beat me for now, so you might as well make the best of it because the minute I turn eighteen I am out of this house, I'm gone, I'm leaving this country and you'll never tell me what to do ever again."

"Go to your room now," my mother said as she reached out and gently touched my father's arm to draw a halt to the situation before it spiraled completely out of control. "Go. Go up to your room. Now."

I went to my room and sat on the bed and for once I felt a moment of calm. I had needed to hear myself speak those words. They had been the white noise I had lived with. I needed to draw a line in the sand and say here it is, this is where Colin begins, the first thin scrawl of an identity forming.

Twenty minutes later my mother came into the room. She closed the door behind her and stood with her back to it.

"Your father and I discussed it, and you're right. We can't make you take the pledge."

"Good."

"We just don't want to see you in the shape your uncle Brendan is in right now."

"He seemed to be in great form the last time I saw him at Dunmoyle," I said, referring to a much-talked-about appearance Brendan had made at my cousin Mary's wedding just a few weeks earlier, when he had shown up so late he missed the ceremony completely. By the time he'd arrived, the crowd had exited the church and were outside flinging confetti and taking pictures. Brendan pulled up in his new Mercedes three sheets to the wind and stumbled out wearing a bright checkered suit with a half bottle of booze in his hand. He proceeded to kiss and hug half the ladies who were on their way out the chapel gates. Then, much to everyone's delight, especially us younger boys in the crowd, he began poking fun at everybody and everything, making a mockery of anyone who appeared to be taking themselves too seriously.

"What are you doing up there, Quasimodo?" he yelled as the photographer climbed on the church pillar to get a better angle of the bride and groom, and the crowd went into peals of laughter. "Hey, Quasimodo, I didn't know you were in the photography business," he continued, and even the normally stern Father McPeake had to concede a giggle. It was the most entertainment I'd ever seen at a church event, people roaring with laughter, other men sparring back with their own barbs to keep him at it. The crowd was elated that something out of the ordinary had taken place. Everybody but my mother and her sisters, that is, who seemed less taken with his outrageous performance than the rest of us.

Brendan was much admired and talked about in Altamuskin. The stories about him were legendary. He might have been drunk as a skunk at noon, but he was as successful, if not more so, than any other man in attendance. It was well known that he owned Northwest Lumber, one of the largest lumberyards in Northern Ireland. There wasn't another Catholic in a ten-mile radius who could afford a new Mercedes, and none within all of Ireland who could have made life look like such incredible fun.

"He's doing a disservice to all you young lads," my mother continued. "Believe me, he's not nearly as much fun as it looks when you get to see him on his own."

"Well, at least he's having some fun with his life, which is more than I can say for everybody else around here."

"Trust me, it looks like fun but it's not fun. We just want you to be careful. You're a lot like him in some ways."

"You drank when you were young."

"I did, and I stopped because I didn't like how it made me feel."

"Maybe you didn't drink enough."

My mother sighed deeply, seeing that she was fighting a losing battle.

"Dad got to drink plenty when he was young. . . ."

"You might have seen your father drunk one time."

"One time? I seem to remember other parties once upon a time in this house, even before that, and as far as I can remember both of you were there."

"That was a long time ago, and you have not seen your father drunk since that one time you seen him sick, is that true or not?"

"It is. Maybe that's the problem, maybe you both need to drink more, lighten up a bit."

"I'll just say this one thing and then I'm done. You have younger brothers and sisters in this house and you will not stagger around here making a fool of yourself for them to see it, and that's that."

But she was wrong about that. At that time I had great admiration for my uncle Brendan because of his drunkenness. In his drunkenness he laughed in the face of conformity. Where my mother saw recklessness I saw courage. It seemed to me then that it was essential that my younger brothers and sisters see me break the rules. It was my duty. I was their older brother; I was supposed to stand up for them, to rebel against my mother's twisted sense of conformity. I was going to do absolutely everything in my power to make sure that she did not taint the joy of their teenage years with her own fears and phobias as she had done to mine. I wanted them to see me drunk, I wanted them to see me wild, I wanted to show them that you could say no and survive my mother's wrath. She had cost me my first love. She would not take away theirs. Not if I had anything to do with it.

Drunk as Angels

My seventeenth year I spent ablaze. I blazed through jobs and girls and fights. I blazed cars into ditches and walls and fields, tore them all to pieces the way only an angry seventeen-year-old boy can do. I was determined to show my younger brothers and sisters that I could not be controlled. I left black strips of tire rubber all over Altamuskin, shredded the tar from the Altar Glen to the Cross and ripped donuts out of every intersection along the way. I was going to pay them back for all the years of keeping me on a leash, I was going to show all the neighbors what a nasty little animal I really was, dissolve all remaining memory of the mammy-won't-let-me's.

Good evening. This is the ITN news for Northern Ireland. It's six o'clock.

*Prime Minister Margaret Thatcher narrowly escaped
a bomb attempt on her life last night*

Fuck.

Colin, God forgive you.

Would yis wheesht till I hear the rest of it?

*. . . although the bathroom of her hotel suite at Brighton's
Grand Hotel was destroyed, she managed to escape completely unscathed.*

Fuck.

Colin. That's quite enough of that language in front of
the wee ones.

*So far there have been five deaths reported in the bomb-
ing, including Conservative MP Sir Anthony Berry
and the wife of Parliamentary Treasury Secretary John
Wakeham. A further thirty-four people were taken to
hospital with serious injuries.*
    *The IRA have claimed responsibility for the attack.
In a statement released this afternoon they declared,
quote, "Today we were unlucky, but remember we only
have to be lucky once; you will have to be lucky always.
Give Ireland peace and there will be no more war."*

In a statement read by Mrs. Thatcher this afternoon, she responded to the attacks by saying, "This attack has failed. All attempts to destroy democracy by terrorism will fail."

Well, God curse on you, ye auld bastard.

Machil, not in front of the children.

They'll get that auld hoore yet.

That'll do, Colin.

She let ten men starve to death because they were Irish and Catholic; she's a friggin' animal and she deserves to be blown to smithereens.

That's enough chat about it now, there was innocent people killed, people who had nothing to do with it, them poor women sleeping in their beds who had nothing to do with it . . .

Well, if they were in that hotel with her . . .

That'll be enough about it now, I said. God have mercy on their souls. Bless yourselves children. In the name of the father and of the son and of the holy ghost amen. Now, everybody just finish up your

dinners and not another word about it. There'll be
none of that chat in this house and that's that.

The energy in our home had shifted drastically since I had
confronted my parents over my right to drink. The air had
been cleared a little. They had been forced to accept a new
definition of who we were as a family. They had held on to
their old image of what they expected us to be until the picture
had strained and cracked in their hands. Some of us were no
longer little children; we could no longer be dismissed with
a clip on the ear and chased off to our bedrooms to cool our
heels. They had been confronted with the reality that they
could no longer control everything we did. My brothers and
I were becoming adults, nearing the age that they had been
when they had first gone off to live in Birmingham. In truth
they too had been little more than children when the story of
our family had begun, when their insatiable youthful desire
had flung them at each other, tossing my older brother Michael into their laps some eighteen years ago. In some respects
my parents bore all the characteristics of two dazed survivors
staggering out of the wreckage of a terrible collision. A family
that stays together under one roof for nearly twenty years has
much ugliness to confront. Maybe we were being rewarded for
not having murdered one another in the process. Whatever it
was, there was a definite shift in the tension, and there was a
certain sense of relief, as if we had managed to survive long
enough to reach some new plateau as a family.

Most mornings I drove my brother Brendan to his job. Brendan was sixteen, a year younger than me—finished with school and working as a carpenter also, but Brendan never kept any money for a car of his own. Every penny Brendan made went into poker machines and Bacardi. The only times I ever saw him were at the dinner table and on our way to work in the mornings. Even then we didn't speak much. Brendan was the open cauldron of rage that bubbled in our midst, whatever noise was going on inside Brendan's head we too could hear it. He was constantly starting fights with anybody else in the house foolish enough to engage, and there were times when nothing gave me more pleasure than to engage.

Michael, who was eighteen now, was the quiet one, the sensible one; he worked as a butcher—a good job, a steady job for a Catholic, a job with a future—and was always gone to see some girl up the country nobody knew anything about. He drove a brand-new car and drank little. As brothers we didn't intrude much on each other's space. We ate dinner together with the family every evening and every Sunday after Mass, but outside of that we didn't spend much time together anymore.

My two younger sisters, Noleen and Louise, and my youngest brother, Gerry, were too far behind in age for us to spend any real time in one another's company but we were close just the same and I knew they looked up to me.

Our parents managed to settle into the background a little. They said little about what any of us did now that their wall of control had been cracked. The younger ones in the house were suddenly free to go to discos and develop attitudes that never would have been tolerated around our house when I was their age. It was as if a spell had been broken in our parents' lives and they, too, were free to relax a little. Although my parents' idea of relaxation was to work.

Our mother took to cleaning the house more, not that she wasn't already a neat freak, but now I would wake up in the morning and find the clothes that I had staggered home in and tossed on the floor washed ironed and folded next to my bed when I woke in the morning. Walls were vacuumed, cupboards were emptied, and dishes that were never used were polished on a regular basis. It was nice to have a house that was clinically clean, a house you could bring people home to without ever having to worry about what sort of a mess it might be in. Our house was always visitor-ready. People in Altamuskin cared deeply about such things; a clean house was talked about and much envied. Any woman who could be seen out pinning a row of wet sheets to a clothesline at eight in the morning could be said to have her affairs in order.

My father disappeared into the garden. He'd never had much time to do much with it since we'd moved in five years before, but it suddenly became his source of solace. He took to landscaping the lawns, digging drainage in the damp spots, building elaborate flower beds and rockeries, planting new trees—beech and pine, and fir. Stone walls were built and fences repaired, a new shed and a greenhouse erected. On Saturday evenings he shaved and put on a clean shirt and went off up the road, where he volunteered for a night every week at the credit union alongside my old schoolteacher Master Cooney. Suddenly it seemed everyone had found something to busy themselves with in the long bright evenings.

. . .

I bought my dream car: a black 1275 GT Mini. My father warned me against it, saying that it was too fast for a boy of seventeen, that I wasn't ready to have that kind of power at my fingertips. It was a fast car, small and vicious, and I treasured it. It was the kind of car other lads would look at and say, "Is that a real twelve-seventy-five?"

"It is."

"I've never seen one as clean."

It was immaculate. I had bought it without a dent and had managed to keep it that way for almost three whole months, a new record for me. Nobody thought it would last. It didn't.

It was winter again. Crows high in the empty trees, cows poking their great big bony heads through the barbed-wire fences to tear at the grass by the side of the road, clouds hanging low and heavy like damp cotton over the Altamuskin hills. When I left the house early in the morning not even a truck from the quarry or a school bus was in sight as silvery threads of chimney smoke vanished into the thin cold air.

I had Brendan with me, as usual, to drop him off at Mickey McCann's cabinetry workshop, where he'd started working. My car wheels spun and slipped on the icy concrete laneway up to the workshop, prompting Brendan to offer a rare moment of concern about my driving: "She's slippy."

By which I heard, "Could you please slow down a little

today, because there's too much ice on the road to drive like you do. I know we don't speak much but you are my older brother and I do care deeply about you and I don't want to see you dead."

"She is," I said in reply, by which I meant, and would have been clearly understood by the tone in which I muttered these two words (such was our mode of communication), that I acknowledged his concern and was appreciative of this rare outburst of affection and love on his part and would do my best to stay alive until I saw him again at the dinner table that afternoon. I was acutely aware that such an overtly emotional outburst must have been an enormous strain for him.

We didn't say anything more after that. I stopped the car at the door to the workshop and he got out carrying his lunch box, a Rover biscuit tin wrapped in the customary black rubber band, and he disappeared into the steel shed without so much as a glance over his shoulder.

It was indeed slippy. Slippy enough that I had to let the car run dangerously fast on the ice going back down the lane, being careful not to dab the brakes until I was on drier concrete for fear of spinning off into the hedge. I wouldn't have done any physical harm to myself had I spun out, but I just didn't need the hassle of being without transportation for the time it would take to repair the car if I wrecked it.

Once I was back on the Altamuskin Road I even paused for a moment to check for oncoming traffic and took off slowly without leaving a trail of smoking rubber in my wake.

I lit a cigarette and popped a fresh cassette in the deck; Dire Straits' self-titled debut album, one of my favorite driving albums of that time. I rolled down Campbell's Hill and kept the car rolling fast for the steep climb out of the hollow and on toward Dunmoyle Chapel on the other side.

Feeling the first waves of warm air finally reach my feet, I reached to turn the fan up a notch as the first bars of "Down to the Waterline" drifted from the speakers. I came over the top of the hill 'round by the Dunmoyle football pitch and there, in the road about a hundred yards ahead of me, was a tractor coming my way. The tractor was wide enough in the back from tire to tire that it filled the road entirely. I wasn't going very fast, not more than fifty miles an hour, when I instinctively hit the brakes a tap to slow myself. The tractor was such a long way off, it seemed I would have plenty of time to figure out a way to get around him. But the road was more slippery than I had anticipated, and maybe I was rolling a little faster than I realized and the tractor was coming up on me a whole lot quicker than I had first imagined. There was no way to get by unless I went for the ditch, but it was too late for that. The car hit a patch of ice and I was drifting sideways, gaining speed as I barreled toward the front of the tractor with the driver's side of the car positioned to take the full thrashing. I braced myself for the inevitable collision when suddenly the car spun again at the last minute, positioning the Mini so that the passenger side would bear the brunt of the crash.

There was an explosion of glass and metal as I made impact. The car seemed to bounce backward and settle. For a moment there was a crystalline white silence. And then there was pain. Pain like I had never felt before. My insides felt like they had been crushed flat. I tried to scream, but no noise would issue from my mouth. I struggled to breathe. Nothing. The driver of the tractor was staring at me through the place where my front window had been and I could see by his expression that he was convinced I was dead. I tried to scream out to him, scream with the pain that was engulfing my whole body, but still nothing. I couldn't move. I couldn't breathe. I was suffocating, or perhaps I was already dead; perhaps this is what it felt like to be dead.

I watched in horror as he turned and ran away. I could see him leave but I could not scream out to him or signal that I didn't want to die here alone like this, could not make him understand that some part of me was still conscious. I struggled to take in air but nothing worked. My body was locked in position and I could not breathe.

Out of the corner of my eye I saw a car pull up alongside me. It was my elderly neighbor Simon Corey. I could see him look at me from his car but he continued to sit there looking away from me and by his expression I knew that I must be dead. I began to pray. *Please God don't take me now. I'm too young. I'm only just beginning. Please don't let this be the end.*

I could see the driver of the tractor come running back down the road with a neighbor who lived nearby, and suddenly the air rushed back into my lungs in a great burst and I was screaming. I just kept screaming to hear my voice, to feel the air, to feel alive.

Then my uncle Matt was there and I was in his arms being carried. I searched his face trying to gauge the severity of my situation and found no comfort. He was terrified.

When we reached our house he pulled into our driveway and from where I was propped across the backseat I could see my mother's face, red and petrified in the kitchen window. She ran outside, opened my door, and cupped my face in her hands so she could see into my eyes.

"What did you do? What did you do?" She wept.

"I'm fine," I said, faking a smile as best I could. "I'm just grand."

"We have to go, Claire," Matt said. "I have to get him to the hospital."

"Machil will be here in a minute. I called him, he's on his way home from work right now."

"Well then wait here for him, and we'll see you at hospital."

"Are you sure you're all right, pet?"

"I've never been better," I told her, trying to mask the fear that I felt that this would be the last time I would see her. My insides were burning. I could feel my skin rising in a fat bubble under my sweater near where my heart was supposed to be. My mother kissed my face and closed the door and Matt sped off down the Altamuskin Road toward Omagh Hospital.

I was silent for the ten-mile ride, gripping my chest, trying to hold the swelling down and trying not to think too much about what must be busted in there.

At the hospital I was lifted into a wheelchair and rushed through the halls, questions, bright lights, the smell of ammonia, passing out, coming to, and then I was in a bed and my parents were there, my father asking me if I was OK, how fast had I been driving, was I on my own side of the road, how much pain was I in. I closed my eyes and slept.

When I woke, my body ached. I put my hand to my chest and felt the bandages.

"Try not to move too much," my mother said. "You broke some ribs and punctured your lung."

"Am I going to be all right?"

"You're going to be fine. Just lie still and try not to move too much."

Over the course of the day I found out through family and friends who stopped by that the first reports from the accident were that I had died. The farmer I collided with had been so convinced that I was dead when he first inspected me that he ran to the nearest farmhouse and told our neighbor that I was dead. The woman, a nurse, had called my mother and told her that I had been killed.

The rumor of my death had even reached my brother Brendan in the workshop, where I had luckily dropped him off just moments before the accident. Had he been with me, we both would have been killed, as the car was crushed so flat that there was room for only one body from door to door. There was no way either of us would have survived if we had been crushed together into that small space.

Later that night I woke in my hospital bed groaning in agony and felt a hand take mine and hold it. When I opened my eyes to the dim light in the ward, I saw a young woman next to my bed in a nurse's outfit. She squeezed my hand when she saw my eyes open and with her other hand she gently brushed back my hair and put her hand on my forehead. She had dark shoulder-length hair, and when she tilted her head a little to smile at me, I was in love with her.

"Is the pain bad?"

"Yes."

"I'm going to get you something for it."

"Am I going to be OK?"

"You're lucky to be alive, but I'm going to make you all better."

"Promise."

"I promise."

"Thank you . . ."

"Angela."

"Angela."

Over the next two weeks Angela did nurse me back to health. At night she would come by and sit on the side of my bed and we'd whisper to each other for hours until she would insist I get some sleep so she didn't get in trouble with the head matron on the ward.

In a couple of weeks I was out of the hospital, bandaged tightly and off to Knocknamoe Castle nightclub in Omagh to find my nurse. When I arrived, I saw her right away, standing with a friend near the end of the bar. Her face broke into a smile the moment I walked through the door, as if she'd been watching out for me. For the first time in my life I had the feeling that I should have stopped somewhere on the way to have a few drinks to brace myself before coming to meet her. I was intimidated by her, or had I already become dependent on the courage a couple of drinks gave me? She was older than me by a few years and she was a nurse, and as anyone could tell you, all nurses were nymphomaniacs. It was common knowledge that they were like wild animals in bed. At least, that was what I had heard.

I was tongue-tied and anxious in her presence. We had

spoken so freely in the hospital, but now that she was standing in front of me I could think of nothing to say. I led her off into a corner and kissed her, but my confidence was nowhere to be found. I could tell she was aware that I was unsure of myself, but I didn't possess the language or the self-awareness to communicate my sense of vulnerability. Instead I made my excuses and went to the bar and ordered a double vodka and another. I needed lubrication, courage, I needed to relax; I got neither. I avoided Angela and continued to drink.

At some point during the night the houselights came up and the DJ and the bartenders started ordering everyone to clear the room because there was a bomb scare. The crowd reluctantly trudged toward the exit doors, swilling the last of their drinks as they were ushered along.

"Come on, everybody!" the bouncers were yelling. "Put the drinks down, now, the place could go up at any second. We've been told there's a bomb in here. Please, folks. Out. Quickly."

Most of us had been through this drill so often by this point that the threat of a bomb represented nothing but a hindrance to good drinking time. Knocknamoe Castle, where the nightclub was situated, had been bombed and burned numerous times over the years. Five British soldiers had been blown to pieces in the parking lot when their booby-trapped car exploded after leaving the bar one night. But that was because they were Protestant, and Protestants were not welcome in Knocknamoe Castle. This was strictly a Catholic club. Those were the unwritten rules in the North, the Catholics stayed in their bars and the Proddies stayed in theirs and God help anyone who walked into the wrong one on the wrong night.

There would be no mingling, no dating young Protestant girls for us, even though it was common knowledge that the Protestant girls were dirty little tramps and they didn't care who they rode.

I looked for Angela outside as the young, half-drunk crowd grew impatient, shouting abuse at the bouncers and shuffling around with their shoulders bunched up in the cold waiting to get back inside to their drinks and the heat. After about half an hour, when the bouncers decided that the threat of an explosion had passed, they let us back in again and the mob rushed the bar to make up for lost drinking time.

By the time the lights came up at the end of the night and everyone stood to attention facing the stage for the playing of the Irish national anthem I had found Angela again. It was customary in all Catholic bars and clubs in the North to stand at attention at the end of the night for the singing of the Irish national anthem in Gaelic. Most of us didn't know all the words but with a few drinks you could wail your way through it with the best of them. It was always a passionate and rousing conclusion to the night, a great burst of nationalistic pride fueled by many drinks turning the key on our anger and lifting the curtain on our oppressed souls for just an instant.

I slipped my arm around Angela's waist and held my other fist in the air as the crowd erupted into a cheer and I overplayed my nationalism holding my two-fingered victory sign in the air and yelling with the crowd *"Tiocfaidh ár lá"*–Our day will come, which were just about the only three Gaelic words I really knew and understood–and whistling for longer than was necessary or even remotely cool. Then she took me by the hand and led me out through the thick crowd and down the driveway to my car.

As I drove out through the town toward the nurses' quarters I ran into a British Army checkpoint on Campsie. It was common practice for the Brits to set up roadblocks on all the roads leading out of Omagh so they could get a good list of all the names of those who attended the dances at the Castle. Knocknamoe Castle had a solid reputation as an IRA bar, meaning it was protected and frequented by members of the Provisional Irish Republican Army. British intelligence were well aware of the bars and nightclubs with a more political bent than others, and strategically placed late-night checkpoints would net them the names and addresses of all those who would attend such places.

"License and insurance, please. Is this your vehicle?"

"Aye."

"Where are you coming from?"

"Hang-gliding lessons."

"You been drinking, then?"

"Aye."

"How many drinks 'ave you had?"

"I lost count after the first five or six."

"And you're all right to drive, are you?"

"I managed not to run you over."

He shone the flashlight into my eyes and then over at Angela's face.

"And wot about you love, 'ave you been drinking?"

Angela looked straight ahead and ignored him as he ran

the light from the flashlight slowly down over her chest and onto her legs then back up at my face again to see if he was getting to me just yet.

"All right then. You gonna get her home safely then?"

I didn't look at him or speak. I could have told him to go fuck himself, of course, but then he would have had both of us out on the side of the road for the next hour. Sometimes you just had to comfort yourself with the thought that there would be a bomb waiting for him under the seat of his car ready to take him to shreds the moment he turned the key in his ignition.

In the parking lot of the nurses' homes I pulled into an out-of-the-way spot and popped a Van Morrison cassette, *Common One,* into the stereo.

"I love this album," I said, buying a little time. The alcohol hadn't worked the way it usually did. Besides the fact that I was still suffering from a mangled rib cage and a badly bruised lung, I still felt stiff and awkward. I had lost all my natural rhythm. "Do you like Van Morrison?"

"I don't really like him, he makes me think of hippies twirling ribbons and other superficial forms of happiness," she said with an air of irritation. I found myself suddenly at a further remove than I had been already. Her disinterest in my musical taste had only served to widen the deep chasm I already felt opening up between us. In the hospital she had been the one taking care of me, I had been helpless, but she was no longer wearing that uniform. I sensed that what she really wanted was for me to take care of her now. I needed to jump in with both feet and just hope that some of the magic would return of its own accord.

I leaned over her and kissed her determinedly as I fumbled down the side of her seat for the recline lever, which was, this being my father's car that I had borrowed for the night, not where it was supposed to be. There ensued a frustrating few moments where I had to break from kissing her and ask her to move this way and that while I tried to locate the lever, all the while losing whatever valuable momentum I had just gained by my emphatic embrace.

When I did finally locate the recline handle and pulled it, the seat collapsed backward with a sudden jolt, causing her to emit a panicked gasp as I fell with her, whacking my not fully recovered rib cage on the gear stick as I keeled over on top of her, and from my lips escaped what I can only describe as a sort of high-pitched squeak. I slowly curled myself back onto my seat with my teeth tightly clenched, grimacing and groaning like a chimp in the throes of labor.

"Oh my God. Are you all right?" she said, straightening herself and placing a comforting hand on my shoulder. "I knew this was a bad idea. You're not ready for this."

"No, I'm fine," I said, straightening myself, trying to ignore the searing pain that gripped my entire chest area.

"Are you sure?" she asked, and for a moment I was reminded that this was exactly why I had fallen for her in the first place; it was because she was so caring and warm. This beautiful girl wasn't scheming to rate my sexual performance on a scorecard. This girl was my angel.

"Yes. I'm sure," I said as I leaned over and kissed her again, determined to ignore all pain and fear of death so I could finally show her what a great lover I really was.

By the time I had hurriedly wrestled both my legs over the center console and past the gear stick between us so I could be in the seat alongside her, it felt like someone had taken a mallet to my rib cage.

Given the sheer lack of space on the passenger seat of my father's car, and the fact that I had more or less landed myself on top of the beautiful Angela, I was faced with the fresh dilemma of how to get at all her bits and pieces, buttons, and zippers, which were very much sandwiched underneath me. It became more and more apparent that I might not have the strength to raise my own body weight again to get at them.

I stalled for time, deepening the passion with which I kissed her to distract her while slowly introducing a little pelvic action into the mix to let her know that I still meant business. I ran my hand down to her waist to see if I could somehow roll myself off a little to one side so I could at least send my hand in there to scout things out between her legs and keep her amused while I figured out my next move, but there was no opening to be found to squeeze my hand casually between us and the pain in my rib cage was so bad that I literally could not find the strength to raise my own body weight to get off her again. I was becoming further alarmed by the fact that I had sprouted what felt like about a third of an erection in my pants, but because of the way it was buckled in the crotch of my jeans it must have felt like I was poking her in the thigh with a child's pacifier. This was a disaster.

I gripped the seat in one last-ditch effort to shove myself off her so I could more smoothly manipulate the removal of her undergarments, but my hand slipped down the side of the seat suddenly and I cracked my forehead into her nose, causing her to yell, "Fuck! What are you doing?"

"I'm sorry, my hand just slipped."

"You're obviously not ready for this," she said with a polite smile as she gripped her nose in one hand and with the other reached for the door handle and proceeded to slip herself out from under me.

"No, really, I'm fine . . ." I said, struggling through the pain and humiliation to affect some kind of devil-may-care smirk on my face as she got out of the car and stood outside the open door looking in at me slumped sideways in the seat.

"I really should be going in now anyway," she said as she stood by the car door straightening her clothes and pulling back her hair. "Are you really OK?"

"I'm fine."

"Are you sure you're OK to drive?"

"I'm great, I'm just going to lay here for a moment and listen to a little Van Morrison before I hit the road."

"OK then," she said as she leaned down and gave me a parting kiss on the forehead, and in her eyes as she turned away I was sure I caught just a hint of sadness as if I were already dead to her.

I lay in the car and smoked cigarette after cigarette until the rest of the Van Morrison cassette played out, feeling sorry for myself, hating how impossible this bruised and cracked teenage body of mine was to navigate.

But there was more to it than that. The more I thought about it, the more furious I was with myself for not having punched that Brit in the face for shining the flashlight on

Angela's breasts and legs. I had just sat there and done nothing to defend her honor. Of course she wanted nothing more to do with me. It wasn't just that I was physically weak; yes, that was part of it, but more important, I felt, it was because I had been proved a coward, too.

What a girl like Angela needed was a real man, someone who could avenge her honor or at least try to. When I failed to defend her against the sexual innuendo of the soldier he had succeeded in undermining the very essence of my manhood. I had done nothing. If I'd been even half a man I would have spat in that soldier's face and took the beating that would have followed it. She might have loved me for it.

I was becoming bitter inside. I wanted revenge. I wanted to see blood on my hands. I'd squared off to my parents already, why not the Brits, too? But the truth was I still wasn't sure if I could live with myself if I deliberately took another human life. I needed to be certain in my heart before doing something as drastic as signing up for the IRA. If I made that decision, I would have to be ready to do whatever it was that they asked of me. I had to be ready to kill, ready to live with the finality of that act. I needed to be one hundred percent sure. It was a certainty I did not yet possess.

So I went to war with myself instead. I bought another car, wrecked it too, got drunk as often as possible, smoked more hash, grew my hair, dyed my hair, pierced my ear, and fought every chance I got.

Larger Than Life

Good evening. This is the ITN news for Northern Ireland. It's six o'clock.

Another civilian has been killed this afternoon near Strabane in County Tyrone, bringing the death toll of civilian informants shot by the IRA over the past five weeks to a total of six. Three of those have been in County Tyrone. Two of the deaths have been accredited to mistaken identity.

And you wonder why I can't sleep until you are all home safe in your beds at night.

Why, because you think we're informants?

Don't be so smart. Two of them lads that were killed had nothing to do with anything either. What about that poor cub over in Pomeroy there a couple of weeks ago, shot driving down the road in his car and him had nothing to do with anybody?

Wheesht.

The IRA have released a statement this afternoon on the latest killing, saying that the dead man had admitted during interrogation to being an informant to the SAS and was responsible for the deaths of three IRA volunteers when they were shot on the victim's property by the SAS earlier in the year.

Good enough for the grass.

That'll do, Colin.

Right.

Over the next few weeks my uncle Brendan's health deteriorated rapidly, to the point that he was admitted to the Royal Victoria Hospital in Belfast. It was the first time I saw my mother look beaten. There were whispered conversations over the phone with her sisters, moments when I might find her staring off blankly out the kitchen window or stepping hurriedly past me into the bathroom with a tea towel clamped to her mouth, her eyes red and glistening.

She came into the bedroom one afternoon when we were playing darts with our cousins Paul and Des McCann and said, "I think maybe you boys should think about taking a run up to Belfast to see your uncle Brendan. He's very ill."

Five or six of us got in my brother's car and made the one-hour drive that night. We arrived just as visiting hours had ended, but when we explained to the nurse who we were there to see and that we had just driven an hour to get there, she agreed to let us in to see our uncle, as long as we didn't cause too much racket or disturb the other patients.

We trudged awkwardly down the polished floor of the hushed ward, glancing at the occupants of each bed as discreetly as possible, but there was no sign of him anywhere. We turned down the far end, convinced we had gotten the wrong ward, and started back out again. We were almost as far as the door when we heard our uncle's voice call from one of the beds.

"Who the hell let this lot into a civilized establishment like this? Nurse, nurse, somebody call security." It was only when he followed his little rant with that great big belly laugh of his that we finally stopped at the foot of his bed and stared at the swollen yellow caricature of the man we knew as our uncle.

My cousin Paul stepped around the bed first with his hand outstretched, holding a bottle of Lucozade we had brought along as a gift. "You're still causing trouble then, I see."

"They can't keep a good man like me down for long, McCann. What is that, a bottle of Lucozade? Is there a child here on the ward you're visiting?" Brendan asked, twisting his head around teasingly in the direction of the other beds. "Do I look like a sick child to you?"

"We didn't want to be bringing anything stronger in case the other patients got jealous," replied Paul, playing along and giving the rest of us time to adjust to the shock of seeing our most jovial, most notorious, most revered uncle somehow transformed from his big pink cherubic self to this monstrosity that lay before us.

"You were always a cheap bastard, McCann, and your father before you," he bellowed, and we all laughed along, fumbling our way up either side of the bed, each man now trying to do his bit to keep the ball in the air. He had always been the larger-than-life joker, the most outrageous export Altamuskin had ever produced, the one to thumb his nose at all convention, the one to find a laugh in every situation no matter how dour. We had never witnessed him speak a serious word. It was a struggle to overcome the sudden wave of nausea I felt rising up into my chest. I lowered myself grinning into the chair beside his bed and let the others fill the air with the great drunk buzz of comedic one-upmanship until I, too, was able to overcome my initial shock at Uncle Brendan's physical state and slip casually back into the theatrics of the dance. Pretty soon we were all so acutely attuned to the general hilarity that an hour had sailed past without a single mention of why we were having this conversation in a hospital in the first place. He regaled us with dazzling stories of his drinking exploits.

In one memorable escapade he had wound up in America. He was in the mountains somewhere, down south, he said, in an old bar that looked like a rundown wooden shack. There was sawdust on the floor; chickens wandered in and out freely. He was drinking moonshine with some old wrinkled hillbilly who'd been sitting in that bar so long his hair had begun to sprout out of the holes in his hat. I was in awe of the details and the wildness of it all. I made a secret vow that I, too, would go to America one day and drink with a hillbilly in a mountain shack. Here was a future I could aspire to.

A nurse came by and tapped the end of the bed with a pen until she had found her way into the conversation.

"I'm afraid it's time to go, boys," she said, smiling pleasantly.

"Is it time for my bath again, nurse?" Brendan offered with a wink and a nudge to Des, who was up on the bed next to him. "This is the last time I'm letting you bathe me today, and that's that."

"I can hardly wait, Brendan. I'll be back with my soapy sponge in two minutes and you boys had better be gone by then."

"There you have it, boys, it's been a pleasure to have you up, but as you can see, duty calls." Brendan laughed as he took each nephew's hand and gave it a tight squeeze, offering a couple of last-minute quips as we parted.

"Go on, McCann, you tight bastard, and take your bottle of Lucozade with you."

"By God, young Broderick, you have hands on you like a ten-year-old girl."

. . .

Little was said in the car on the long ride home. It was clear to me why my mother had wanted us to go see him for ourselves. She had wanted to impress on us the physical implications of a life of drinking. I couldn't help but feel it was for me, in particular, that we had been sent.

When the phone rang later that same night just after we'd all gone to bed I was still wide-awake, picturing him as he had appeared to me when we had turned upon hearing his voice in the ward: jaundiced and swollen unlike anything human I had seen before, the skin on his hands and face stretched tight as a drum, rendering him almost featureless—unrecognizable but for the two eyes still ablaze with childish mischief. I could hear my parents' bedroom door open, footsteps hurry down the hall, the last ring seeming to sing on through the long, dark corridor of silence that followed before the receiver was set back on its perch. The door to my bedroom opened and my mother was there with the face of a little girl again, whispering.

"He's gone."

Brendan's funeral was the largest funeral I had ever seen. A stream of bitterly bereaved strangers rolled through the wake to view his body in his new luxurious house that he had just recently built outside of Omagh. For the three days and nights the procession of people never stopped. A group of children stood vigil in front of a massive aquarium recessed into the living-room wall, openmouthed at the glittering array of exotic fish that Brendan had acquired.

It was like being the nephew of Elvis. Strangers arrived from all over Ireland. The house and the yard outside were filled with little groups of people sharing Brendan stories, each one more daring, more outrageous, than the next. On the day we buried him, we went to Knocknamoe Castle bar with his sons, my cousins, Sean and Ian, and toasted him until the lights went out.

He had been forty-two when he died. It did not occur to me then how young he had been. Forty-two didn't seem such a terrible fate. What was more important to me was that he'd thumbed his nose to convention, in particular to my mother's demands of him. He'd been courageous enough to be his own man right to the very end. I admired his courage. He didn't give a damn what people thought of him. So what that he'd died a little younger than most? As far as I could see, most people weren't living at all. Most of the adults I knew were already stiffs and none stiffer than my own parents. At least Brendan had taken the bull by the horns and enjoyed the short time he'd had on this planet. He might have been dead at forty-two, but at least he'd been fully alive for the short time he was here. That was success enough in my book. Give me a handful of years ablaze over a century of pedestrianism any day.

A Gathering of the Clans

Good evening. This is the ITN news for Northern Ireland. It's six o'clock.

Wheesht, everybody. Brendan, turn up the television till I hear this.

Two RUC men are dead after the Provisional IRA attacked a police station in the town of Ballygawley in County Tyrone last night.

Go on, Tyrone . . .

Brendan, be quiet.

A group of armed men began shooting at the barracks at around seven o'clock last night, killing two members of the police force before entering the police station and stealing a quantity of rifles and ammunition. They then planted what is estimated to be a two-hundred-pound bomb in the building before making their escape. The building was completely destroyed in the massive explosion. Many houses in the small village had their windows shattered and some of the nearby houses received some structural damage, but there have been no reported civilian casualties at this time.

Look at the shape of the place, look, not a stick left standing.

Look, look, there's Master McSorley's house. Look . . .

I see it, Noleen.

Can you imagine what it felt like for them right beside it when the rattle nearly broke our own windows down here?

By God, they showed the bastards . . .

Colin. Enough. Not in front of the children, please.

Sorry, children.

For my eighteenth birthday, my parents gave me a silver watch as a present. It was a difficult gift to receive at a time when I felt so much disdain for them, when my only thoughts were of getting as far away from them as humanly possible. It was obvious that the watch must have cost a good chunk of my father's paycheck. When you lived in a house with six children, such gifts were rare, or unheard-of. I was acutely aware of what the gift represented for them emotionally. We were not given to hugs or declarations of love in our house. But the gift bore all the weight of a warm, teary embrace.

I strapped it onto my arm right away and stood in our kitchen admiring it.

"So you like it?"

"I love it. Thanks, Mum. Thanks, Dad."

"You're welcome to it," my dad said, matter-of-factly. "It might be a bit loose. You probably want to get a link or two taken out of it before you wear it out."

"No, I think it's fine for now," I said, rattling it around on my wrist, showing it off to my brothers and sisters.

"It's beautiful," my baby sister Louise said, her innocent little face aglow, sensing perhaps the rare envelope of familial affection in the moment.

"Anybody need to know the time? I have it right here," I asked, immediately grabbing my eight-year-old brother in a headlock, messing his hair, making comedy out of the moment to defuse the discomfort of such intimacy. "Gerard, you need to know the time?"

"Leave me alone. I can see the clock on the wall. I don't need to see your stupid watch to know the time."

"Oh, I think you do," I said, grabbing him and pinning him to the couch and tickling him into a giddy mess, much to the delight of Noleen and Louise, who squealed when I got up to chase them, too.

I went out to Kelly's Inn the next night, determined to make this the best birthday ever. As usual, there was an entire corner of the bar devoted to a small army of my first cousins. We had a reputation around Kelly's of being clannish when we were out for the night. We had the entire corner booth and three or four of the surrounding tables commandeered before the crowd got too thick. It was a good feeling to have such a large family circle in public. It could be useful in times of trouble, and there was always some kind of trouble.

Our clan was known as the McClean clan, as we were direct descendants of Frank McClean. Some of us were Broderick, some were McCann, some were Mullin. But our mothers had been McClean, daughters of Frank McClean of Altamuskin. There might have been twenty of us together on any given night in Kelly's Inn or Knocknamoe Castle, although the clan itself was much larger, numbering upward of a hundred first and second cousins.

In a time when Catholics were not represented by a police force, the clan was an important element of public protection. As Catholics we policed ourselves in the North of Ireland. The police force was Protestant; they operated under English law and they were loyal to the English Crown. They were our enemy and never to be trusted. If there was a disagreement, we settled it ourselves. If there was a car accident involving only Catholics, we solved it ourselves if at all possible: if there was a report of abuse or violence, we took it upon ourselves to take care of it. Any disturbance within the community that posed the threat of outside law enforcement was dealt with by an IRA tribunal. The culprits were spirited away to a safe house, where men in balaclavas questioned them and dealt the punishment. Sometimes a beating was administered, or a threat. Sometimes it was worse: kneecapping or banishment from the country. As a result, petty crime was almost nonexistent. You did not need to lock your door, ever. You could leave your car running and unattended while you popped into a grocery store.

In a community where secrecy was tantamount to survival, a sideways glance could be as threatening as a gun. This was all understood without ever having to read a brochure about it. We had a language of communication that transcended mere words. Entire pools of thought were communicated nonverbally. A simple grunt, a nod, a wink, or a rub of the face could convey more than an entire paragraph of speech. You didn't need to be tutored for a semester or two on the mechanics of the operation and neither did your parents ever explain it any more than they would have explained the birds and the bees; you simply grew up knowing it in your blood and you respected it. We lived with a secret in our midst; any threat to that secret was eliminated.

In general we Catholic lads respected one another's clans also, but when we didn't, all hell was likely to break loose. One clan no one liked to mess with was the Galbally clan. These lads were from "up the country a little bit," as we liked to say.

Galbally, about ten miles away from Altamuskin. On the night of my eighteenth birthday, they were all there at Kelly's Inn.

Galbally was renowned as one of the fiercest republican strongholds in all of County Tyrone, or in the entire North of Ireland, for that matter. The clan of lads who hung out together was made up of the members of two notoriously nationalistic families. These were hard men and nobody in their right mind got in their way. It was common knowledge that the Donnelly and Arthurs families came with the backing of the East Tyrone Brigade of the Provisional Irish Republican Army. Although specifics were never discussed, it was safe to assume that if you were from that part of the country in the late 1980s you were involved in a direct effort to rid the northern six counties of Ireland from the English occupation. This meant that they brought with them a reputation as being just about the most dangerous clan of lads in the entire county. Not that Altamuskin didn't have its own militant republican reputation; we had the Bards and the McCann clan, after all, but our local crowd had a fairly firm reputation for stability. The Galbally crowd, on the other hand, were about as volatile a crew of lads as you were likely to find in the North. This was a nest of bees you would do best not to poke with a stick.

Now that I had been coming to Kelly's Inn for a couple of years, it was beginning to eat away at me that these guys would be considered any tougher than we were. As far as I was concerned, Kelly's Inn was on our turf, not theirs. It bothered me that they were considered the most fearsome crew around. It was not an issue any of my cousins wanted to hear mentioned. Nobody wanted a part in a fight that might wind up

with somebody being beaten to death. So there was an unspoken agreement that we just stayed away from one another. We
never spoke to them, or they to us, and as long as things were
left that way we could all enjoy the general revelry of Kelly's
Inn, get drunk, and pick up girls in peace.

That particular night I was out celebrating my birthday,
their very presence agitated me more than usual. I tried to
block them out of my mind, but the more I drank the more
they bothered me. I tried to remind myself that this was my
birthday. I was eighteen. I was now legally free of my parents'
control. My mother had been reminding me of her legal rights
of guardianship over me since I was fifteen. But no longer. I
was officially free to do whatever I wanted to do and to go
wherever I wanted to go for the rest of my life, and no one
could ever make me feel trapped or limited ever again. This
was the moment I had been waiting for my whole life. I was
free of their constraints. I could go to England, or America if
only I could afford it. I could go directly to the airport and
fly to China first thing in the morning if I so chose, providing
I got a passport approved before breakfast, of course. I had
another drink and tried to veer my thoughts away from the
slow burn of rage that I could feel rising toward the Galbally
crew, who were off down the other end of the bar bothering
no one at all.

I had noticed this sense of rage as a side effect almost from
the first night that I'd been drunk. This self-righteous anger
of mine seemed to start to bubble up after about three or four
drinks. The booze unlocked a well of anger within me that was
hard to control. It was as if there was a psychotic genie in that

third or fourth bottle of beer; once the top was uncorked he was staying out until he hurt someone. I tried to steer my attention away from the Galbally crew . . . but just who did they think they were on tonight of all nights, coming into our bar and making us, me, feel like I had to kowtow to them in any way? On my birthday? It just wasn't on, it was not cool and it just wasn't going to happen, not anymore.

I was in the bathroom by myself a little later. I was turning from the urinal when the door opened and into the narrow hall came the two youngest of the Donnelly-Arthurs clan. The moment we made eye contact I knew there was going to be trouble; perhaps I made it abundantly clear with the way that I glared at them that I was looking for trouble, that I was finally ready for it. One of them moved past me and shoved me aside with a look that I assumed was supposed to leave me quaking in my shoes. I sprang at him like a snake out of a pit, smashing his head into the tiled wall and turning on his friend with my fists, until the two of them were sprawled on the floor. The whole thing happened in a flash. The genie was out. Then I strolled on out of the bathroom and made my way casually back over to where my cousins were sitting.

As I sat down, I could see the two boys exiting the bathroom, hurriedly twisting their heads around as they marched straight up to the older boys in their crowd.

"Listen, lads, I think there's about to be a wee spot of bother here in a minute," I said, and a couple of my cousins stopped and stared at me, waiting for me to enlighten them.

"What did you do now?"

"They started it."

"Who started what?"

"The young lads, Arthurs and Donnellys crowd."

As my cousins all turned their heads to take a look down the end of the bar, one of the young lads had spotted me and was pointing me out to his older brothers. It looked like he was bleeding from his forehead.

"Oh shit," Paul said. "What the fuck did you do?"

"I told you, they started it."

"You punched one of the Arthurs clan?"

"Two of them."

"Are you out of your mind?"

"Fuck it," I said, draining my pint. "Don't worry about it. I started it. I'll sort it out."

I got up before another word was spoken. It would have been unfair to drag my whole family into a fight with the Galbally crew. There was going to be payback. We Tyrone men were not in the habit of letting things slide. Somebody was going to have their head kicked in; that's just the way things worked for us. I decided that I might as well just go on over there and get it over with as quickly as possible. Besides, there was more of a chance that I would survive whatever it was they were going to throw at me if there was a crowd around to witness it. If I left it until later and they got me outside, it would be much worse.

As I walked toward them, the two eldest brothers stepped in front of the boys I had beaten and the others, about seven or eight of them, all stood in a semicircle waiting for me to approach.

"Did you fuckin' hit my brother in the bathroom?" the

oldest one, a boy of about twenty-three or -four, asked me, an angry scowl on his face. I stopped in front of them well within swinging range so they would know I was there to face the music.

"They started it," I said, nodding to the two youngest–boys of sixteen or seventeen–who stood behind them.

"Naw, we fuckin' didn't. This fucker shoved me up against the wall the minute I walked in the door. I never laid a finger on him." The boy who spoke had a trickle of blood running from a crack in his forehead. He was almost dancing on the tips of his toes with rage. But these boys were soldiers; it was obvious they were not going to react until the older brothers gave the command.

"They said you started it," the other older boy said to me. I looked him in the eye. He was suppressing a smirk, as if he just couldn't believe that I wasn't on my knees apologizing to them. "What do you have to say to that?"

"All I know is that little fucker right there–" The minute I raised my finger to point at him, the young guy with the cut on his forehead threw a punch over his brother's shoulder and hit me square in the face. I exploded at him, getting one good shot at his face again before they were all on me. They were standing so close that most of their blows were coming in soft, but one or two of the boys who were standing farther back were making it through the fray and connecting with my face, so I put my hands up and tried to block the barrage as best I could. They kept at it hard and fast for a bit; I was powerless and surprisingly content with the battering I was receiving. They could do their best. I felt nothing.

It went on for a bit until I could feel someone's arms wrapping around my waist from behind and I was yanked in one quick swoop from the middle of the fray. A man's arms held me upright and clamped tightly as he ran with me to the main door of the bar and when he dropped me outside, I turned around to see that it was one of the bouncers and he was yelling at me.

"Run and hide as quick as you can. I'll lock the doors and try and keep them on the inside as long as possible. Run, for fucksake!" Then he slammed the door behind me and I was standing outside the bar alone.

In front of me was the main Ballygawley-to-Omagh dual carriageway. The road to Altamuskin went up the hill directly in front of me. No matter which road I took, they would find me, and the thought of running into a wet field to hide in the dark didn't seem appealing, even though I could hear the doors being rattled and kicked directly behind me and voices yelling at the bouncers to open the door.

There was a recessed doorway about ten feet to the left of the main doors. I stepped into it just in time to hear the main doors shattering as they managed to kick it open and spill out into the front parking lot.

"Where'd he go?" one of the older brothers yelled. "Where the fuck did he go?"

I backed into the corner of the doorway so I was hidden in a line of shadow and watched in amazement as one of the boys ran up to a parked car not thirty feet in front of me and without pausing to reach for his keys, smashed his fist straight through the passenger-side window and reached in to open the door from the inside, yelling, "Somebody get in the other car. He can't have gone far. Find the fucker!"

The entire crowd was filing out into the parking lot. Small skirmishes broke out all over the place. The bouncers were running around, trying to keep order. My steady Friday-night girlfriend, Noleen Campbell, came out of the bar and stopped about four feet in front of the doorway with her back to me casting her head about to try to locate me in all the commotion.

"Don't turn around," I whispered, just loud enough for her to hear. "Get one of the lads to pull a car up here by this doorway so I can get out of here."

She nodded and I watched her walk away, and in a few minutes my buddy Brendan McNamee pulled up in front of me and my brother Michael threw open the back door. I ducked into the car and we were gone.

When I tried to pry my eyes open in the morning, they were almost caked shut. I crawled out of bed and sneaked my face up in front of the mirror on the dresser. I was face to face with a stranger. Both eyes were almost swollen shut, my chin was scuffed, and it looked like my nose was a little off to the left. It was a relief not to see myself. I liked this new mask. I was in no mood to see the real me. I held up my arm and took a long, painful look at the place where my new watch had been, then I crawled back into bed again and pulled the blankets up around my head.

Before the end of the day I had received word that the

Galbally crew were going to destroy me the first chance they got. They were looking for me, and there was a very real possibility that they might show up at our house to finish what they had started. This was not some idle threat. It was well known that there were lads who had crossed their paths and had wound up in hospital. Under advice from my cousins and some close friends, it was decided that it would be best if I didn't go out anywhere in public for a few months in the hope that it would all blow over.

But I would have suffered any beating gladly, death even, over the look of disappointment on my father's face when I confessed to having lost the watch I had just received as a gift two days before. He pursed his lips, and just when I thought he was going to berate me, he stopped. He sighed deeply, shaking his head as he turned away and walked out of the kitchen without a word. There was only one thing worse than receiving a beating from my father, and that was not to have been worth his rage at all.

Good evening. This is the ITN news for Northern Ireland. It's six o'clock.

An off-duty British Army UDR soldier was killed in an explosion this evening when he triggered a booby trap attached to his car near Castlederg in County Tyrone.

Good enough for the bastard.

Colin, that will do.

The Provisional IRA have claimed responsibility for the attack.

Good stuff. He's UDR, it's good enough for him.

What's a UDR?

Never mind what it is, Gerard. . . .

A UDR man is a member of the Ulster Defense Regiment, which means he's a dirty Protestant who grew up here in Northern Ireland and he works for the British Army–

That'll do, Colin, there's no call for that kind of chat in this house in front of the children–

–and at night he puts on his filthy British Army outfit and he goes out on the road with a gun and a bunch of his buddies and they stop Catholics like me and you going down the road–

Colin–

–minding our own damned business, and they abuse the shit out of us and they get away with whatever the hell they like because they're Protestants and we're just Catholics trying to go about our daily business in our own country. They all deserve to be blown to smithereens in their cars, every last filthy one of them. In fact, even that'd be too good for the bastards.

Machil, are you going to sit there and let your son talk like that in front of the wee wans?

Now, have you any more questions, Gerard?

That'll do, Colin.

OK, Dad.

By the following weekend I was done with being a prisoner in my own house. I left alone on foot to go and try to find the Galbally crew and get it all over with. I was sick of waiting. Rumor was they all liked to get together for a good drink up in Knocknamoe Castle bar on a Sunday evening. I hitched my way down and walked on in by myself, and sure enough there they were, the whole crew taking up one end of the bar: the two older brothers on stools beside each other, engrossed in conversation; the rest of the brothers, including the two I had fought with, were behind them standing around with their pint glasses, chatting away to one another. I walked on over and shoved my way in between the two older brothers at the bar so I could order a beer.

I turned from side to side to let them get a good look at me. The younger one, who was standing behind me, suddenly recognized me. Just as he was about to take the first swing, his older brother stopped him.

"Just leave this to me here for a minute, boys."

He was staring at me with a quizzical, amused expression, glancing over at his brother on the other side of me.

"Just what the fuck do you think you're doing?" he asked.

"Ordering a beer."

The bartender stopped in front of me, pointing his finger at me to let me know he was ready to serve.

"Shout," he said, turning an ear toward me to catch my order in the general din.

"I'll have a pint of Harp."

As he walked away I got the same question again.

"I said, just what the fuck do you think you're doing?"

"Listen," I said. "I know you boys have been looking for me, you want to give me a beating, well, here I am, beat away and let's get this thing over with. I'm having a pint. I'm right here anytime you want to begin."

At this, he laughed and shook his head and looked at his brother, who was also thankfully smiling.

"You've got some balls on you, boy."

"I'm just fed up waiting."

The bartender stopped back over and set the drink down in front of me, and when I reached for my money the older brother stopped me.

"You want to have a drink with us?"

"Yes."

"All right, I got this." He paid the bartender and turned to the others. "Nobody touches him . . . What's your name?"

"Colin."

"Lads, this is Colin, and nobody touches him, it's over. He's one of us. Go on, shake hands and let that be the end of it."

I turned around and shook hands with each of the lads. Everyone was very civil about the whole thing. They were dignified soldiers. There were drinks bought back and forth, the two younger lads, Declan and Seamus, and I toasted a pint together and before long we were all chatting and laughing together like we were old friends. More drink was ordered and talk wore 'round to girls and to getting out of the North to go live in London for a little while to make some fast money. That's where the real money was, they told me. Carpenters making two hundred pounds a week; brickies, even more. That was five times what I could make working in Northern Ireland. A lad could go to London, work for a year, and make enough money to come back and buy his own house or a farm if that was the kind of work you were into. That kind of money was unheard-of anywhere in Ireland. We might have been accustomed to poverty, but that didn't make us any more fond of it. There was no shame in taking the Englishman's money, neither was there any stigma attached to living in London; the war was being fought there, too, angry young lads like me from the North of Ireland would have no trouble finding a home and a job, I was assured.

London was suddenly in the throes of one of the greatest building booms in history and contractors were literally crying out for skilled manual laborers. Boys from every corner of Ireland were pouring across the Irish Sea to try to grab some of the easy money. If you could drag your ass out of bed and could hold yourself upright and awake for an eight-hour shift, there was a fortune to be made in the Big Smoke.

The lads told me that they had people that they knew over there, areas where the Northern lads looked out for one another, places you could live for free. I had cousins who were already over there also. London sounded like heaven, and it might have been were it not situated in the heart of England. But still, with that kind of money available I could save enough to get out to America in no time. If I stayed in Tyrone, I would never make it to New York, where I'd decided I really belonged; on the wages I was making it would take me at least two years to save enough to make a move like that. If I was making two hundred pounds a week, I could be lying on a beach in America in a mere matter of months.

I left the bar that night determined to get out of Ireland with my next paycheck. I needed to make the move out of my parents' house. I had been delaying the inevitable for long enough. I had passed my eighteenth birthday; it was time to flee the nest.

No Fixed Abode

The night before I left for London my father shoved forty pounds in my hand.

"Here, take that."

"No, I don't want it."

"Take it."

"I don't need it, I have my own money."

"Here . . ." he said, forcing it into my hand. "You never know, you might be glad of it."

I took it reluctantly and stuck it in my pocket, frustrated at how ill equipped I was to deal with any gesture of affection from my old man and uncomfortable at having to partake in this charade of manners we performed in lieu of a hug.

"Do you know where you're staying when you get there?"

"I have Padge's address in my pocket," I lied.

"And he'll be able to get you set up with work?"

"That's not a problem."

"Have you packed everything?"

"All ready to go."

"Right, then . . ." He put his hand out for mine. We never had reason to shake hands before then. Never had occasion to make some small declaration of our emotional attachment to each other. I gave him my hand and we shook rigidly without eye contact.

"I'll say good-bye now then," he said. "I'll probably be gone to work in the morning before you get up. Watch yourself out there." And then he turned without another word and left the room.

"Good-bye, Dad," I called after him as he was closing the living-room door behind him. "Thanks."

My mother slipped about the house like a stranger that night. She would drift into the living room intermittently, pause for a moment, clench her lips tightly as if she were trying to brace herself for a speech she had prepared, then leave again, apparently unable to trust that whatever word she chose to lead with would not trigger some internal domino effect, dismantling the skeleton that kept her body in an upright position, sending her crashing to the floor like some blubbering mass of deranged flesh.

I was angry with myself for not having disappeared quietly without a word to anyone, angry for not having slipped away a few months earlier on the night of my eighteenth birthday, as I swore that I would, and saved myself all of this anguish and a perfectly good watch into the bargain. I was angry for not at least spending my last night in a bar somewhere getting hammered with the lads so that I wouldn't have to deal with this long good-bye.

Before my little sisters, Louise and Noleen, and my little brother, Gerry, went off to bed, my mother marched them into the living room to say good-bye to me also. The girls cried openly as they clutched my waist.

"I don't want you to go away," Louise whimpered. "Don't go away."

"I'm only going over to England. I'll be back before you know it."

"You promise?" Noleen sobbed through deep, bone-rattling sniffles.

"I promise," I said, struggling to keep my composure, having to witness my mother now behind them, red-faced, tears rolling down her cheeks.

"Come on now, girls. That's enough now. Kiss your brother good-bye and off to bed. Give your little brother a chance to say good-bye, too."

I put my hand out to shake Gerry's hand, determined to brace myself against any more emotional outbursts.

"Will you take care of these girls when I'm away?"

"Aye. Bye-bye, Colin."

"Bye-bye, Gerry. Now, go on to your bed so you can get up for school in the morning, and I'll be back to see you in no time."

"All right."

"And will you look out for all my stuff? You can take my records and tapes and anything else I've left in the room."

"All right," he said, but I could see that he wanted more

than just a handshake, that he was just an innocent young boy, and that I was being unfair and selfish in denying him at least a little hug.

"Come over here," I said as I grabbed him in my arms and held him and let him hold me for the first time in our lives. "Don't you worry about a thing, I'll be back before you know it, you hear me?" I could feel his fingers dig into my back as he gripped me tightly with his face buried in my chest.

"I'm going to miss you," he said.

"I'm going to miss you too, Gerard," I said, struggling to block the reservoir of tears now threatening to breach the banks of my eyes.

"How come that wee shite gets all your records?" Brendan called from where he was lying on the couch watching snooker on the telly, giving me a conspiratorial wink when I glanced his way so I would know that he was only feigning his anger as a way of bolstering our little brother's sense of himself. "What do I get out of the deal, that's what I want to know."

"Gerry gets anything I leave behind." Gerry gave me a little smile and I could see that he was proud that I had given him special status over Brendan for the first time, that he had suddenly, in this last moment, been elevated in status to "brother" and not just the kid of the house anymore. He went off then with a proud little smirk on his face and I, seeing my mother ashen-faced and teary, bundling my young siblings out of the room, felt for the first time like I might be the one to collapse.

.   .   .

By the time we got into Belfast Airport, I was stoned. I'd smoked a joint in the parking lot after saying good-bye to my brother Michael, who had driven me there. My cousin Noel, who had decided at the last minute to come with me, guided me to the bar and ordered us the first pint of the day. I bought the next and before we had time to order a third, they were calling for us to board the plane.

Noel had brought his Walkman along and he handed me one of his earplugs so we could both listen to U2's *Unforgettable Fire* as the plane thundered down the runway and roared into the air. We were finally off Irish soil.

We squeezed our heads together in the tiny window as the plane blasted into the sky to peer down at the cartoonish green patchwork quilt of fields unfurling beneath us and the cold slate gray of the North Channel and the way it scribbled a thin border of white surf against the ragged shore line as we left Ireland behind for the first time.

The stewardess came by and we ordered double gin and tonics and we lit our smokes as I felt the first waves of freedom wash over us as the clouds cleared and we rose into a startling ocean of blue. I had finally made it out. There was no one to tell me what to do, or where to go, no one waiting up for me when I got home at night, no one to tell me I had to get up and go to Mass on a Sunday morning, or to get on my knees for a decade of the rosary before bed, no one to tell me when to comb my hair or polish my shoes. I had served my time. I was a free man at last.

A big, burly-looking lad who introduced himself as Martin

Donnelly from Armagh struck up a conversation halfway through the flight.

"Where are you boys from?"

"Tyrone."

"Oh aye, what are your names?" he asked as a way of pinpointing which side of the fence we were on. He knew that by announcing himself as Donnelly he had cleared up for us what religion he was; Donnelly was a very Catholic name, and any Northern boy would know that right away. Our surnames were Broderick and McClean—two surnames that fell on either side of the fence, meaning they could be Catholic or Protestant. So he had to delve deeper; the next obvious question, though not nearly as subtle, was "What school did you attend?" If we were Catholic, our school would in all likelihood be named after a Catholic saint; if we were Protestant it might be an academy of some sort. If the name of the school still failed to reveal your religion, then you simply asked "Church or Chapel," and that would clear the matter up entirely, church being a Protestant house of worship and chapel being Catholic.

Being from the North, this conversation felt as natural as saying "Lovely weather we're having." It was imperative to establish a person's allegiance right off the bat. Had we been Protestant, he would have gone back to his drink and we to ours and in all likelihood all communication would have been dropped immediately. As a Catholic you didn't go around speaking to Protestants. Protestant boys had Protestant relatives who were policemen or military men, whereas every Catholic boy knew something about how the IRA operated within the community and there was an unspoken rule that everybody just better stay to themselves.

"St. Ciaran's," I said, clearing the matter up instantaneously. The conversation could proceed.

"Great stuff. Where are you headed?"

"London."

"First time?"

"Yes."

"What the hell took you so long? I got out of that hole the minute they let me out of school; dropped me schoolbag and went straight to the airport."

"You like it over there, then?"

"Love it. I'm just on my way back over after buying my second house at home in two years. I just had to go back home and sign the papers."

"You own two houses already?" I was astonished. He was a big lad, but Martin didn't look like he was any older than Noel or me.

"Two houses in two years. There's a fortune to be made in London. The cash is literally fallin' out of the trees. You'll never go back, wait till you see."

"You don't miss living at home at all?" inquired Noel.

"Home's an hour away on a plane for godsake, if you get lonesome you can jump on a plane on a Friday evening at Heathrow and be back in your local pub with a load on before closing time and all on a day's pay. What did this flight cost you today?"

"Forty-five pounds."

"That's what I make a day as a shuttering carpenter in London, a day's bloody pay and you're home in an hour. How the hell would the likes of us"—he said, meaning Catholics like us—"ever make that kind of money in Northern Ireland?"

"Never."

"That's right; never. Go to London, work like a whore for a few years, and come home and live like a king for the rest of your life. That's my plan anyway. All my pals are already in London. There wasn't one of us stayed at home. Five of us got a flat together so it costs hardly anything. Do you have a place to stay yet?"

"I think so."

"What part?"

"North London. Harlesden."

"Who do you know up there?"

"Cousins, Padge McCann and John McCann."

"I know them, all right."

"You do?"

"Know them well, a pair of headers."

"Do you know where they live, then?"

"I don't know their house. I know the housing estate they were squatting in about six months ago. They might still be up there. You don't have an address?"

"We have a general area, but not a house number or a phone number or anything like that."

"No bother, stick with me and we'll track them down."

"Great."

"We'll head into Shepherd's Bush first and have a few

pints. I'll have to get my hands on a car to take yis up there. Better order another couple drinks here quick before they shut the bar on us."

I was astonished that the entire flight from Belfast to London took only an hour. There is only a thin slip of water dividing the two countries. It was no wonder England spent so much time and energy trying to knock the vinegar out of us; we were practically living on their front lawn.

We followed Armagh Martin in a haze of inebriated wonder through Heathrow and onto the tube for the ride into Shepherd's Bush.

When we exited the train station and came up onto the street, it was just as I had pictured it, the gray bustle of London, red double-decker buses, black taxis, a smattering of bowler hats and stern-faced businessmen marching along with umbrellas for walking sticks. We ducked into an old pub with battered red leather booths, blackened wood rails, and smoky ancient mirrors. I half expected to see Sherlock Holmes drawing on a hooked pipe in the corner.

Instead, there were a few grunts from the lads at the bar when they noticed their friend Martin back among them. They eyed Noel and me with threatening, angry scowls until Martin nodded in our direction.

"A couple of stragglers I picked up on the plane, Tyrone men, cousins of John and Padge McCann's," he said, vouching for us as good staunch Catholics. If you were from County Tyrone and you were Catholic, you carried with you a certain air of notoriety. It was an understood fact that Tyrone was on the front lines of the war. Tyrone had lost just as many souls to the Troubles as either Belfast or Derry and the East Tyrone Brigade of the IRA was widely recognized as being one of the most courageous and daring of any in the North. "It's their first day in the Big Smoke."

"What're yis drinkin', boys?" the roughest of the three barked in our direction, his face scrunched sideways as he bit down on his cigarette.

"A pint of Harp."

"Two."

"Two pints of piss water there, Mick, and throw this other bollox up a drink as well," he said, nodding at Martin as he dug down into his pocket and pulled out a ball of cash and held it in the air so the bartender could get a look at it before he started to pull the order. "And you might as well give me another when you're on yer feet," he said as he hoisted a pint of Guinness in a big, meaty fist and drained it in a swallow.

There was talk of counties and town lands, football teams and work, and then in hushed tones, with lips buried behind cupped hands and jacket collars, of the bastard English invaders and the hell our boys were giving them back home.

A car was located and Martin flung us up and down small narrow streets, the windows down, the radio blaring away, and within half an hour we were pulling into a great monster of a low-income housing estate. It was still early in the evening and bright out as we rolled down the narrow concrete paths past rows and rows of drab four-story buildings, dull redbrick, battered cream siding, dark stairwells to the narrow walkways of the second-floor apartments, the charred remnants of a car on blocks, windows and doors boarded with plywood here and there.

"Welcome to Church End Estate," said Martin. "This is where they were squatting the last I saw of them. You're sure you don't have an address?"

I dug a crumpled piece of an envelope out of my pocket and read, "Church End Estate, Harlesden. That's all I have."

"Well, at least we're in the right townland," Martin said, stopping the car. He stepped out and stood with one foot still in the car, keeping his hand on the horn for a good twenty seconds and then roaring at the top of his lungs, "McCann . . . John McCann. Padge McCann . . ." He was making such a ruckus that everyone who happened to be walking nearby stared, but no one paused or shouted back. A couple of women in aprons drying their hands on tea towels leaned over the rail on the second-floor walkway to take a good look at Martin before stepping back into their open doorways. A pair of young black boys slowed on their BMX bikes and then hurried on again over the cracked sidewalks and barren lawns.

Suddenly, on the balcony above us, not fifty feet away, John McCann appeared, yelling down, "Is there somebody looking for me?"

"McCann!" Martin yelled up. "I have visitors for you from across the shuck."

"Who do ye have?"

Noel and I stepped from the car.

"That redhead looks like a McClean." John laughed.

"Welcome to London, boys. You might as well come on up, now that you're here."

Martin helped us unload our bags onto the sidewalk and without further ado, he was gone again.

I was pleasantly surprised to find the interior of John McCann's second-floor home clean and tidy. I had conjured up all manner of degradation and slummy visuals to the word "squat," but once we were inside, it was a relief to see the place looked like a normal home, comfortably furnished, curtains on the windows, a TV in the corner, the smell of dinner cooking on the stove, Talking Heads on the record player, an attractive girl on the couch rolling a joint.

"Adeline, this is Noel and—I'm sorry, what did you say your name was again?" John said, giving me an inquisitive look.

"Colin," I grunted defensively. "Colin Broderick."

I had never met John before, although I had heard about him often. Before he had even left for London, he had already achieved somewhat legendary status locally in his willingness to serve as the outcast, the unrepentant pot smoker and castigator of all forms of religion. From what I'd heard about him, he was known as a man of peace; he wanted nothing to do with the war. The fact that he did not want to be associated with Catholicism was, to many, tantamount to saying he had abandoned his people. He was a true independent, which in the closed-shop Catholic community of Northern Ireland at the time was almost the equivalent of announcing you were with the other side. Just saying I was his friend bore the very real possibility of guilt by association.

That's what it was to be from the North; every new relationship, every new introduction had to be weighed politically. I had to remain vigilant, paranoid of all people, of strangers. I was suddenly acutely aware of these traits that had been so deeply ingrained in my psyche but were only becoming evident now that I was in an unfamiliar situation away from home. I had spent my entire life up until that very day living, more or less, within the cocoon of Catholicism. Almost every interaction I had ever had in my entire life was exclusively with Catholics. If you stopped for gas you stopped at a Catholic-owned gas station, if you went for a drink you drank in a Catholic bar. The schools, youth clubs, football games, and street fairs I had attended were all exclusively Catholic. Even Bundoran, where we went for the occasional day at the beach, was considered Catholic-approved. Bundoran was in the Free State. We never once visited a beach on the Northern coast within the six counties, and there were some beautiful beaches, but they were Protestant beaches in Protestant beach towns.

I had been effectively brainwashed. These defense mechanisms that were springing into my conscious mind were so deeply ingrained that anything unfamiliar seemed threatening to my very mode of existence. I had been trained this way without any memory of an official lesson. To a more learned stranger I must have appeared anxious, uneasy, broken.

Who was this beautiful new girl who nodded to me as she licked the glued edge of the skin and packed the end of the joint with a matchstick? What if she was a Protestant? Adeline could be. I had to be careful about what I revealed about myself to her. Who knows what kind of company John McCann was keeping these days. I'd never been friends with a Protestant before, apart from our postman, that is, but it was generally accepted that the postman was fairly harmless—and necessary—and you were given a pass for liking him, unless of course he turned out to be a member of the UDR, in which case he would be promptly assassinated. But a real-live Protestant girl . . . a girl who would sleep with you at the drop of a hat, a girl with no scruples whatsoever, well, that was something to be fearful of, no doubt about that; and I was.

"You might as well have a seat, boys," John said, leaning in the doorway of the living room, "now that you're here. Did Padge know you were coming over today?"

"Naw, we had no way of telling anybody we were coming. We didn't have an address, or a phone number, we just met that lad Martin on the plane and he took us here."

"Well, we'll have to get you sorted out with your own place after it gets dark out. We have a full house here at the minute. I don't think we have room for any more. Adeline's on the couch here as it is; she just got here from Dundalk yesterday."

"I don't know if we have enough money to rent a place just yet," Noel said, voicing my own immediate concern about being rushed out to meet a real-estate agent.

"Nobody said anything about renting a place." John laughed. "Sit down and relax, you two, and have a smoke and don't worry about it, you boys want a beer . . . forget that . . .

stupid question . . . I'll get the beers," he said, grinning as he turned away and sauntered off to the kitchen, rubbing his hands in a tea towel draped casually over his shoulder.

Later that same night after dinner, drinks, and another smoke, we went out armed with a hammer, a nail bar, and a pair of vise grips, a couple of screwdrivers, and a new door lock. We followed John and Padge and listened to them discussing a ground-floor unit farther down into the heart of the housing estate that they felt might be a suitable first home for us newcomers.

Noel and I were placed fifty feet away on either side as lookouts while Padge and John went about ripping all the plywood off the windows and front door of the ground-floor unit. They then replaced the barrel of the front-door lock. The entire operation took them less than forty minutes. John produced an industrial-strength fuse from his back pocket and after jimmying open the external fuse box in the concrete stairwell, he placed it in the empty slot and our little house sprang to life.

"Ta-da," he said with a great theatrical flourish, leading us in through the front door. "Oh, this place is nice. This is perfect for you boys."

"Come here and see this," Padge called from the living room. When we went in, he was hunkered down in the corner by the window and he was holding a phone receiver out to John with a grin.

"It's working?" John said, taking the receiver and putting it to his ear.

"Sure is."

"You guys got lucky."

"We have a working phone?"

"You know how much beer and hash this is worth?"

"We can sell it?"

"You can sell the use of it for long-distance phone calls for as long as it lasts. There's a little community of Irish and Australian squatters here in Church End Estate; you'll get to know them all soon enough. We'll put the word out you have a phone, and then all you do is charge a six-pack or a few joints to let them stay on for an hour or so to call home, and then you kick them out again. But me and Padge get to use it for free 'cause we found it."

"Sounds good to me."

"Colin, you come on back to the house with us. I'll give you boys a couple of blankets. You have to stay in here for forty-eight hours without leaving and it's legally yours."

"And if they don't kick you out in twenty-four hours," Padge continued, helping John give us a brief rundown of the legalities of owning our very first house, "then it's yours until they go through the legal process of evicting you, and that could take anywhere from four to six months. That's if they even bother to try. We've been in our place for over a year now and nobody's said a word."

"A year?" Noel said, incredulous at the apparent simplicity of it all. "No rent, no electric bills . . ."

"Squatters' rights," Padge added. "You'll get used to it. If the peelers show up, don't let them in. They have no right unless they have court papers, and there's no possible way that they could have them so soon. If you get stopped by the cops walking around, give them a false name and when they ask for your address, tell them, 'No fixed abode.'"

"What's that?"

"It means you don't live anywhere."

"And on Thursday I'll show you boys where the dole office is so you can get signed on and start claiming for your wife and kids."

"I don't have a wife or kids," I said, thinking he must have mistaken me for someone else he knew by the name of Broderick from back home.

"You do now." John laughed. "We'll talk about it Thursday. Until then, you boys lay low, stay here, drink beer, get stoned, call your parents and tell them you've arrived safely, and we'll sort out the rest as it comes. Welcome to Church End."

Over the following months, our apartment became known as the Kiosk. Every squatter in Harlesden filed through that place at one time or another. We pinned the phone bills to the wall in the living room to show the progression—three hundred pounds, twelve hundred pounds, three thousand four hundred pounds owed, and still no one paid us a visit from the telephone company, no one thought to switch off our service.

I bought a false birth certificate for fifty quid and went down to the dole office and put in a claim for my wife and two young daughters. When they told me they didn't believe me and asked to see them in person I paid an Irish girl I knew another fifty pounds to bring the two English children she was babysitting to the dole office with me and I got my first check right there on the spot.

I bought some carpentry tools, a hammer, a handsaw, a couple of wood chisels, a Yankee drill, and a square, threw them in a bag, stuck a pencil behind my ear, and called myself a carpenter for thirty-five pounds a day. I took to selling hash to subsidize my own burgeoning habit. If I could move two ounces a week, I was never short of a smoke. I finally had enough money and freedom to get drunk every single night of the week, and I did. My uncle Brendan was the only one who'd had the right idea, it seemed to me. It didn't make sense why anyone would want to live any other way. Everything felt better with a little bit of a buzz on.

I unsuccessfully pursued Adeline for the first six months, but my deep animal hunger scared her. It scared me. I had never wanted a girl so physically before then; all the repression of my sexual self, the constant reminder by the Church of how evil and dirty my natural desire to procreate was, had instilled in me a lust akin to violence. I was terrified of what I might do to her if she let me near her.

My frustration was magnified by the arrival of a new disease called AIDS. The word was that it was spreading like wildfire. You got it the same as you got the clap or crabs and you died a horrible death within months. Everyone was talking about it. It arrived overnight, coinciding with my first few weeks away from home. I was incensed that the first great sexual plague had chosen to smite the planet during the very pinnacle of my sexual potency. It was so unfair. Girls crossed their legs and said no thank you.

Back home I had never been without a girlfriend, or numerous girlfriends, but in London I had regressed somehow. In this new environment I was demoted to the role of cute skinny kid with spots. The kind of boy a girl might be thrilled to knock around with as a best friend. Sex was out of the question. Any of the girls who were brave enough to date, were dating older men, or at least boys older than me. The wild, swinging madness of the '80s had screeched to an abrupt halt; and it was still only 1986. I drank heavily and blacked out regularly.

Over the next few months I ran into a bunch of the crew from Galbally. It seemed half of County Tyrone had moved to Church End Estate—at least anybody who was halfway cool, that is. My cousin Seamus shared a house with Paul Arthurs and Damien Donnelly, and Paul's brother Patrick also arrived and lived in another house nearby with a couple of carpenters from Cork. Damien's bubbly little sister Martina arrived with her long, shimmering cascade of auburn hair, and eyes that sparkled like sun on fresh dew. She was just about the prettiest Irish girl I'd laid eyes on since I arrived in London. But she was with her boyfriend, an equally long-haired guitarist named Terry Campbell—a sweet, likable boy who quickly became one of my better friends, which meant that over the next year and a half I got to spend as much time with Martina as I liked, only in the painful role of the frustrated best friend.

On weeknights we drank in the White Horse Tavern down at the bottom of Church Road. Before long it had the comfort of Kelly's Inn on a Friday night with all the clans present and commingling, now that we had gotten to know one another. In London, the Tyrone lads looked out for one another; in Church

End we had become one clan. The Tyrone clan consisted of the Donnellys, the McCleans, the McCanns, the Arthurs, the Campbells, and the Kellys.

There were about fifteen of us at any given time from Tyrone, which meant we could operate with some level of safety, because if you messed with one of us, you messed with the lot. We were a formidable platoon. The only other county in the housing estate with as solid a representation was Derry, and because there were so many of them and because we had been spawned with the same distrustful gene, the Tyrone lads and the Derry lads gave one another a wide, respectful berth. We were cordial enough with one another, but we kept to our own corners of the bar, much like the Altamuskin crew and the Galbally crew had done back in our days at Kelly's Inn.

There were a few skinheads from Belfast, but they seemed less dangerous when you saw them out standing by themselves at the bar, and once you got past that threatening husk, they were the sweetest, most vulnerable lads of all. Fear is a wonderful makeup artist.

County Cork had a decent representation, as did Kerry and County Meath and a few sweet-natured Donegal heads, but it became apparent there was no fight in the Southern lads. The Southern lads were happy enough to just drink their beer, have their smoke, and listen to In Tua Nua. For them, the war in the Northern six counties might as well have been happening in the Middle East, for all they knew or cared about it. They heard about it on the six o'clock news every evening and digested it with their spuds and turnips like they would any other news of trouble in the world, Belfast, Beirut, Jerusalem:

who the hell cared? It was all happening somewhere else, to someone else. Life in the Free State of Ireland was rolling along without a hitch.

But the lads from the North kept one eye open for trouble all the time. We stood like sentries at the bar. We walked with our fists clenched and our heads cocked like roosters, radiating a suicidal sense of readiness to defend wherever we went.

The only Irishman to watch out for in the bar was the Dub. The Dubliner knew everybody's name, he was the first one with a joke, the first one with the need-to-know information; he was the go-to guy if you needed a forged birth cert or a clean driver's license or a passport or an ounce of opiated hash or a bag of speed. To the Dubliner, we were all just a shower of muck savages, farm-fresh off the bog, uncivilized, uncouth, uneducated, and unwashed. Of course, there was an element of truth to his opinion of us. But his air of superiority had more than just a hint of Englishness to it, so we kept one wary eye propped open specifically for him at all times.

The only man not present in the White Horse Tavern was the Connemara man. The Connemara man in London was a breed unto himself: part savage, part mystical shaman. Here was the original Irishman, undiluted and lost. There were boys who arrived from that remote part of the West Coast of Ireland in those days who could barely speak a word of English. They were raised in thatched cottages on desolate farms and spent their days tending sheep, communicating with one another primarily in our native Gaelic language. Many couldn't read a street sign or write a letter home to their mothers. Here was the closest semblance of our heritage left standing in all of Ireland: a man hewn together out of rock and fern, hair as thick and reckless as seaweed, a tongue as rich as an oar being dipped in saltwater.

The Connemara men I met in London in 1986 seemed to live nowhere, know no one; they neither asked nor gave, they could be found standing on a busy street corner up by the Crown Clock in the middle of the afternoon, head down, swaying to the rhythm of some internal ocean crashing wave upon wave against a ragged shoreline, or by the street in Cricklewood at seven in the morning, disheveled and dispassionate but still hardy enough that they were the first men loaded into the back of trucks by the Irish gangers who were on the hunt for brutes to shovel blue English clay for the obligatory twenty pounds a day. But when the Connemara man got paid, he didn't drink with the rest of us Irish; we were as foreign to him, it seemed, as the Englishman. He suffered the work in silence and went off to drink alone.

On Saturday nights, my hunger for female company might drive me up to the National in Kilburn. The National Ballroom on a Saturday night was where you could go to see bands like the Smiths and the Pogues, or maybe Elvis Costello, and even if there wasn't a band, there were still about a couple thousand drunk Irish crashing into one another on the dance floor hoping that some crude semblance of a connection might be forged before the lights came up and we were all tossed out onto the Kilburn high road again before morning.

More than likely someone would hurl a bottle or a chair into the crowd around midnight and that would ignite the entire latent savagery in the place, and every man fought with the man who was standing closest to him. Women were punched and they punched back, furniture was smashed and beer glasses were hurled, the whole place would roar like a furnace as all our self-hatred and the seeds of our repression blazed for a few ferocious moments. And then it would all be over again as quickly as it had begun, and more beer would be bought and the entire congregation would sail out into some cosmic unified blackout and come-to in jail cells and doorways, lawns, and strange mattresses all over North London. I saw a mob set upon an Englishman who happened to be walking by one Saturday night as the crowd poured onto the sidewalk at closing time. They didn't stop kicking until he was dead.

The days turned to weeks and time thundered along the way it does when you are eighteen and drunk seven nights a week. I dropped acid and snorted speed and smoked joints like cigarettes, and every night was a party in somebody's squat. I stopped sleeping altogether and began crashing out instead. I ate little and stopped going to Mass completely.

On the job I had my first guarded conversations with English carpenters. These were lads my own age from up the country, boys from Lancashire and Yorkshire who'd come down to London for the work and the party and to escape their parents, same as I had. To my astonishment, most of these lads didn't seem to really care about the North of Ireland at all, They were much like the lads from the South of Ireland; it was just another mindless war they heard about on the news. My bitterness for the entire population of England was being undermined. But I could not trust them entirely. That little voice continued to whisper in my ear as I smiled and laughed at their jokes and smoked their cigarettes: *Don't get too close to this bastard. He's still your enemy.*

I staggered from day to day like someone still half asleep. I was in a state of semiconsciousness most of the time. I was smoking too much hash, and if I didn't have a drink in my system to accompany it the faint blur of paranoia followed me everywhere I went. I saw a young Irish lad lose four fingers off his right hand one day when the pulley rope he was holding was yanked too quickly during a practical joke by two of our workmates on the job. I stood three feet in front of him as we both stared at the place where his fingers had been just a second earlier and the blood came in powerful spurts out of the front of his hand in a crimson arc that stained the muck at my feet and turned the toes of my boots an oily carmine hue. Nothing about it seemed real. Not his loss, or the terror I saw in his eyes before he passed out. I stood there completely unmoved by the sight as two men I didn't know rushed out and carried him off toward the canteen. I sauntered back to my place on the job and continued working for the day as if nothing had happened.

I had no template for how any of this was supposed to feel. What amazed me most was that I felt almost nothing at all, or perhaps I did but had no name to define it. Can an emotion exist without a name? Isn't it the name itself that defines the existence of an emotion? It seemed I was living with the thought of the thing rather than the thing itself; the boy had lost his fingers. That had to mean something to me. Intellectually, part of me understood that I should feel one way or another about it. But I couldn't decide what that should be. Had I been desensitized to the very idea of violence and bloodshed? Had a lifetime of news reports of killings and tortures deadened my nerve endings? Had the thrashings at home and at school completely obliterated my ability to feel? Perhaps I was smoking too much hash? Yes, that was it. I would have another drink. That would stop the noise.

I felt as if I was watching the world through a smoky gauze. A good friend, a lad from Belfast, lost an eye to a smashed beer glass in a fight in our local bar. He had to get a hundred and twenty stitches in his face to close the wound. Another two friends, an Australian brickie and an Irish carpenter, were both killed in separate accidents on the train: one stumbled, drunk, in front of the tube on his way home from work one afternoon during rush hour, the other was crushed between two cars when he tried to take a whiz on a moving train and misjudged his footing. Both lads had been regular visitors at the Kiosk, we'd drank and smoked and laughed together often, but when I heard that they died I went about my daily life as if nothing had happened at all. They had been unlucky. They were dead. What more needed to be said about it?

There were other accidents–stabbings and beatings, drug overdoses, deaths, friends sent to prison for years. Concerned Irish parents were showing up in Church End Estate, knocking on doors looking for their runaway daughters. The police made random arrests looking for information in an effort to infiltrate the burgeoning community of Northern Irish lads who were squatting in the estate. When I was held for the night I was interrogated relentlessly for hours for information about who I might know in the IRA. They kept me up all night screaming in my face, told me I was a useless piece of Paddy shit, threatened to throw me in prison for years, threatened to arrest members of my family. After thirty hours or so I was released again onto the street. Rather than fear, I found the entire episode comical.

I had become a hard man.

One night at a party in my cousin Padge's apartment, somebody picked up the coffee table and, holding it out the window by the leg, flung it through the kitchen window of the unit downstairs, where a bunch of the Derry lads shared a squat. Within seconds they had stormed upstairs with bats and knives, ready to murder all of us in the apartment. It turned out they had been cobbling together a bomb on their kitchen table at the very moment when the table had been launched through their window. The bomb had almost detonated, killing all of us in the building. It was a tense standoff with threats issued, but ultimately no one was brave enough to take the first swing. There would have been all-out war had it begun. Besides, we all knew we couldn't take the chance that the police would show up and find the evidence downstairs. It would have been enough to send us all away for a very long time.

Following that particular incident, tensions between the Tyrone lads and the Derry lads reached a fever pitch. When we passed one another in the street or saw one another down at the White Horse, we no longer acknowledged one another at all with a nod of the head. Threats had been made against one another's lives, and neither side would forget completely the words that had been spoken. We were Northern Irishmen, after all.

To make matters worse, in the following weeks I got involved with a girlfriend of one of those very same lads from Derry. It was a suicidal act, but the danger of it thrilled me. It was a relief to feel anything at all. My cousin Padge came to the Kiosk to tell me that one of the Derry crew had approached him on the street and told him in secrecy to warn me that the girl's boyfriend had discovered the affair and he was going to kill me. Padge advised that I get out of town as quickly as possible. It was a warning that finally sobered me up long enough to acknowledge the danger I was in. Within days I was on a plane and returned home again to Tyrone in the hope that things would blow over. I might have been acting suicidally, but some other part of me very much wanted to live.

Exile

Back at home again in Tyrone, the first restless pangs of the exile announce themselves. I miss London. I miss the boys I have gotten to know in my new family back in Church End Estate. I miss having my own flat to go home to and the freedom I had there to come and go as I pleased. I have never been fully at home in Altamuskin, and neither have I been fully at home in London. There is poison in them both for me, but maybe there is a little medicine, too. I realize that both places exist for me now, and that my definition of home has been forever fractured. No matter which I choose, the ghost of the other will gnaw at me always.

I am back in my parents' house in my old bedroom, sharing a bed with my younger brother Gerry again. I am on the dole and picking up odd jobs here and there and drinking whatever bit of money I make. I have little enthusiasm in working at all now that I have had a taste of earning four or five times as much for doing the same job just a couple of hours away in London.

I get my hair cut and buy new clothes and begin to feel a little healthier now that my mother is feeding me again and I am removed from the routine of getting stoned and drunk every day. I spend a little time with Gerry and my sisters, Noleen and Louise. It's as if I am only seeing them now for the first time. I get the first inkling of responsibility when I realize that they are beginning to look up to me; I am the big brother, back home from England with all these exciting stories. I am the outside world brought home to them. I don't want them to view the world with the same cynicism as I do. I feign interest in a life I feel little for.

My brother Brendan and I take a job painting the outside of a neighbor's house. It's the first time we've worked together, and we begin to form the brotherly bond we never had growing up. He wants to hear my stories of London. He wants to know if I will take him with me the next time I go. We even manage to go out for drinks together and share a few laughs.

It's summer and the long, bright afternoons have a tranquil and timeless air about them. I sense for the first time an enormous quiet to the countryside. The damp aroma of freshly cut lawn grass seeps into my pores. It soothes me.

Brendan and I are in no hurry to finish the house we are painting. We are working for ourselves, so we can come and go as we please. We are listening to the radio as we work one day when the news breaks that there has been a shoot-out in Loughgall the previous evening. Eight members of the Provisional IRA have been shot and killed in an ambush by the SAS. We put down our paint buckets and rush to the small radio on the windowsill and stand there frozen, paintbrushes in hand, waiting for more, waiting for the names. It had happened so close to home that we were sure to know at least some of them. The lads I knew from Galbally, the Arthurs and Donnelly clans, were all from that same area. There would be a chance that we would know at least some of the names, or that we would have some connection to them one way or the other, but the names were not released, not just yet. We would hear them soon enough.

We had no sooner heard the newsflash when we heard the first signs of a British Army helicopter in the distance rising out of the army base in Omagh. We watched it, the buzz growing into a more definable *chopa-chopa-chopa* as it approached, and we tilted our heads back to stare up at its dark-green belly as it passed directly over our heads not more than a couple hundred feet off the ground, a gunner perched in the open side door scanning the countryside for the flash of a rocket launcher or a gunman's barrel in a bush, and on it went toward Loughgall.

We put our things away, unable to continue working without knowing more, and started out the lane to the road. I had the sick feeling of death in my gut. Of course I would know some of the names. I looked up suddenly, hearing the low, mournful bray of an animal in pain. In the next field stood a tall black horse, her belly was swollen, and she was tipping her head back throwing her great cry into the air. Our neighbor Sean Donnelly hopped a fence on the far end of the field carrying a length of rope and hurried toward the horse as he called out for to us to come.

We climbed the gate and hurried toward the horse, meeting him midway. She stood silent and you could see her belly clamping against it, but the foal would not come.

"I might need some help with her," Sean said as he tied a slipknot on the rope. "She's stuck in there."

"What do we do?" I asked. I had never witnessed the birth of a foal, much less one in trouble.

"Just watch her for now," he said as he worked his hand up inside her with the rope and she dipped her head and pushed, sending a great gusher of greenish-yellow water out along his arm, soaking him from the neck down. "That's just her water breaking, she's all right," he said, responding to the shock on my face. "I almost have it."

I swatted a dung fly from her face and put my hand on her neck and gave her a rub to let her know we were there to help.

"Got it," Sean said, taking his hand out and rubbing the thick slime and blood off on the front of his shirt. He got a hand on her haunch and leaned back, pulling the rope and directing Brendan to the other side of her to hold the tail up as the two front hooves started to show. The legs came out and the head between them in a transparent envelope of skin. She started to go down then, the big horse, her back legs buckling, the front folding too.

"Just watch she doesn't come down on you," Sean said,

taking a step away from her to let her settle. "Just let her roll onto her side, it'll be easier on her."

When she was all the way down she lay panting and you could see the muscles wrestling for the last big push and the foal slipped from her easily then, settling motionless on the wet grass behind her.

Sean untied the rope from the foal's ankles and hooked his fingers into her nostrils, clearing the slime from her nose and her mouth to make sure she could breathe.

"Is it alive?" Brendan asked.

"It's alive, all right."

"Is it all right?" I said, not seeing any movement. The horse lay silent too, her belly shuddering, her legs treading the air.

"We'll see in a minute," Sean said, standing away from her now that she was cleaned, and we watched as the foal rolled a little and put her two front legs under her and pushed herself up, bringing the back legs into position as she stood.

"By God, she's a fighter," Sean said with a gleam of pride in his eyes.

"She might have been better off where she was," I said.

"What the hell's going on today?" Sean asked as we watched another helicopter appear from over beyond Foremass in the direction of Carrickmore. It was a black dot in the sky no bigger than a fly, but there was no mistaking that sound. We looked away from the foal for a moment and watched it as it grew larger, off beyond Dunmoyle Chapel in the distance and on toward the Rabbit Burrow, to Loughgall.

"You didn't hear the news?" I said.

"Naw. What happened?"

"Eight IRA shot dead in Loughgall," Brendy said.

"Holy fuck. When?"

"It happened last night. We just heard it on the radio now."

"No names?"

"Not yet."

We turned for a moment, the three of us in silence, to watch the foal make her way to her mother's head to rub their noses together for the first time and stare at each other as the noise of the helicopter faded off into the distance. She cocked her head toward us too and seemed to regard us for a moment: the three somber faces of the men who'd help deliver her into this peculiar new world. Here was how all life began in the gray North; we slipped from our mothers in innocence and joy, but when we opened our eyes to see, there was death too in this fragile inheritance.

We turned and headed back across the field for home so we could hear the names of those we had lost.

Within a matter of hours, everyone in the British Isles would know of Loughgall. Eight young IRA men had been slaughtered. Two innocent civilians who just happened to drive into the massacre accidentally were also riddled with bullets by the SAS. The two brothers Anthony and Oliver Hughes were on their way home from work. Anthony died on the scene. Oliver was taken to the Royal Victoria in Belfast, where he recovered.

The massacre at Loughgall represented the largest loss of life for the IRA in a single incident in the history of the Troubles.

Upon hearing the first names announced my mind went blank for a moment as if a white sheet had been flapped in the air and draped over my memory. Then in the clear white of the past I could see the faces of the two young boys I had first wrestled with in Kelly's Inn not two years before, boys I had fought and drank and laughed with and whose families I had come to know and love: twenty-one-year-old Declan Arthurs and nineteen-year-old Seamus Donnelly were dead.

I'd just spent the previous year living in London with some of their older brothers: Paul, Patrick, and Damien were all part of our close-knit circle of friends on Church End Estate. These boys were among my best friends. Just weeks earlier we had all been together in the White Horse Tavern like a family, the whole group of us sitting around a table by the open fire on a Saturday morning, taking turns buying rounds of beer, smoking cigarettes, telling yarns, and laughing while we waited for our clothes to dry in the Laundromat across the street.

I thought immediately of Martina; Seamus Donnelly was her brother. I thought of calling the Kiosk in the hopes that I might be able to get in touch with her. I wanted to tell her how sorry I was, how angry I was. But it was pointless; she and Damien would have been on their way home by then, or perhaps she was back already—back to Tyrone for the wakes and burials.

My mother had us all kneel to say a decade of the rosary for their souls. Prayer was the language she knew best to convey to me that she acknowledged the pain I must be in. My stomach churned at the thought of what my good friends must be going through and my mind began to race with thoughts of rage and bloody revenge. I went back to the list of names again and again, hoping for a different result, but no matter how many times I visited it the list remained the same:

Patrick Kelly, 32.
Padraig McKearney, 32.
Jim Lynagh, 31.
Gerry O'Callaghan, 29.
Eugene Kelly, 25.
Tony Gormley, 25.
Declan Arthurs, 21.
Seamus Donnelly, 19.

The day of the wakes, the sky over Tyrone was heavy with the brattle of British helicopter blades. They hung in deliberate provocation in the air over the small cottages of the deceased, low enough that we had to lean in to one another to hear what was being said as we huddled in small groups, smoking and talking and moving gravel with our toes as we waited our turn to pay our respects.

There were cars crammed bumper to bumper all the way down the lane and up the road a half mile on either side of the Donnelly house by the time we arrived. It had been the same over at the Kelly and Arthurs households. The narrow roads around Galbally were littered with parked cars. The turnout was enormous. The families of the dead boys had agreed to leave the caskets open so that we might bear witness to the carnage that had taken place.

When my time came to enter the Donnelly house, I joined the queue and took the hands of those who were on the receiving line; the family members whom I did not know personally were easily discernible by the measure of grief their faces bore. I was not prepared to see my close friend Damien in this surreal scene, just as I had not been ready to see Paul and Patrick standing next to their younger brother's coffin over at the Arthurses' house moments before. These were my good friends, tough men—the very toughest. To witness their pain and the dignity with which they bore it, greeting every guest with a warm handshake and a smile and a sincere "Thanks for coming," was almost too much to bear.

I entered the small, dim room where the coffin lay, draped in an Irish flag and bookended by a pair of IRA men in full uniform bearing rifles, their identities concealed in the traditional black balaclavas. The remaining family members, the women and the elderly, sat around the perimeter of the room with somber faces, their hands clutching handkerchiefs in their laps. Martina leapt from the chair and threw her arms around my neck and sobbed.

"Look what they did to him, look what they did to my brother. . . ." I held her tightly and forced myself to see over her shoulder as she sobbed. I took a good long look at what was left of the boy's face, Seamus, this beautiful nineteen-year-old boy all shot to bits like the others. Young men slaughtered mercilessly when they could have just as easily been taken alive.

Witnesses from the village said that the boys were never given an opportunity to surrender, even though they were surrounded by an SAS ambush squad.

This was how justice worked under Thatcher's shoot-to-kill policy. The SAS had obviously picked up information well in advance of the attack, long enough to conceal themselves in the bushes surrounding the Loughgall police station so that they could lie in wait for the vanload of boys to arrive. They had many hours to contemplate the arrival of these young Irish rebels. They could just as easily have used that time and information to arrest the boys long before they reached their destination. There were whispers of villagers who had witnessed the event, saying that the boys had been taken alive and lined up alongside the road and shot one by one in the face then dragged and kicked and beaten, guns placed in their hands for the British propaganda pictures.

These were tactics the SAS had used elsewhere. There were similar assassinations taking place all over the North, but not all of them had witnesses to verify the slaughter. But we knew. We, the neighbors of these boys, knew. We understood that what had happened here in Loughgall was calculated, premeditated slaughter. We didn't need to wait for a court's decision or a team of forensic experts or lawyers or an English courtroom to verify what was blatantly obvious. The British government wanted these boys dead, so they killed them.

These were not innocents who lay before us; everyone in this room understood that this was war, but the boy in this box should have still held breath, should have still played and fought and dreamed—*should have,* if justice had any place in what had happened here.

"I can't take it, Colin, I can't take it," Martina cried. "I want Seamus back. I want my brother back." The room was filling up behind me as she clutched me tightly and I whispered useless hollow words in her ear.

"I'm sorry. I'll call you soon. It's going to be OK."

I put my head down and turned to leave, out the narrow hall, down the graveled street, past the hordes of mourners and the long row of cars, with a fresh and bleeding hate and the virgin heart of a killer.

We Know Who You Are

After the massacre at Loughgall I spent the next year drifting back and forth between London and Altamuskin. I was more lost than ever. My cousin Padge had managed to patch things up with the Derry crowd after arranging a meeting where I apologized for dating one of their women, and they consented to let me live. They had been warned that if I wound up dead, the Tyrone crew would kill one of theirs. It was business as usual in Church End Estate.

I was working construction, dealing hash, running errands for a crew of Irish gangsters in London's East End who were smuggling vanloads of hashish into Scotland and pounds of cocaine into London from Amsterdam by motorbike. The head of the crew, a guy called Mike, had a car-parts store he used as a front. I would ferry trays of Guinness all afternoon long from the pub across the street to whoever happened to be hanging about. Stolen cars had to be driven from one location to another. Sealed envelopes delivered from point A to point B with no questions asked. I had to build a secret compartment under the bathtub in Mike's home where he could store his cash, drugs, and guns. In return I got to hang out with whatever celebrities might stop by for their weekly drug supply. Some were actors I'd grown up watching on TV; more than once I found myself rolling joints and getting stoned with just about the entire cast of *EastEnders*. I was valued for my ability to keep a secret. As a Catholic child of Northern Ireland I was somewhat of an expert in this particular field.

Occasionally I would pop back home to Altamuskin for a few weeks to straighten myself out and spend some time with my younger brothers and sisters. I had begun to feel guilty that perhaps I had been too selfish where they were concerned. I had taken the little knowledge I had gleaned in my short life and I had abandoned them without a single serious conversation. I began to feel a need to cement some small bond so that they understood that I cared for them. I knew what it felt like to be alone and misunderstood, and the thought of any one of them feeling as I had deeply horrified me.

While at home I had started working for my neighbor Brian Mullin, or Brian the Bard as he was better known. Brian, my friend Mark's older brother, was a big, round-faced lad of about twenty-five. I hadn't known him at school, but I knew him well enough. Everybody knew Brian. It was no secret in the community where his allegiance lay. He was one of the Bards after all. On Sunday mornings he'd be standing outside the chapel gates selling copies of the *An Phoblacht* newspaper, and if Gerry Adams happened to be around to give a little speech you could be sure the loudspeaker was strapped to the roof of Brian's car. He was a hard man and a staunch Irish nationalist. He carried the reputation of a man to be either feared or respected, and he was both. He was also one of the sweetest lads I ever knew. He was funny and generous and showed great patience when I would screw up mixing a load of mortar. He never once yelled at me or made me feel small and I loved him for that.

For the first few weeks I worked with him, he grilled me for information about London. And he had plenty of time to grill; it was just him and me together working side by side nine hours a day, five days a week. There was no escaping the barrage of questions. Who did I know? How well did I know them? What did I do when I was over there? Who were the lads I knew from Derry and Belfast? I was well aware of his status as a major player in local IRA affairs. Well aware that if I allowed it to happen, he could open that door for me, too.

When we were stopped by the Brits or the police at the random roadblocks, Brian was nearly always waved through without them even stopping to have him verify his identity. It became evident that they were not interested in busting Brian Mullin on something as inconsequential as a driving infraction. They weren't going to waste a whole lot of time grilling him about where he was just coming from and where he was planning on going. Brian was a big fish; they weren't even going to check the trunk of his car for guns. When they were ready to take him down it would be big-time.

I was careful not to divulge any information about London

to Brian that would make me look like I was a lad who might not be smart enough to keep the kind of secret that could cost someone their life. I wanted Brian's trust and his respect. There was a game being played here, he had asked me to go work for him, and I had accepted. That in itself was a mark of respect. We were engaged in the dance. He was weighing my character and by going along and verbally jousting with him all day long I was, in effect, asking for his approval.

Much like the thrill I had when I'd put my life in jeopardy by dating the girl from Derry, I thrived on the danger of the game I was playing. What was at stake was the very real likelihood that I might be asked to kill a man. If I joined the IRA, that's what it might lead to. If I joined, I was leaving myself open to that alternative. There wasn't a day that went by when I didn't seriously consider the consequences of that action. But I still wasn't sure if I could go there. There was something still holding me back and I didn't quite know what it was. At times it felt like fear; what if I wound up dead like the lads in Loughgall? The very idea that I might be afraid sickened me. I despised myself for even allowing the thought to enter my mind. Real men were not ruled by fear. It was weak. Those boys I knew who had died at Loughgall, those were real hard men. The Donnellys and the Arthurs, they were hard men. And here was another, my good friend Brian Mullin. Given Thatcher's current shoot-to-kill policy in the North, Brian walked around every day with the threat of assassination hanging over his head. And make no mistake, it was a very real threat. Brian was a big deal in County Tyrone; if there was a hit list, he was on it. And never once did he even betray a hint of fear in his demeanor. Not once. Brian smiled from one end of the day to the other, I never knew a lad so happy. That was real bravery. But still I could not commit.

Every day there was a fresh thicket of inquiries to maneuver through. It was like stepping through a minefield. He quizzed me endlessly about the local drug scene—a particularly dangerous conversation to get involved in because to slip up and give the wrong answer could cost me my kneecaps, or possibly much worse. It was well understood among anyone who dabbled in hash that there was only one safe place to buy your stuff, and that was directly from an IRA-run bar in Belfast. As long as they were in control of the supply, all was well with the world, but if you happened to be caught shipping in your own supply across the border or across county lines or, God forbid, you were discovered selling hash unauthorized locally, you ran the very real possibility of critical punishment. The cops in Northern Ireland may have been a little green when it came to drugs, but the Provos were not.

"Do you like to have a wee smoke?" Brian would ask casually as we worked, trying to playfully tease information out of me.

"I love to smoke. Do you want one?" I would say, offering him a cigarette and knowing full well what the real question was.

"Not a fucking cigarette, you bollox, you know, the other stuff."

"What other stuff?"

"Don't act dumb with me, Broderick. You know what I'm talking about."

"Oh, you mean rolling tobacco, no I don't have any, I can't stand the stuff. I can't roll them properly, the tobacco always gets stuck in my teeth."

"Right, right, oh you're a smart one all right."

"That's what they told me in school."

"Ha, if you'd been half as smart at school as you think you were you wouldn't be out here lying on the handle of that shovel all day."

"How is that batch of mortar? Is it wet enough for you this time?"

"It's as dry as a camel's hole, wet it up a bit for godsake. The water's free, you know, you don't have to worry about splashing a bit in there from time to time."

And he would let it go for the day, knowing that he would have to wait for another day now to catch me off my guard. All the time we were growing closer. He would swing by our house after work in his little blue Toyota Celica and he and I would go off down to Knocknamoe Castle for a few pints. He introduced me to his girlfriend. The three of us went out together for drinks on occasion. He would buy me dinner and throw me a pack of smokes once in a while. These little tokens of his affection meant more to me than a day's pay. We laughed hard and often, we sang together on the way to and from work, and as the weeks passed working together, we became fast friends.

"Hi, Broderick, where would I get my hands on some drugs?"

"What's the matter, Brian, do you have a headache?"

The longer I evaded telling him what he knew to be the truth, the better he could trust that I would hold up under intense interrogation.

"No, I don't have a headache you little bollox, I want some good drugs. Can you get them for me?"

"What is it, your tummy? I'm not surprised, the way you eat; you need to go on a diet, have you tried lettuce?"

"Aye, you're one smart little fucker all right, Broderick," he would say, laughing. "Seriously though, where do you get your drugs? I know you know where to get them. Do an auld friend a favor and tell me."

"All right then, I'll tell you."

"Good man yerself, where do I go?"

"It's not much of a secret, though: I get mine in the chemist in Sixmilecross, same as everybody else. Usually I just get Mammy to get them for me. I'll tell her to pick up some aspirin for you tomorrow if you like."

When Brian laughed, the whole scaffolding shook and you had to laugh along with him. He had the big, happy countenance of a little boy and the reputation of a man who could shoot you in the face and never miss a meal over it, and I grew to love him.

That afternoon as he was dropping me off outside my house, we sat in his car as I finished my cigarette. We had been singing along to "Sylvia's Mother" by Dr. Hook, his favorite song at the time.

"All right then, I'll see you tomorrow then," I said, reaching for the door handle to let myself out.

"Wait a minute," he said, and he paused as he contemplated what he was going to ask me for a moment or two as if to impress on me that it was not without serious deliberation that he was going to ask me what he was going to ask me.

"I need you to do me a little favor tomorrow," he said, looking at me now with an expression that had not a trace of his usual tomfoolery.

"Anything, whatever you need me to do," I said, making it clear that I was ready for the next step no matter what that might be.

"Anything?"

"Absolutely, whatever it is just tell me and it's done."

"You're sure about this now?" he said, and paused again to give me all the time I needed to grasp the severity of the situation at hand.

"Anything. Tell me what it is and it's done," I said, staring him right in the eye so that there was no doubt about my allegiance.

"All right then," he said. "I need to go for a little drive tomorrow down south; we'll have to leave early in the morning and I need a driver no questions asked."

"What time do we leave?"

"Early. I'll pick you up at about seven thirty."

"I'll be ready."

"Good man."

Once my mother found out that I would be rising before her to go to work in the morning at seven thirty, it was as if her radar went into high-alert mode. She was up before me in the morning with the kettle on, popping a couple of slices of bread into the toaster for me as I came quietly though the kitchen door.

"What are you doing up?" I asked, sitting on the couch to tie my boots, knowing well the expression of concern on her face. I had grown accustomed to that expression over the past couple of years since I'd first left home to go off to London. She said little about my comings and goings anymore, but her face bore all the weight of a mother on the verge of losing her children.

"Oh, I just couldn't sleep, I thought I'd get up and make you a wee bite of breakfast."

"I could have gotten it myself."

"I could use a wee cup of tea myself, anyway." Out the kitchen window the first pale-gray light was beginning to bleed though the clouds over beyond Dunmoyle. A row of black crows sat on a telephone wire. The first of the trucks from the gravel quarry rolled by down the Altamuskin Road.

"Where's the job today?" my mother asked, not looking at me for an answer.

"Same job," I lied. "Down by Omagh."

"It's early to be off to Omagh. I thought you usually left a little later than this." There was the sudden sound of a car arriving around the side of the house. "Looks like Brian is here early," she said, waving to Brian out the kitchen window, and as I stood I could see Brian waving back at my mother with that big, friendly grin of his.

"Right, I'm going to run."

"Here, take a slice of toast with you."

"Thanks. Bye."

"Come here and give your auld mother a hug," she said, and she wrapped her arms around me and pulled me to her in a desperate motherly way that I gave in to for a moment, sensing her need and knowing that she understood full well the implications of leaving early with Brian Mullin under suspicious circumstances. You did not spend your whole life living in Altamuskin and not understand the conversation that was at hand here; we all did, and everybody was playing their part dutifully by saying nothing about it.

As soon as he pulled around the front of the house out of sight of my mother, Brian got out of the car and had me get in the driver's seat.

"Where to?" I said.

"Head towards Monaghan town."

On our way down through the British Army checkpoint at Aughnacloy they had us slow and the Brit gave Brian an angry, murderous scowl. It was obvious that they recognized his car. Brian grinned back and chortled a little, seemingly satisfied that his presence had been sufficiently acknowledged. Then they waved us on through without checking for my driver's license or insurance, which was standard enough procedure when leaving the North.

In Monaghan town Brian got out of the car, saying only, "Wait right here."

I turned off the ignition and I waited. It was three hours before I saw him again. When he came back he wasn't carrying

anything that might cause suspicion. No bags, no bulky envelopes or violin cases. He simply got back in the car and said,
"Home."

We were coming up on the south side of the border checkpoint at Aughnacloy when he asked me suddenly to pull over
and stop just about two hundred yards south of the British
Army lookout post.

"I'll drive from here," he said, and once we had swapped
seats he sat for a moment with the motor idling before turning
to me. "Are you ready for this?"

"Sure."

"This is going to be a little crazy going back through here
now, you realize that?"

"No bother."

"Good enough."

The moment we pulled up at the checkpoint, two soldiers
stepped in front of the car and trained their rifles at us through
the front windscreen. I had crossed the border many times
in my lifetime; I had never seen a reaction like this. Another
stepped out and waved the car into a closed-in car bay area,
where we were immediately surrounded by about another
fifteen soldiers all bearing their weapons. My heart began to
pound with the threat of it all.

It was instantaneously apparent just how big a deal Brian
Mullin really was to the Brits. This was a military operation.
These soldiers were on high alert. They were circling the
car and shouting orders like they'd just apprehended Attila
the Hun.

The doors of the car were flung open and we were dragged

out and made to stand with our hands on top of our heads while we were frisked; meanwhile a green military Land Rover was backing into the bay and another was pulling in behind the car. We were separated, and I was grabbed and shoved roughly into the back of the Land Rover in front, surrounded on all sides by about five British soldiers who kept their weapons trained on me at close range at all times. Brian was bundled into a jeep farther back, and once they had a soldier behind the wheel of Brian's car, we were driven out on the road again and up through Aughnacloy in a convoy of about five military vehicles, gunners perched out of the roofs, a helicopter suddenly hovering low overhead, shadowing our every movement. The convoy slipped down a side street near the bottom of the town and we were driven about a half mile out to an enormous military warehouse as big as an airplane hangar.

Once all the vehicles had pulled inside, the enormous steel doors were closed behind us and we were marched up separate staircases at either end of the hangar into separate interrogation booths with glass walls that faced down onto the floor, where a team of mechanics started dismantling Brian's car immediately as I was sat at a desk. The grilling began.

"How do you know Brian Mullin?"

"I don't know him."

"Where are you coming from?"

"I can't remember."

"Do you realize how much trouble you're in right now?"

"I have no idea what you're talking about."

"How long have you known Brian Mullin?"

"I never heard that name before."

"Where did he pick you up?"

"At a dance."

On and on the questioning went. I had been through a similar interrogation just months earlier in London. Nothing about the experience frightened me. I knew they already had an answer to almost every question they were asking me. I'd been stopped at various checkpoints locally with Brian in the time we had worked together, so I knew that they would know my name, where I lived, who I worked for previously, where I stayed in London, the color of the wallpaper in our front hallway. The level of sophistication employed by British intelligence in Northern Ireland was legendary. It was commonly known and accepted that they were watching and listening all the time. You just acted and spoke accordingly, never betraying even an iota of your internal dialogue, even in a whisper to your closest friend, and then you had nothing at all to worry about.

I watched the mechanics down below as they stripped the car of its wheels, seats, floor mats, headlights, and indicator covers. The tires were removed from the rims, removable parts were taken off the motor, the air filter and hose pipes were checked, and after a couple of hours of searching they began to put it all back together again just as efficiently and methodically. In all, they held us for more than three hours. When the car was reassembled they told me to stand up and get the fuck out.

"We know who you are: Colin Broderick, aged nineteen,

one of six children, neighbor of Brian Mullin, we know where you work, where you drink, who your friends are . . ."

"So what are you wasting your time questioning me for then?"

"We'll be keeping a close eye on you, son. I'd be very careful if I were you."

Once we were a couple hundred yards away, Brian gave me a little sideways smirk and I smiled back knowing he was pleased with how I had handled myself. I was over another hurdle and his approval filled me with pride. He popped Dr. Hook back in the cassette deck and turned it way up and we both sang along with "Sylvia's Mother" as we headed on home to Altamuskin.

In the days that followed I realized that I was finally ready to follow Brian wherever he might lead me. I was ready to accept any offer he might make. The feeling of solidarity I'd had with him that day we were interrogated was something I wanted more of. For the first time in my life I'd finally felt worthwhile. I had won the approval of one of the hardest men in our community. I'd held my cool over the first hurdle. If I was man enough to follow it through to its ultimate conclusion, I, too, could earn my place in that league of heroes. My destiny was clear to me now. It was inevitable that I pick up a gun; my whole life had been funneling me into this very moment. If I wanted to think of myself as a true Irishman, it was time to start acting like one. I could not shake the images of the Loughgall boys with half their heads missing. What more incentive did I need? We were a people living under the abusive rule of a foreign invader and I was of fighting age. I was angry with myself for waiting so long. When Brian called on me next I would be ready to go.

Good evening. This is the ITN news at six o'clock.

A lone gunman has attacked the congregation gathered in Milltown Cemetery today to bury the three Irish Republican Army members who were shot just days ago by the SAS in Gibraltar.

The man approached the crowd and started shooting, before launching an estimated four grenades into the crowd of Catholic mourners.

Oh my God, the dirty bastards.

Gerard, get up and turn up that television.

Among the victims who have been killed are a seventy-two-year-old grandmother and a ten-year-old boy who was shot in the back.

In the footage that follows you can see the confusion where it seems the crowd was unaware at first that it was being attacked, and then pandemonium as the gunman hurls grenades into the crowd and begins to shoot. As the gunman made it to the perimeter fence Sinn Fein president Gerry Adams can be seen raising his arms as he appealed to the crowd for calm . . .

Well, the dirty filthy black bastards.

Colin. We don't know who did it.

Of course we know who fucking did it; another
Protestant piece of scum slaughtering unarmed
Catholics is all it is. The three that are being buried
were all slaughtered in the same way three days ago
in Gibraltar, unarmed, approaching a checkpoint
for godsake. This is Thatcher's shoot-to-kill policy,
it's bullshit. It's slaughter. Just the same as the lads
at Loughgall. We're like sitting ducks around here,
the fucking Brits are slaughtering us and we're
sitting around eating our dinner minding our
friggin' manners and watching the damned news
like nothing's going on. This is our country . . .
Our country.

Right, that will do now.

No, it won't do. Why does that have to do? The
children should hear this . . .

Colin, stop it.

I'm sick of being told to be quiet.

Colin.

I've had it. Fuck it. I can't take it anymore.

Colin, sit down and finish your dinner . . . come back
here . . . Colin . . . Children, everybody bless themselves. In the name of the father and of the son and of
the holy ghost amen.

It was later that same evening that my mother took me by the
arm and led me into the living room and closed the door.

"Sit," she said.

"I don't need a fucking lecture right now about my language in the house," I said, standing my ground. "I really don't
need it, Mum, so if that's what this is, forget it right now, OK?
I'm done, I'm done up to fucking here."

"I know you are, pet, now please sit down with me for a
minute so I can talk to you, just a little bit, please," she said
very calmly.

I sat.

"OK," she continued, clasping her hands in her lap,
straightening her back and raising her chin a little to look at
me directly. "I'm only going to say this one time and then I'm
never going to say another word about it, OK?"

"Good," I snapped, wanting the lecture to be over and
done with as quickly as possible.

"Believe it or not, I understand what you are going through
right now. You're my son, I know these things, and I know exactly what you are thinking about doing right now."

"You don't–"

"Just let me finish. Please . . . I know how angry you are and
how frustrated you are and you're seeing young lads you know

get killed and there's a certain pressure on you to do something about it, and you're thinking about it. I'm your mother. I don't need it spelled out for me. I just want to say that I understand your anger and I know what you want to do with it. I really do. I know you're on the verge of taking that step. I just want you to know that if you do decide to do that, that will be your own decision; you are an adult now and there's nothing I can do to stop you, but I will ask you to think about one thing before you pick up a gun."

And here she paused to take a breath. I was listening intently now. I felt a sudden surge of relief to see her formulate the truth into language. She had finally allowed the very real possibility of a gun into our home. The word "gun" had popped on her lips like a shot and snapped me back to the center of things, away from the tattered fringe of my sanity. She was speaking the truth and I could hear it loud and clear, and it grounded me there on that couch next to her, there on our couch, in the living room of our home, the home that my father built with his bare hands on the Altamuskin Road. And I was a boy called Colin Broderick and this was my mother, Claire, speaking to me—a woman who was a little girl herself once upon a time, a little girl who played in the very field where our house now sat with her own brothers and sisters without a care in the world, years and years ago before she fell deeply in love with a farmer's lad called Michael who looked the spitting image of a young Paul Newman, a boy she kissed to the very edge of eternity, a boy she loved enough to run away with once upon a time before we were all born. And for the first time I really did understand where I came from; I came from love, a love that had traveled to England and back, a love that had lost its temper and its sanity from time to time, but a love with such strength and such an endurance that it had the power to raise a family of six unruly children through times when they couldn't even afford to buy us a pair of shoes, never mind a pair for themselves. It was a love that had raised my cousin Roisin when she had lost her own mother as a child, a love that was large enough to encompass my other brother, Fergal, the Vampiro, yes, for he too was my mother's child. This was the love from where I came: a big, imperfect, unwieldy, messy, beautiful love, and I could see it now and how it had survived in a troubled place called Northern Ireland with every manner of difficulty thrown as an obstacle into its path. This was the woman who bore me on a bed without painkillers or her mother's hand on her brow. And I could see her now in all her humanness and she was telling me the truth about myself, acknowledging the person I had become, was becoming, and it made me whole again.

"You have two younger brothers in that other room right now, watching TV. Two younger brothers who look up to you and admire you and who will follow you into whatever trouble it is you lead them into, because they love you. I need you to understand that if you make this decision, you are making it for all three of you. Whatever you decide to do, they will do. If you decide to do this, you are deciding for all of us as a family; you bring all of us down that road with you. As I said, if you decide to join the IRA and pick up a gun, I will respect your choice—God knows it seems like a good idea even to me sometimes—but if one of those young boys signs up after you do and something happens to one of them because of the decision you are about to make, it will be on your shoulders and your shoulders alone, do you understand that? Their lives are in your hands."

I was speechless as I stared at her. She had stopped me dead in my tracks. She had taken my heart and held it up for me to see it. She had shown me that it could break in ways that no fixing would ever make right again. She had laid my young brothers' lives at my feet and asked me to look: Look at your brothers. What she was telling me was that she understood that *I* would never be able to forgive myself if anything happened to those boys. *I* would be broken, our family would be broken, and it would all come down to this, this one simple decision that *I* was about to make.

I sat next to her on the couch in stunned silence, staring at her, unable to fully comprehend right away the power of her words. And after she got up and left the room I sat there for a long while letting the full impact of what she'd said settle within me. I had been staggering around so blindly in my rage for years that I had forgotten that I belonged to a family.

I got up and walked into the kitchen, where they all were: my mum ironing clothes in front of the stove; my dad with the day's newspaper stretched out on the table in front of him; Michael peacefully asleep in an armchair with his arms folded high across his chest; Brendan sitting with a scowl on his face, concentrating on some movie playing on the TV in the corner; my two little sisters, Noleen and Louise, with their homework books in their laps, scribbling away, and Gerard next to them, all in a row on the couch, dressed in their pajamas, ready for bed. I knew then, in that instant, that my mother was right;

I couldn't live with the risk of harming a single hair on any one of their heads. I could not be the one held responsible for destroying this family. That was a hell I was certain I could not endure. Finally, there was one thing I could be certain of. And here was another: for whatever it was worth, I loved this roomful of strangers. I would have to take those two truths and start from there.

How could I take another human life when I could not yet make sense of the one that I had? This head of mine needed clarity, and I was never going to find it there in that country. Not in the North of Ireland. Everywhere I turned, my thinking was clouded with hate. I was living in a society that demanded my silence, but I needed to talk this childhood through. I needed to scream it at the top of my lungs if I was ever going to get to the bottom of all this noise. And if I survived long enough to get to the bottom of it all, to understand myself more clearly, perhaps I wouldn't have to raise my voice at all. Perhaps I would never need to hold a gun, I could just say it all instead. Write it all down. That might be just as powerful in the long run.

It was time to go to America.

Acknowledgments

I am going to try and keep this very short and to the point. Here are the people I need to thank who supported and carried me in one way or another while I was writing this book over the past four years.

My agent Jane Dystel who urged me to write this book in the first place, who knew I was ready for it, before I knew it myself. Thank you Jane. My agent Miriam Goderich who helped me formulate the original idea into a cohesive narrative. Thank you Miriam. You two ladies are my champions.

My first editor, Philip Patrick, who said yes and gave this book its home at Random House. Thank you Philip for believing in me in the early days of this process and for giving me the freedom to run with it. You are awesome, my friend.

My second editor, Heather Lazare, who came along and started knocking it into shape and who helped me see that I needed to think about translating my Northern Irish experience into English. Thank you for your patience, Heather.

Meagan Stacey, who came along just when this book and I both needed her to be there, with her compassion, insight, and understanding. You gave me the courage and belief in myself to bring this baby home. Thank you so very much.

Renata, who suffered through the first two years of darkness, witnessing me open old wounds with this book, and who helped give me the courage to face it head-on and deal with the poison. You will always be close to my heart. Thank you. And your boyfriend, Jamie, who has helped in a million little ways since then, thank you too, my brother.

My immediate family: my parents, Michael and Claire; brothers, Michael, Brendan, and Gerry; and sisters, Noleen and Louise. Your significant others, Dympna, Sylvie, Caroline, Brian and Stephen, and yes Anna and Nicky too (I include you with my immediate family also). This is a book about family, and without each of you this book wouldn't exist, especially you, Gerry; you have been a rock for me.

My close friends who listened and listened to me going on about this book until they were ready to throw me under the wheels of a bus, especially Tony Caffrey, but also Jon Greenhalgh, Josh Brolin, Dermot Kenny, John Hyams, Karl Geary, Chris Campion, Stephen Smallhorne, Don Creedon, Brendan O'Shea, Leo Hamil, John Duddy, Mike Kelly, Josh Lucas, Kevin Patrick Dowling, Eric Branco, Jody McGrath, Dermot Burke, Packie Joe Gilheany, Cal Kelly, Des and Paul McCann, Dermot Corrigan, Budgie, Chris Temple, Christy Kelly, and Martin McKenna. You are my family too. Thank you all, my brothers.

Eugene Callum, Paul Schmitz, and Danil, your belief in me and support, when I was in need of it, helped too my friends, and I am indebted to you all. I do not forget, ever.

There are a few others I also need to mention who helped talk me through many a dark night of self-doubt: M.M., Natasha, Dalia, Emma, Martina, and Barbara, without your warmth and support I may have crumbled entirely. From the bottom of my heart, thank you ladies.

And finally, and most important, Erica, my darling angel daughter, who was born four years ago, the same month I started this book, and who has taught me more about the power of love in that time than I ever knew was possible. You are my living breathing heart angel face. Your smile cures me. Thank you.

And *That*, as they say, is *That*.

About the Author

COLIN BRODERICK was born in Birmingham, England, but raised Irish Catholic in the heart of Northern Ireland, the second eldest in a family of six kids. He has a four-year-old daughter and lives in Manhattan.

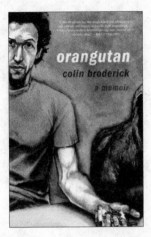